LIFE SAVING

WHY WE NEED POETRY

INTRODUCTIONS TO GREAT POETS

JOSEPHINE HART

virago

VIRAGO

First published in Great Britain in 2012 by Virago Press

A CIP catalogue record for this book
is available from the British Library.

ISBN 978-1-84408-871-3

Typeset in Goudy by M Rules
Printed and bound in Great Britain by
Clays Ltd, St Ives plc

Papers used by Virago are from well-managed forests
and other responsible sources.

MIX
Paper from
responsible sources
FSC® C104740

Virago Press
An imprint of
Little, Brown Book Group
100 Victoria Embankment
London EC4Y 0DY

An Hachette UK Company
www.hachette.co.uk

www.virago.co.uk

To the boys

ACKNOWLEDGEMENTS

Thanks to:

Lennie Goodings; The Very Reverend Dr John Hall; Dame Harriet Walter; Dr Non Vaughan-O'Hagan; Ed Victor; Robert Browning; Sir Richard Eyre; Simon Callow; Angharad Wood; Dan Stevens; Sir Evelyn de Rothschild; Louis Susman; Sir David Hare; Marjorie Susman; Sir Tom Stoppard; Brian Cox; Michael Grandage; Jean Cardot; Lord Bragg; Professor Roy Foster; Kenneth Cranham; Michael Gough; Sir John Major; Lord Salisbury; James Bierman; Dame Gail Rebuck; Gary Bond; Sir Peter Stothard; Lord Gowrie; Dame Eileen Atkins; Sir Stephen Lamport; Lady Bakewell; Zoe Gullen; Alan Bates; Tom Burke; Rory Daniels; Sally Emerson; Lord Chadlington; Paul Kavanagh; Dame Lynne Brindley; Sir Roger Moore; Jon Fawcett; Roger Walshe; Matt Caswell; Quentin Smith; Julian Glover; Arabella Warburton; Ralph Fiennes; Malcolm Dolbear; Douglas Slater; Lord Ryder; Tom Hollander; Angus MacKechnie; Lord Strathclyde; Caroline Michel; Ronnie Taylor; Sian Wilson; Deborah Findlay; Sarah Mowat; Lord Wakeham; Alan Yentob; Guy Staight; Bobby McDonagh; Sir Nick Hytner; Didier Bernheim; Lady Antonia Fraser; Victoria Gray; Edna O'Brien; Professor Alistair Buchan; Joy Davies; Nancy Carroll; Tim Duffy; Simon Gray; Helen Ramscarr; Alan Cox; Lord Sainsbury; Edward Fox; Geordie Greig; Fiona Shaw; Sinéad Cusack; Jeremy Irons; Carlos Lopez; Helen McCrory; Chloe Kirton; Nicholas Soames; Seamus Heaney; Professor Kevin Nugent; Charles Dance; Prudence Peat; Dominic West; Charles Smallwood; Juliet

Stevenson; Hugh Dancy; Jo Carr; Marianne Faithfull; Sonny Mehta; Claire Bloom; Bono; Joanna David; Valerie Grove; Brian Dennehy; Lindsay Duncan; Peter Florence; Emilia Fox; Sir Bob Geldof; Paul LeClerc; Alper Simmons; Rupert Graves; Robert Hardy; Daniel Lopez; Felicity Kendal; Max Irons; Damian Lewis; Susan de Soissons; Ian McDiarmid; Elizabeth McGovern; Jo Danvers; Sir John Mortimer; Professor Stephen Greenblatt; Dusan Hamlin; Charlotte Rampling; Mark Strong; Eleanor Ryan; Greg Wise; Beth Boxall; Vita Paladino; Maddie Sexton; Kelly Reilly; Charles Collier; Phil Georgiades; James Hilton; Jacquetta Adams; Harold Pinter; Elton John; Daithi O'Ceallaigh; Michel David-Weill; The Dowager Marchioness of Salisbury; Monique Henry,

whose dedication and scholarship made this book happen.

Thank you
Maurice Saatchi

CONTENTS

PART II: THE POET IN THE GARDEN

INTRODUCTION

Each of the essays in this book was the introduction to an extraordinary event. Each heralded an hour of great poetry read by great
actors in London, Dublin or New York over a quarter of a century.
Josephine Hart was Britain's greatest impresario of poetry in modern
times. At each show, before any of her actors performed, before Bob
Geldof growled out the lyrics of W. B. Yeats, or Harold Pinter intoned
Philip Larkin, or Roger Moore played Kipling, the audiences heard
Josephine Hart's introductions. Each one was integral to the performance, no longer than was necessary to appreciate what was to
come, essential for appreciating it at its best.

This book preserves them as she delivered them.

These are short introductions – to W. H. Auden, Robert Lowell,
John Milton and Christina Rossetti among others of her favourites.
Hart did not make poetry simple: as she said of Emily Dickinson,
'Short does not mean sweet. Short does not mean easy.' But these
pieces remain the perfect preparation for reading the poems aloud
and for hearing them read aloud.

Josephine Hart was an acknowledged master of minimalism in her
own fiction. She was just as ruthless a ringmaster of the poem in performance. She was famed for seven intense and personal novels
including *Damage*, which was filmed by Louis Malle in 1992. But she
poured an equal intensity into many hundreds of hours of equally
spare, precise and passionate readings of words by others.

Great poems, she believed, came to life when they were heard.
She often cited Auden's maxim: poetry is 'memorable speech'. She
sometimes called it 'the Eliot effect'. The darkest, most daunting

1

parts of *Four Quartets* became clearer, crystalline, in the voices of Edward Fox, Jeremy Irons and Eileen Atkins. The 'ice writing' of Elizabeth Bishop would always be 'less than seductive', she warned, but fine reading could release 'one of literature's most frightening, and frightened, voices – that of the terrified child'.

Josephine Hart's Poetry Hours were both education and entertainment, performances played in libraries and theatres before audiences of devoted students and fashionable society. Hart herself was an unmistakable figure, never seen in the city except in black and white – usually by Chanel – always on performance days in the same pompom-heeled 'lucky shoes'. She could persuade and charm like few others, ensuring that the best of English and American poetry be read aloud and recorded by the best actors of her time. Each show was under Hart's firm and knowing directions, all of them delivered from the black ring-binder that always sat on her knee and where this book began.

Josephine Hart was born in 1944 in Mullingar, County Westmeath, in Ireland, the daughter of parents whose business was the ownership of a garage but whose legacy to their bookish daughter was a catalogue of family catastrophes and the death of three siblings, two of them within six months of each other when she was seventeen years old. Her last novel, *The Truth About Love* (2009), which sets the history of modern Ireland against a family struggling with dismemberment in all its forms, came as close as she ever did to addressing these tragedies directly. *Damage*, her first, told of a moderately successful, purposeless politician who meets destruction through a woman who warns him of the deeper truths that he cannot see: 'Damaged people are dangerous. They know they can survive.'

She was a pupil at Catholic schools where the learning and reading aloud of poetry were compulsory and writing, too, was praised and encouraged as God's work. She lost her convent Catholicism but kept the nuns' belief in the transformative power of poetry – for good and ill. If life could be damaging, so could art. She considered an acting career but instead became a unique impresario. She loved Robert Frost, not just for his power of 'cutting along a nerve' but because, as Allen Ginsberg put it, he literally created the audience for poetry readings in his time.

Her work lives on not just here but in CDs distributed free to schools, anthologies of the performed poetry and an app that has so far attracted almost forty thousand users. Audiences have always been amazed at whom they heard. Would great actors work for no pay before small audiences, reading Milton and Gerard Manley Hopkins and other writers who rarely figure in a life on stage? They would, it seemed, if Josephine Hart asked them to. In 2005 Sir Roger Moore gave a rendering of Kipling's ballad 'The Mary Gloster' at the British Library; the Hollywood star had not been expecting to perform a piece that was quite so long; the audience, made up of sceptics and the star-struck, was barely more certain what would transpire. Under Hart's hardest gaze, Moore proved his seemingly effortless power over Kipling's story of the helpless shipping magnate disappointed in his son, using no accents, no grand gestures or regional burrs – and he left the rows of his audience in tears.

There was no house style for the Poetry Hours. When Kenneth Cranham took on the Kipling duties (he had met Hart through a shared passion for Elvis Presley) it was as an equally potent, but very different, character part. Harold Pinter was never offered Kipling; Hart knew who would do what and why. Pinter did Larkin. A controlled encouragement of variety was the key. When Bob Geldof had his rock star's pick of early Yeats – 'The silver apples of the moon, / The golden apples of the sun' – there were the sights and sound of crouching concentration. The Boomtown Rat and campaigner for Africa was allowed to luxuriate before his fans in the familiarity of 'I have spread my dreams under your feet; / Tread softly because you tread on my dreams.' When the actor Sinéad Cusack took over, she gave the 'The Circus Animals' Desertion' a more classic tone: 'Now that my ladder's gone, / I must lie down where all the ladders start / In the foul rag and bone shop of the heart.'

In the Ireland of Hart's youth there had been 'Holy hours' when it was wiser not to be seen entering or leaving a bar, and when the trapped drinkers would perform – each to their own individual standard of excellence under the landlord's guidance. To some this was the key to her style, as much as the convent and the classroom. She understood well the perils. In her third novel, *Oblivion* (1995), there is a rhetorically gruesome scene in which a director sets out his skills before a documentary-making journalist, showing how he fires up his stars into 'giving life to the dead'. Not every performance was a masterpiece. Not every actor repaid Hart's faith in his or her power to make poetry understood. But so many did – and surprised even themselves in what they did.

Josephine Hart died on a Thursday afternoon, of a cancer whose existence few of even her closest friends had known. She recognised herself as a connoisseur of death and had chosen her way to meet it. Four hours later, on the bare black-bricked stage of the Donmar Warehouse in Covent Garden, the actor Deborah Findlay carried on stage the familiar black binder. With her was Cranham, representing the older generation of her cast; Ruth Wilson and Rupert Evans representing the younger, and with them Max Irons, son of Cusack and Jeremy Irons, the star of *Damage* and probably the most loyal of all Hart's players over three decades.

There was a short, shocked exhalation from the audience when the news of the death was announced. Then there were readings, as planned, of war poetry – by Yeats, Owen, Sassoon and Brooke, and epitaphs by Kipling. This book – with poems by each of her chosen writers selected by her husband, Maurice Saatchi – provides a permanent reminder of events that those who have experienced them will never forget.

Peter Stothard

PART I

THE COMPLETE INTRODUCTIONS

Accompanied by extraordinary actors, Josephine Hart introduced remarkable programmes of poetry. *Life Saving* is dedicated to preserving these introductions. It was important to include the poets' voices too, and the poems have been chosen by Josephine Hart's husband, Maurice Saatchi.

These introductions are as she delivered them, from platforms in London, Dublin, New York; from the British Library, the National Theatre, the Donmar Warehouse, the American Embassy, the National Library of Ireland to the New York Public Library. Some of the poems referred to in the introductions are not included here, but we hope that readers will be inspired by this book to make their way back to all of the poems she loved.

W. H. AUDEN

Wystan Hugh Auden was born in York in 1907. A poet,
playwright, librettist and critic, his 1930 collection *Poems* brought
him instant fame. Awarded the Gold Medal for Poetry in 1937 and
the Pulitzer Prize in 1948, he was Professor of Poetry at Oxford
University from 1956 to 1961. He died in 1973.

W. H. AUDEN

Truth Out of Time

'One Sunday afternoon in March 1922, a school friend casually asked me if I wrote poetry. I, who had never written a line or even read one with pleasure, decided at that moment that poetry was my vocation.' Just like that. And therein lies the mystery of Auden. The critic and novelist John Bayley writes: 'That he turned out to be a brilliant poet ... does not alter the arbitrariness of his decision to become one.' Art and will conjoined; fame and success followed. *Poems*, published in 1930 by Faber and Faber (T. S. Eliot's initial rejection had been a great disappointment), made his name and almost immediately. Edward Mendelson in his introduction to *The Collected Poems* points out that, in the history of English literature, only Byron became famous more quickly. Two further collections, *The Orators* (1932) and *Look Stranger!*, led to two Gold Medals for Poetry, one from the Queen, one from the King – George VI. During a lifetime as a poet, playwright, essayist and librettist, W. H. Auden garnered further awards and honours on both sides of the Atlantic. In America he won the Gold Medal for Poetry, the National Book Award and the Pulitzer Prize. In 1956 he was elected Professor of Poetry at Oxford University.

'Poetry', he once wrote, is 'memorable speech'. His poems contain some of the most succinct, elegant and unforgettable lines in literature. His psychological and philosophical insights into the workings of time, the nature of love, of isolation, the ethical choices of the

9

state and the individual, sear themselves into our consciousness. A poetic inquisitor, he drills deep in 'the deserts of the heart'. His poems throw down a moral challenge – can we win 'Truth out of Time'? Even in the gladiatorial arena of love and sex, an arena in human life in which self-deception often rules, he remains clear-sighted. His love for Chester Kallman, 'the wrong blond' (so named because Auden, who was expecting another male guest when Chester turned up at his hotel room, exclaimed, 'But it's the wrong blond!'), lasted on its own terms, mostly Chester's, for the rest of his life. 'The triple situation of being sexually jealous like a wife, anxious like a nanny, and competitive like a brother, is not easy for my kind of temperament. Still, it is my bed and I must lie on it.' He knew the cost when he wrote 'If equal affection cannot be / Let the more loving one be me.'

Auden, like Kipling, had a purpose. 'In so far as poetry, or any of the arts, can be said to have an ulterior purpose, it is, by telling the truth, to disenchant, and disintoxicate.' And yet he himself as Edward Mendelson points out had been 'enchanted'. One night in 1933, 'something happened': his 'Vision of Agape', captured in a Dali-like image, in the poem 'Out on the lawn I lie in bed'. Of this seminal experience Auden wrote, 'I felt myself invaded by a power which, though I consented to it, was irresistible and certainly not mine. For the first time in my life I knew exactly – because, thanks to the power, I was doing it – what it means to love one's neighbour as oneself.'

The disenchanter as an ecstatic points less to fierce internal conflict than to what John Bayley describes in his essay 'The Flight of the Enchanter' as a 'dualism' in Auden. Bayley notes that a certain vulnerability in the poet is cited in both Humphrey Carpenter's biography and Edward Mendelson's critical study as the possible cause. Charles Osborne in his biography notes the same lifelong trait. Evidently a favourite quotation of Auden's was that of Montaigne: 'We are, I know not how, double in ourselves, so that what we believe, we disbelieve and cannot rid ourselves of what we condemn.' Certainly it is impossible to miss the almost carefully balanced contradictions.

Born in York, in 1907, the youngest of three sons of a middle-class professional family, Wystan Hugh Auden became an Anglo-Catholic Communist and volunteered to fight in Spain in the Civil War. Many believe he left the battlefield when England was itself at war (in fact, he left with Christopher Isherwood, in January 1939, before war was declared, volunteered in America and was turned down). He was a hugely disorganised man, one of the most sartorially challenged in literature, often wearing his socks on his head – yet his working hours were monastically disciplined. A homosexual, he married Thomas Mann's daughter Erika, who had been declared an enemy of the Nazi state. Marriage to Auden provided her with a passport. Christopher Isherwood, who had been initially approached, had rejected the idea. Honourably, Auden stepped in. 'Delighted,' he said. He may have believed that his dominant faculties were 'intellect and intuition', his weak ones 'feeling and sensation', yet he wrote one of the loveliest lyrics in the language: 'Lay your sleeping head, my love, / Human on my faithless arm'. An independent man, he nevertheless, even in his forties, feared loneliness. 'I shall,' he wrote, 'probably die alone at midnight, in a hotel, to the great annoyance of the management.' He did just that. In the Altenburgerhof, in Vienna, on 28 September 1973, Auden died of a heart attack, which he'd once told Charles Osborne was 'the nicest way' to go; 'it's cheap and it's quick.' He was definitely alone. The reaction of the management is not recorded.

The poetry of such a man should confuse. In fact, it has powerful simplicity. It is his pursuit of truth that gives his poetry its moral tone. His poems sound a warning bell. As they summon us to undo 'the folded lie, / The romantic lie in the brain / Of the sensual man-in-the-street' they also remind us: 'We must love one another or die.'

The Poems

'When I find myself in the company of scientists, I feel like a shabby curate who has strayed by mistake into a drawing room full of dukes.' Not the hierarchical position most poets award themselves. However, in these poems, Auden, the man who'd initially read Natural Sciences at university (before switching to English) and whose father was a doctor, uses language forensically and to the same purpose as the scientist: the revelation of truth. This pursuit is not necessarily driven by a Keatsian belief that 'Beauty is truth, truth beauty', rather more by conviction that we must bear witness to what is real. Heaney describes his poetry as 'magnificently sane'.

In 'Musée des Beaux Arts', the ship in Breughel's painting *Icarus* witnessed the fall, 'the white legs disappearing into the green / Water', yet 'sailed calmly on'. 'The dreadful martyrdom must run its course' while we are 'eating or opening a window or just walking dully along'. Perhaps down Bristol Street, with the clocks chiming out 'You cannot conquer Time' as they do in 'As I Walked Out One Evening'. The poet reminds us 'In headaches and in worry / Vaguely life leaks away, / And Time will have his fancy / To-morrow or to-day.' Less *carpe diem* than acceptance that 'Life remains a blessing / Although you cannot bless.' And, even tougher, 'You shall love your crooked neighbour / With your crooked heart.' Philip Larkin noted the genius that allowed Auden to convey 'the inimitable Thirties fear, the sense that something was going to fall like rain' and, he added, 'The poetry is in the blaming and warning.' In 'September 1, 1939' the warning couldn't be clearer: 'I and the public know / What all schoolchildren learn, / Those to whom evil is done / Do evil in return.'

In 'Song of the Devil' contempt for man's ego and vanity drips from every mocking phrase. Three further poems are gentler but never soft. It's not his style. Of 'O Tell Me the Truth About Love' Auden said, 'For me, personally, it was a very important poem. It's amazing how prophetic these things can be, because it was just after that that I met the person who did really change things for me completely.' (Enter Chester Kallman, bearing the gifts of beauty and, as a gifted librettist, brilliance.) In 'The Love Feast', Saint Augustine's cry of 'Give me chastity ... but not yet' echoes in 'an upper room at midnight' as the narrator spots 'Miss Number in the corner / Playing hard to get'.

Auden writes, 'If I Could Tell You', but he doesn't. He can't. The reason? Love ... In the poem 'In Memory of W. B. Yeats', Auden writes of his fellow poet whom 'Mad Ireland hurt ... into poetry', and who 'disappeared in the dead of winter: ... What instruments we have agree / The day of his death was a dark cold day.' Another line from the poem is equally appropriate to Auden. His 'gift survived it all'.

Musée des Beaux Arts

About suffering they were never wrong,
The Old Masters: how well they understood
Its human position; how it takes place
While someone else is eating or opening a window or just walking
    dully along;
How, when the aged are reverently, passionately waiting
For the miraculous birth, there always must be
Children who did not specially want it to happen, skating
On a pond at the edge of the wood:
They never forgot
That even the dreadful martyrdom must run its course
Anyhow in a corner, some untidy spot
Where the dogs go on with their doggy life and the torturer's horse
Scratches its innocent behind on a tree.

In Breughel's *Icarus*, for instance: how everything turns away
Quite leisurely from the disaster; the ploughman may
Have heard the splash, the forsaken cry,
But for him it was not an important failure; the sun shone
As it had to on the white legs disappearing into the green
Water; and the expensive delicate ship that must have seen
Something amazing, a boy falling out of the sky,
Had somewhere to get to and sailed calmly on.

In Memory of W. B. Yeats

(d. January 1939)

I

He disappeared in the dead of winter:
The brooks were frozen, the airports almost deserted,
And snow disfigured the public statues;
The mercury sank in the mouth of the dying day.
What instruments we have agree
The day of his death was a dark cold day.

Far from his illness
The wolves ran on through the evergreen forests,
The peasant river was untempted by the fashionable quays;
By mourning tongues
The death of the poet was kept from his poems.

But for him it was his last afternoon as himself,
An afternoon of nurses and rumours;
The provinces of his body revolted,
The squares of his mind were empty,
Silence invaded the suburbs,
The current of his feeling failed: he became his admirers.

Now he is scattered among a hundred cities
And wholly given over to unfamiliar affections,
To find his happiness in another kind of wood
And be punished under a foreign code of conscience.

The words of a dead man
Are modified in the guts of the living.

But in the importance and noise of to-morrow
When the brokers are roaring like beasts on the floor of the Bourse,
And the poor have the sufferings to which they are fairly accustomed,
And each in the cell of himself is almost convinced of his freedom,
A few thousand will think of this day
As one thinks of a day when one did something slightly unusual.

What instruments we have agree
The day of his death was a dark cold day.

II
You were silly like us: your gift survived it all:
The parish of rich women, physical decay,
Yourself. Mad Ireland hurt you into poetry.
Now Ireland has her madness and her weather still,
For poetry makes nothing happen: it survives
In the valley of its saying where executives
Would never want to tamper, flows on south
From ranches of isolation and the busy griefs,
Raw towns that we believe and die in; it survives,
A way of happening, a mouth.

III
Earth, receive an honoured guest:
William Yeats is laid to rest.
Let the Irish vessel lie
Emptied of its poetry.

In the nightmare of the dark
All the dogs of Europe bark,
And the living nations wait,
Each sequestered in its hate;

Intellectual disgrace
Stares from every human face,
And the seas of pity lie
Locked and frozen in each eye.

Follow, poet, follow right
To the bottom of the night,
With your unconstraining voice
Still persuade us to rejoice;

With the farming of a verse
Make a vineyard of the curse,
Sing of human unsuccess
In a rapture of distress;

In the deserts of the heart
Let the healing fountain start,
In the prison of his days
Teach the free man how to praise.

ELIZABETH BISHOP

Elizabeth Bishop was born in Massachusetts in 1911. Her four short collections, *North and South* (1946), *A Cold Spring* (1955), *Questions of Travel* (1965) and *Geography III* (1976), won many literary awards including the National Book Critics Circle Award, the National Book Award and the Pulitzer Prize. She died in 1979.

ELIZABETH BISHOP

She came. She saw.
She changed the view.

'Everything has written under it – I have seen it.' Randall Jarrell is right. However, *what* Elizabeth Bishop saw was never quite what the rest of us see, nor indeed was it *how* we see it. And she knew it. She challenges us to look again. Her declared intention to combine 'the natural with the unnatural' gave us poetry as 'normal as sight ... as artificial as a glass eye'. Well! It's hardly surprising that it takes us some time to adjust to the view. The landscape is unfamiliar. The temperature is arctic and is therefore less than seductive. However, deep treasure lies within the extreme geography of Elizabeth Bishop's 'ice writing'. She gifts us what few other poets ever have, a strange, exact hallucination of 'the always more successful surrealism of every-day life'. It is thus – after the necessary period of adjustment – that she becomes not just compelling but addictive. She is the poetic equivalent of a Dalí or de Chirico. Like them, she disturbs the universe and our limited perception of it. We are indeed 'far away within the view', longing to understand, if a little nervous of revelation. In 'Love Lies Sleeping' she word-paints, perhaps, inert terror in her portrait of the man ... 'whose head has fallen over the edge of his bed, / whose face is turned / so that the image of / the city grows down into his open eyes / inverted and distorted. No. I mean / distorted and revealed, / if he sees it at all.' Is he, eyes wide open, in some hypnotised dream-state, a state she declared vital to the creation of her poetry? Is he dead? Miss Bishop herself is less than certain. She is the poet of question marks and when she answers it is rarely reassuring. 'I *think* [my italics] the man at the end is dead,' she told a rather startled Anne Stevenson. She'd been reading Newton's *Opticks* during the writing of the poem – 'Reflections, Refractions . . . and Colours of Light' were as much her obsession as the subject of his masterpiece. (Is Bishop uniquely the only poet to have worked grinding binoculars at a US Navy shop?) Newton, whose work of discovery inspired eighteenth-century poets, is not normally a presiding figure in twentieth-century poetry. Nor indeed is Darwin, whose continued literary influence lies more within fiction. Bishop, the poet of vision, deeply admired his 'heroic observations . . . his eyes fixed on facts and minute details, sinking or sliding giddily off into the unknown' and they became scientific inspiration to her own poetic discoveries. Though Elizabeth Bishop's four small collections, *North and South*, *A Cold Spring*, *Questions of Travel* and *Geography III*, would in time win many awards, including the National Book Award and the Pulitzer Prize, the first was, in 1940, firmly turned down by Random House, Viking and Simon and Schuster. It was finally published by Harcourt Brace in 1947. Originality comes at a price. James Merrill famously commented on her 'instinctive, modest, lifelong impersonation of an ordinary woman'. Perhaps she felt she needed the disguise. Her beginnings were traumatic. 'Although I think I have a prize "unhappy childhood" almost good enough for text-books – please don't think I dote on it.' She didn't. That does not mean she ever escaped it either. Her need for 'mastery', which Bonnie Costello sees as an 'urge for order and dominance confronting a volatile inner life', is wholly understandable. She was born on 8 February 1911 in Worcester, Massachusetts, to William T. Bishop and Gertrude Bulmer [Boomer] Bishop. Her father died, aged thirty-nine, in October of that same year. Mother and child moved to Boston, and then to the charmingly named Great Village, Nova Scotia, in Canada, where Elizabeth's young life was, sadly, less than charmed.

In 1916 when she was five, her mother, after a series of nervous breakdowns, was admitted to a state mental institution. Though Gertrude Bishop did not die until 1934, Elizabeth never saw her again. She was eventually returned to live with her mother's sister in Boston. Much was lost and far too early. In 'One Art' she notes that 'things seem filled with the intent / to be lost' and, with admirable, defiant courage, 'The art of losing isn't hard to master.' It wasn't easy either. Her adult life was one of often alcohol-fuelled departures, both emotional and geographical. The poetry survived it all. She started writing at Vassar, the exclusive women's college in New York, where she befriended Mary McCarthy, whose novel *The Group* would profile her classmates. There remains considerable controversy as to whether the lesbian Lakey, played in the film by the ethereally beautiful Candice Bergen, was based on Bishop. Though Elizabeth Bishop had six intense, sometimes concurrent, often tumultuous lesbian love affairs (one with Brazilian aristocrat Lota de Maceda Soares that lasted, on and off, for decades) love is not really her subject. Loss, deep-rooted in her personal history, and a subdued though multi-layered pattern of essential distancing, haunts her work. Her compulsive travelling inspires her poetic eloquence of elective rootlessness. But despite telling Randall Jarrell that 'Exile seems to work for me' she remained uncertain of its purpose. 'Is it lack of imagination that makes us come / to imagined places, not just stay at home? / Or could Pascal have been not entirely right / about just sitting quietly in one's room? ... Should we have stayed at home, / wherever that may be?' From whichever perspective, in real or imagined landscapes, Bishop contains their discovery, and loss, within an ever-steely elegance of vision. 'I lost my mother's watch. And look! my last, or / next-to-last, of three loved houses went ... I miss them, but it wasn't a disaster.' In truth the abyss was closer than she allowed. Though she was never, in the Lowell sense, a confessional poet (and profoundly disagreed with her old friend over what she saw as the cruel intimacy of 'Dolphin'), in her own later poems, particularly in her prize-winning collection *Geography III*, she returned – a poetic Livingstone – to the source. 'In the Waiting Room', itself a provocative title, is a masterpiece of existential terror. As the seven-year-old Elizabeth sits quietly reading *National Geographic*: 'Suddenly, from inside, / came an *oh!* of pain / – Aunt Consuelo's voice – ... What took me / completely by surprise / was that it was *me*: / my voice, in my mouth ... I knew that nothing stranger / had ever happened, that nothing / stranger could ever happen.' She was ill and in her sixty-sixth year when this poem was published. Baudelaire is right, 'genius is nothing more than childhood recovered at will'. Elizabeth Bishop, whose work Marianne Moore described as 'beautifully formulated aesthetic-moral mathematics', died in 1979 of a cerebral aneurysm. She asked that 'Awful, but cheerful' should be inscribed on her tombstone. Which changes the view. Again. The secondary characteristic of the glass eye is its incapacity for tears. Which leaves us with language – if we can find the words.

The Poems

She once said, 'we are driving to the interior'. One has been put on high alert. Perhaps, like 'The Gentleman of Shalott', we find the uncertainty exhilarating. After all, he 'loves that sense of constant readjustment'. Eliot, as C. K. Stead brilliantly observed, used his 'nerves' in 'Prufrock'. Bishop's is also an art of the nerves, in her case optic. 'Love Lies Sleeping' does not denote repose. As dawn comes we must 'clear away what presses on the brain' as 'the day-springs of the morning strike ... alarms for the expected'. No going back to sleep, then.

Le Roy, in 'Songs for a Colored Singer', probably sleeps soundly. Though his woman wonders 'Le Roy, just how much are we owing? / Something I can't comprehend, / the more we got the more we spend.' An eternal mystery and not just in the Le Roy household. Well, 'life's like that', a line from 'The Moose' (twenty years to complete – 'revise, revise, revise', a trait noted by her friend, the arch-reviser himself, Lowell), and it is sometimes in opposition to Art, compelling us to choose. Would we, as she insists in 'The Imaginary Iceberg', 'rather have the iceberg than the ship, / although it meant the end of travel'? Art, like icebergs, which 'behoove the soul', is part-hidden, 'self-made from elements least visible', and is often dangerous to the ship of life, being as it is an obsession.

'Crusoe in England' knows obsession, knows it well and also knows its price. He remembers the moment: 'Just when I thought I couldn't stand it / another minute longer, Friday came.' Perfect. This blindingly brilliant poem was inspired by Darwin, about whose obsession Bishop wrote, 'What one seems to want in art, in experiencing it, is the same thing necessary for its creation, a self-forgetting, perfectly useless concentration.' Defoe was also self-forgetting, publishing his masterpiece as being that of an anonymous survivor of a shipwreck. He knew we'd find him out.

Bishop's Larkin-like genius for the sense of place – often most powerful in those who fear displacement – is again clear in 'Filling Station': 'Oh, but it is dirty!' Attention. 'Be careful with that match!' And in that line she's got us. Beyond the dirt and possible danger, she notes with heartbreaking accuracy, 'Somebody embroidered the doily.' And continues her enumeration of small graces in unexpected places: 'Somebody / arranges the rows of cans / so that they softly say: ESSO–SO–SO–SO / to high-strung automobiles.' She ends with an almost casual elegy: 'Somebody loves us all.'

'One Art' and 'In the Waiting Room' are late poems. They afford us no place to hide. 'Lose something every day . . . – Even losing you (the joking voice, a gesture / I love) I shan't have lied. It's evident / the art of losing's not too hard to master / though it may look like (*Write* it!) like disaster.' It's lines like that that make one, initially a reluctant convert, tremble. The congregation grows larger day by day; one notes in pews marked 'reserved' a Nobel Laureate, Heaney; a Poet Laureate, Motion; Fenton, winner of the Queen's Medal for Poetry. It's perfectly possible that Elizabeth Bishop, who avoided myth and grand statements but who found 'In the Waiting Room' one of literature's most frightening, and frightened, voices – that of the terrified child – is one of the greatest poets of the twentieth century. And that is perhaps what frightens us: in our own blindness we might have missed her.

Songs for a Colored Singer

I
A washing hangs upon the line,
    but it's not mine.
None of the things that I can see
    belong to me.
The neighbors got a radio with an aerial;
    we got a little portable.
They got a lot of closet space;
    we got a suitcase.

I say, 'Le Roy, just how much are we owing?
Something I can't comprehend,
the more we got the more we spend . . .'
He only answers, 'Let's get going.'
Le Roy, you're earning too much money now.

I sit and look at our backyard
    and find it very hard.
What have we got for all his dollars and cents?
    —A pile of bottles by the fence.
He's faithful and he's kind
    but he sure has an inquiring mind.
He's seen a lot; he's bound to see the rest,
    and if I protest

Le Roy answers with a frown,
'Darling, when I earns I spends.
The world is wide; it still extends . . .
I'm going to get a job in the next town.'
Le Roy, you're earning too much money now.

II

The time has come to call a halt;
     and so it ends.
He's gone off with his other friends.
He needn't try to make amends,
     this occasion's all his fault.
Through rain and dark I see his face
     across the street at Flossie's place.
He's drinking in the warm pink glow
     to th' accompaniment of the piccolo.*

The time has come to call a halt.
I met him walking with Varella
and hit him twice with my umbrella.
Perhaps that occasion was my fault,
but the time has come to call a halt.

Go drink your wine and go get tight.
     Let the piccolo play.
     I'm sick of all your fussing anyway.
     Now I'm pursuing my own way.
I'm leaving on the bus tonight.
     Far down the highway wet and black
     I'll ride and ride and not come back.
     I'm going to go and take the bus
     and find someone monogamous.

The time has come to call a halt.
I've borrowed fifteen dollars fare
and it will take me anywhere.
For this occasion's all his fault.
The time has come to call a halt.

*   Jukebox

Filling Station

Oh, but it is dirty!
—this little filling station,
oil-soaked, oil-permeated
to a disturbing, over-all
black translucency.
Be careful with that match!

Father wears a dirty,
oil-soaked monkey suit
that cuts him under the arms,
and several quick and saucy
and greasy sons assist him
(it's a family filling station),
all quite thoroughly dirty.

Do they live in the station?
It has a cement porch
behind the pumps, and on it
a set of crushed and grease-
impregnated wickerwork;
on the wicker sofa
a dirty dog, quite comfy.

Some comic books provide
the only note of color—
of certain color. They lie
upon a big dim doily

draping a taboret
(part of the set),
beside a big hirsute begonia.

Why the extraneous plant?
Why the taboret?
Why, oh why, the doily?
(Embroidered in daisy stitch
with marguerites, I think,
and heavy with gray crochet.)

Somebody embroidered the doily.
Somebody waters the plant,
or oils it, maybe. Somebody
arranges the rows of cans
so that they softly say:
ESSO—SO—SO—SO
to high-strung automobiles.
Somebody loves us all.

ROBERT BROWNING

Robert Browning was born in London in 1812. He achieved fame late in life with *The Ring and the Book* (1868/69). His earlier works – *Dramatic Lyrics* (1842), *Men and Women* (1855) and *Dramatis Personae* (1864) – testify to his mastery of the dramatic monologue; many of the poems are recognised as enduring works of genius. He was married to the poet Elizabeth Barrett Browning. He died in 1889.

ROBERT BROWNING

The Company He Kept . . .

'Within his work lies the mystery which belongs to the complex and within his life the much greater mystery which belongs to the simple.' G. K. Chesterton, his biographer.

Henry James, who noted everything, noted the essential doubleness in Browning. There are, he said, 'two Brownings – an esoteric and an exoteric. The former never peeps out in society, and the latter has not a suggestion of *Men and Women*.' 'The esoteric' sought his own company. Characters who lived 'on the dangerous edge of things. / The honest thief, the tender murderer, / The superstitious atheist'. They echo Nietzsche's 'pale criminal' and prefigure Freud's criminal 'from a sense of guilt – the utilisation of a deed in order to rationalise this feeling'. His characters, his Dramatis Personae, his Men and Women speak out to us in all their moral complexity in some of the greatest monologues in English literature: 'My Last Duchess', 'Porphyria's Lover', 'Bishop Blougram's Apology', 'Fra Lippo Lippi' ('You understand me: I'm a beast, I know'), 'Rabbi Ben Ezra', 'Karshish', 'Andrea del Sarto'. Their souls are revealed, unvarnished. 'Little else,' he said, 'was worth study.' Oscar Wilde said of Robert Browning (who would also write glorious love poetry and the ultimate hymn to nature, *Pippa Passes*: 'God's in his heaven – All's right with the world') that 'considered from a point of view of creator of character [Browning] ranks next to him who made Hamlet'.

He was born in Camberwell, London, into a harmonious and

intellectual household on 7 May 1812 (the same year as Dickens: they are, according to Harold Bloom, the two great masters of the grotesque) to Sarah Anna Browning and Robert Browning Snr, a banker in the Bank of England, himself an aspiring poet with a passionate love of books, avidly collecting first editions.

Browning was educated mostly at home, learning music, languages, science, and – *mens sana in corpore sano* – boxing, fencing and riding, while, crucially, devouring everything in his father's magnificent library. This habit of intensive reading 'while it gave him knowledge of everything else left him in ignorance of the ignorance of the world', in Chesterton's telling phrase. In his early teenage years Shelley became an obsession and though he would later attempt to erase his manic scribbles in the margins of his treasured copy, he would also recall 'the passionate impatient struggles of a boy towards truth and love ... growing pains accompanied by temporary distortion of the soul also', which his initial reading of *Queen Mab* inspired. There was nothing temporary about Browning's decision, aged eighteen, to become a poet and nothing else. His parents supported him in what must have been a less than reassuring career choice, however noble the vocation of poet would have seemed to Browning's father, whom Edmund Gosse believed saw in his son the realisation of his own thwarted ambition. There was a small allowance, Browning had 'the singular courage to decline to be rich' (though he would later change his mind!). These things are relative. 'My whole scheme of life,' Browning wrote, 'with its wants – material wants at least – was closely cut down and long ago calculated ... So for my own future way in the world I have always refused to care ...' That took self-belief. He needed it. Success came slowly, very slowly. In 1832, aged twenty, he published *Pauline*. Ten thousand words, some excellent reviews – but many were hostile, and alas, not a single copy was sold. Three years later *Paracelsus* (1835) brought him favourable attention from Carlyle and Wordsworth, and a comparison (from Fox) with Shelley. However it was not a major success. Ten years later he would recall those who 'laughed my Paracelsus to scorn'. Worse was to come. 'Sordello', published in 1840, took him seven years to write and though it became a cult text for the Pre-Raphaelites it was savaged by the critics. He was almost thirty and almost finished. Two years later in 1842 *Dramatic Lyrics*, which includes some of his best work, went largely unnoticed. He continued to write, but he would be middle-aged before he achieved the success he deserved, with the publication of *The Ring and the Book*. This success came shortly after the death of his wife, one of England's most revered poets, Elizabeth Barrett Browning. He was married to her for sixteen years. Her star shone so high in the firmament that when Wordsworth died her name was canvassed as Poet Laureate, while his was not mentioned, 'even satirically'. 'I love your verses with all my heart,' he wrote to her in January 1845, months after she'd published *Poems 1844* to enormous critical acclaim. She read on and halfway down the second page she read the astonishing declaration 'and I love you too'. Their story is well known: 547 letters, then secret meetings which finally led to an elopement and then flight to Italy. His invalided wife defied her deeply strange and controlling father to take her chances (which would include late motherhood) with the love of her life. 'Determined, dared, and done', one of his favourite lines from an eighteenth-century poem (Christopher Smart's 'A Song to David'), and which is quoted in a more sinister context in *The Ring and the Book*, applied to her as much as to him. The love poems did not come into being as mysteriously as the dramatic monologues did. They were open celebrations of their deep love and in his case this love came from an uncommonly capacious heart. He never resented her glory. *Men and Women* is dedicated to her with the words 'Here they are – my fifty men and women / Take them, Love / the book and me together: / Where the heart lies, let the brain lie also.' In 'Love Among the Ruins' he sets the whole panoply of heroic endeavour and monuments to ambition beside the human joy of an arranged meeting with the love of one's life and declares 'Love is best.' He meant it.

After Elizabeth's death Robert Browning's output continued to be prodigious and, at last, he was revered. 'Do you object to all this adulation?' he was asked once when surrounded by admirers. 'Object to it? I've waited forty years for it!' He died in 1889 aged seventy-seven from a heart condition, appropriately shortly after his son read out a telegram from his publisher to say that *Asolando* had received excellent reviews. He was satisfied. He was buried at Westminster Abbey, an occasion of which Henry James wrote, 'A good many oddities and a good many great writers have been entombed in the Abbey but none of the odd ones have been so great and none of the great ones have been so odd.'

The Poems

He was, said Chesterton, 'the poet of desire'. John Bayley agrees. Indeed, Bayley believes that even Proust, had he come across it, would have been 'enchanted ... by the astonishing concentration of desire' in Browning's 'Meeting at Night'. The 'desire' in that poem resolves itself delightfully in Blakeian satisfaction. However, as Browning knew, desire can be perverted. He understood 'the Corruption of Man's Heart'. In his sinister masterpiece 'My Last Duchess' and in 'Porphyria's Lover', each narrator is a cold-blooded murderer. The cliché 'cold-blooded' understates the case. They are icy in their cruelty. They are unforgettable.

The poet, according to C. Day Lewis, 'listens in to his universe'. Another memorable voice in Browning's auditory universe is that of Andrea del Sarto – 'the Faultless Painter'. His *Madonna of the Harpies* hangs in the Uffizi Gallery in Florence, in a room dedicated to his work. As Browning ponders in this monologue whether faultlessness is in itself a fault in art he muses also on the price of love. Love, Vasari implies in *Lives of the Painters*, cost del Sarto his position at the French court. Del Sarto, on receipt of a letter from his wife Lucrezia, speedily left the court. Did she hint at infidelity? Hers? We do not know. Neither do we know who the 'cousin' is who waits for her, as del Sarto paints. The tension between love and art is examined by Browning in this wondrous masterpiece, a subtle web of questions to which the answers may be dangerous.

'The Lost Leader' is not subtle. Browning came to regret the ferocity of his condemnation of political betrayal, in this case of Wordsworth, who'd abandoned the Liberal cause. However, as a poem of disillusionment with a hero, it is lacerating. 'Just for a handful of silver he left us / Just for a riband to stick in his coat.' 'The Patriot', with its equally memorable opening line, 'It was roses, roses, all the way', tells of the savage reversal of fortune which can change today's hero into the criminal on his way to the gallows. It's an old story and an old warning. 'Memorabilia' catches beautifully the poet's delight as he looks in wonderment at the man who may once have seen 'Shelley plain'. Heroism, this time of the horse (Browning was an animal lover and a member of the Anti-Vivisection Society), triumphs in the galloping 'How They Brought the Good News from Ghent to Aix', its technically dazzling rhythms reminiscent of Auden's 'Night Train'. Browning once wrote, 'Grow old along with me! / The best is yet to be.' His beloved Elizabeth did not grow old with him. However in one of his last poems, 'Prospice', he challenges death and proclaims, 'For sudden the worst turns the best to the brave ... Then a light, then thy breast, / O thou soul of my soul! I shall clasp thee again, / And with God be the rest!' One hopes.

My Last Duchess

Ferrara

That's my last Duchess painted on the wall,
Looking as if she were alive. I call
That piece a wonder, now: Frà Pandolf's hands
Worked busily a day, and there she stands.
Will't please you sit and look at her? I said
'Frà Pandolf' by design, for never read
Strangers like you that pictured countenance,
The depth and passion of its earnest glance,
But to myself they turned (since none puts by
The curtain I have drawn for you, but I)
And seemed as they would ask me, if they durst,
How such a glance came there; so, not the first
Are you to turn and ask thus. Sir, 'twas not
Her husband's presence only, called that spot
Of joy into the Duchess' cheek: perhaps
Frà Pandolf chanced to say 'Her mantle laps
Over my lady's wrist too much,' or 'Paint
Must never hope to reproduce the faint
Half-flush that dies along her throat': such stuff
Was courtesy, she thought, and cause enough
For calling up that spot of joy. She had
A heart – how shall I say? – too soon made glad,
Too easily impressed; she liked whate'er
She looked on, and her looks went everywhere.
Sir, 'twas all one! My favour at her breast,

LIFE SAVING

The dropping of the daylight in the West,
The bough of cherries some officious fool
Broke in the orchard for her, the white mule
She rode with round the terrace – all and each
Would draw from her alike the approving speech,
Or blush, at least. She thanked men, – good! but thanked
Somehow – I know not how – as if she ranked
My gift of a nine-hundred-years-old name
With anybody's gift. Who'd stoop to blame
This sort of trifling? Even had you skill
In speech – (which I have not) – to make your will
Quite clear to such an one, and say, 'Just this
Or that in you disgusts me; here you miss,
Or there exceed the mark' – and if she let
Herself be lessoned so, nor plainly set
Her wits to yours, forsooth, and made excuse,
– E'en then would be some stooping; and I choose
Never to stoop. Oh sir, she smiled, no doubt,
Whene'er I passed her; but who passed without
Much the same smile? This grew; I gave commands;
Then all smiles stopped together. There she stands
As if alive. Will't please you rise? We'll meet
The company below, then. I repeat,
The Count your master's known munificence
Is ample warrant that no just pretence
Of mine for dowry will be disallowed;
Though his fair daughter's self, as I avowed
At starting, is my object. Nay, we'll go
Together down, sir. Notice Neptune, though,
Taming a sea-horse, thought a rarity,
Which Claus of Innsbruck cast in bronze for me!

Andrea del Sarto

(Called 'The Faultless Painter')

But do not let us quarrel any more,
No, my Lucrezia; bear with me for once:
Sit down and all shall happen as you wish.
You turn your face, but does it bring your heart?
I'll work then for your friend's friend, never fear,
Treat his own subject after his own way,
Fix his own time, accept too his own price,
And shut the money into this small hand
When next it takes mine. Will it? tenderly?
Oh, I'll content him, – but tomorrow, Love!
I often am much wearier than you think,
This evening more than usual, and it seems
As if – forgive now – should you let me sit
Here by the window with your hand in mine
And look a half-hour forth on Fiesole,
Both of one mind, as married people use,
Quietly, quietly the evening through,
I might get up tomorrow to my work
Cheerful and fresh as ever. Let us try.
Tomorrow, how you shall be glad for this!
Your soft hand is a woman of itself,
And mine the man's bared breast she curls inside.
Don't count the time lost, neither; you must serve
For each of the five pictures we require:
It saves a model. So! keep looking so –

My serpentining beauty, rounds on rounds!
– How could you ever prick those perfect ears,
Even to put the pearl there! oh, so sweet –
My face, my moon, my everybody's moon,
Which everybody looks on and calls his,
And, I suppose, is looked on by in turn,
While she looks – no one's: very dear, no less.
You smile? why, there's my picture ready made,
There's what we painters call our harmony!
A common greyness silvers everything, –
All in a twilight, you and I alike
– You, at the point of your first pride in me
(That's gone you know), – but I, at every point;
My youth, my hope, my art, being all toned down
To yonder sober pleasant Fiesole.
There's the bell clinking from the chapel-top;
That length of convent-wall across the way
Holds the trees safer, huddled more inside;
The last monk leaves the garden; days decrease,
And autumn grows, autumn in everything.
Eh? the whole seems to fall into a shape
As if I saw alike my work and self
And all that I was born to be and do,
A twilight-piece. Love, we are in God's hand.
How strange now, looks the life he makes us lead;
So free we seem, so fettered fast we are!
I feel he laid the fetter: let it lie!
This chamber for example – turn your head –
All that's behind us! You don't understand
Nor care to understand about my art,
But you can hear at least when people speak:
And that cartoon, the second from the door
– It is the thing, Love! so such things should be –

Behold Madonna! – I am bold to say.
I can do with my pencil what I know,
What I see, what at bottom of my heart
I wish for, if I ever wish so deep –
Do easily, too – when I say, perfectly,
I do not boast, perhaps: yourself are judge,
Who listened to the Legate's talk last week,
And just as much they used to say in France.
At any rate 'tis easy, all of it!
No sketches first, no studies, that's long past:
I do what many dream of, all their lives,
– Dream? strive to do, and agonize to do,
And fail in doing. I could count twenty such
On twice your fingers, and not leave this town,
Who strive – you don't know how the others strive
To paint a little thing like that you smeared
Carelessly passing with your robes afloat, –
Yet do much less, so much less, Someone says,
(I know his name, no matter) – so much less!
Well, less is more, Lucrezia: I am judged.
There burns a truer light of God in them,
In their vexed beating stuffed and stopped-up brain,
Heart, or whate'er else, than goes on to prompt
This low-pulsed forthright craftsman's hand of mine.
Their works drop groundward, but themselves, I know,
Reach many a time a heaven that's shut to me,
Enter and take their place there sure enough,
Though they come back and cannot tell the world.
My works are nearer heaven, but I sit here.
The sudden blood of these men! at a word –
Praise them, it boils, or blame them, it boils too.
I, painting from myself and to myself,
Know what I do, am unmoved by men's blame

Or their praise either. Somebody remarks
Morello's outline there is wrongly traced,
His hue mistaken; what of that? or else,
Rightly traced and well ordered; what of that?
Speak as they please, what does the mountain care?
Ah, but a man's reach should exceed his grasp,
Or what's a heaven for? All is silver-grey
Placid and perfect with my art: the worse!
I know both what I want and what might gain,
And yet how profitless to know, to sigh
'Had I been two, another and myself,
Our head would have o'erlooked the world!' No doubt.
Yonder's a work now, of that famous youth
The Urbinate who died five years ago.
('Tis copied, George Vasari sent it me.)
Well, I can fancy how he did it all,
Pouring his soul, with kings and popes to see,
Reaching, that heaven might so replenish him,
Above and through his art – for it gives way;
That arm is wrongly put – and there again –
A fault to pardon in the drawing's lines,
Its body, so to speak: its soul is right,
He means right – that, a child may understand.
Still, what an arm! and I could alter it:
But all the play, the insight and the stretch –
Out of me, out of me! And wherefore out?
Had you enjoined them on me, given me soul,
We might have risen to Rafael, I and you!
Nay, Love, you did give all I asked, I think –
More than I merit, yes, by many times.
But had you – oh, with the same perfect brow,
And perfect eyes, and more than perfect mouth,
And the low voice my soul hears, as a bird

The fowler's pipe, and follows to the snare –
Had you, with these the same, but brought a mind!
Some women do so. Had the mouth there urged
'God and the glory! never care for gain.
The present by the future, what is that?
Live for fame, side by side with Agnolo!
Rafael is waiting: up to God, all three!'
I might have done it for you. So it seems:
Perhaps not. All is as God over-rules.
Beside, incentives come from the soul's self;
The rest avail not. Why do I need you?
What wife had Rafael, or has Agnolo?
In this world, who can do a thing, will not;
And who would do it, cannot, I perceive:
Yet the will's somewhat – somewhat, too, the power –
And thus we half-men struggle. At the end,
God, I conclude, compensates, punishes.
'Tis safer for me, if the award be strict,
That I am something underrated here,
Poor this long while, despised, to speak the truth.
I dared not, do you know, leave home all day,
For fear of chancing on the Paris lords
The best is when they pass and look aside;
But they speak sometimes; I must bear it all.
Well may they speak! That Francis, that first time,
And that long festal year at Fontainebleau!
I surely then could sometimes leave the ground,
Put on the glory, Rafael's daily wear,
In that humane great monarch's golden look, –
One finger in his beard or twisted curl
Over his mouth's good mark that made the smile,
One arm about my shoulder, round my neck,
The jingle of his gold chain in my ear,

I painting proudly with his breath on me,
All his court round him, seeing with his eyes,
Such frank French eyes, and such a fire of souls
Profuse, my hand kept plying by those hearts, –
And, best of all, this, this, this face beyond,
This in the background, waiting on my work,
To crown the issue with a last reward!
A good time, was it not, my kingly days?
And had you not grown restless . . . but I know –
'Tis done and past; 'twas right, my instinct said;
Too live the life grew, golden and not grey,
And I'm the weak-eyed bat no sun should tempt
Out of the grange whose four walls make his world.
How could it end in any other way?
You called me, and I came home to your heart.
The triumph was – to reach and stay there; since
I reached it ere the triumph, what is lost?
Let my hands frame your face in your hair's gold,
You beautiful Lucrezia that are mine!
'Rafael did this, Andrea painted that;
The Roman's is the better when you pray,
But still the other's Virgin was his wife –'
Men will excuse me. I am glad to judge
Both pictures in your presence; clearer grows
My better fortune, I resolve to think.
For, do you know, Lucrezia, as God lives,
Said one day Agnolo, his very self,
To Rafael . . . I have known it all these years . . .
(When the young man was flaming out his thoughts
Upon a palace-wall for Rome to see,
Too lifted up in heart because of it)
'Friend, there's a certain sorry little scrub
Goes up and down our Florence, none cares how,

Who, were he set to plan and execute
As you are, pricked on by your popes and kings,
Would bring the sweat into that brow of yours!'
To Rafael's! – and indeed the arm is wrong.
I hardly dare ... yet, only you to see,
Give the chalk here – quick, thus the line should go!
Ay, but the soul! he's Rafael! rub it out!
Still, all I care for, if he spoke the truth,
(What he? why, who but Michel Agnolo?
Do you forget already words like those?)
If really there was such a chance, so lost, –
Is, whether you're – not grateful – but more pleased.
Well, let me think so. And you smile indeed!
This hour has been an hour! Another smile?
If you would sit thus by me every night
I should work better, do you comprehend?
I mean that I should earn more, give you more.
See, it is settled dusk now; there's a star;
Morello's gone, the watch-lights show the wall,
The cue-owls speak the name we call them by.
Come from the window, love, – come in, at last,
Inside the melancholy little house
We built to be so gay with. God is just.
King Francis may forgive me: oft at nights
When I look up from painting, eyes tired out,
The walls become illumined, brick from brick
Distinct, instead of mortar, fierce bright gold,
That gold of his I did cement them with!
Let us but love each other. Must you go?
That Cousin here again? he waits outside?
Must see you – you, and not with me? Those loans?
More gaming debts to pay? you smiled for that?
Well, let smiles buy me! have you more to spend?

While hand and eye and something of a heart
Are left me, work's my ware, and what's it worth?
I'll pay my fancy. Only let me sit
The grey remainder of the evening out,
Idle, you call it, and muse perfectly
How I could paint, were I but back in France,
One picture, just one more – the Virgin's face,
Not yours this time! I want you at my side
To hear them – that is, Michel Agnolo –
Judge all I do and tell you of its worth.
Will you? Tomorrow, satisfy your friend.
I take the subjects for his corridor,
Finish the portrait out of hand – there, there,
And throw him in another thing or two
If he demurs; the whole should prove enough
To pay for this same Cousin's freak. Beside,
What's better and what's all I care about,
Get you the thirteen scudi for the ruff!
Love, does that please you? Ah, but what does he,
The Cousin! what does he to please you more?

I am grown peaceful as old age tonight.
I regret little, I would change still less.
Since there my past life lies, why alter it?
The very wrong to Francis! – it is true
I took his coin, was tempted and complied,
And built this house and sinned, and all is said.
My father and my mother died of want.
Well, had I riches of my own? you see
How one gets rich! Let each one bear his lot.
They were born poor, lived poor, and poor they died:
And I have laboured somewhat in my time
And not been paid profusely. Some good son

Paint my two hundred pictures – let him try!
No doubt, there's something strikes a balance. Yes,
You loved me quite enough, it seems tonight.
This must suffice me here. What would one have?
In heaven, perhaps, new chances, one more chance –
Four great walls in the New Jerusalem,
Meted on each side by the angel's reed,
For Leonard, Rafael, Agnolo and me
To cover – the three first without a wife,
While I have mine! So – still they overcome
Because there's still Lucrezia, – as I choose.

Again the Cousin's whistle! Go, my Love.

LORD BYRON

George Gordon Byron, Lord Byron (he inherited the title at the age of ten) was born in London in 1788. A poet, playwright, essayist and campaigner for Liberal causes, he exerted a profound influence on Romanticism. His collection *Childe Harold's Pilgrimage*, the first cantos of which were published in 1812, brought him worldwide fame. His satirical and controversial masterpiece *Don Juan* was published in 1819. He died of fever at Missolonghi in 1824 during his campaign for Greek independence.

LORD BYRON

Not Laughing But Weeping

'I will cut a swathe through the world or perish in the attempt': Byron, aged sixteen. Well, he cut a swathe through the world and perished in the attempt. He died, one of the most celebrated poets in Europe and the most infamous in England, aged thirty-six, a hero and a soldier fighting for Greek independence. It was an act of remarkable courage and self-sacrifice. The historian Macaulay coupled Byron's name with the hero of his youth, Napoleon: 'Two men have died within our recollection, who had raised themselves, each in his own department, to the height of glory. One of them died at Longwood, the other at Missolonghi.' Carlyle considered Byron 'the noblest spirit in Europe' and also linked him with Napoleon. In Bertrand Russell's *History of Western Philosophy* Byron has a chapter all to himself. The Byronic myth, in which, as John Updike says, 'the poetry projected a Personality – a personality Napoleonic in its insatiability and capacity for ruinous defeat', was to inspire painters – Delacroix, musicians – Berlioz, writers – Pushkin, Nietzsche, Goethe (who, according to the American critic Harold Bloom, developed a kind of infatuation for Byron) and the Brontës, most particularly Emily. His arrival in the world, on the twenty-second of January 1788, was as dramatic as his departure. He was born with a caul over his head and talipes (a form of club foot) to the Laird of Gight, Scots heiress Catherine Gordon, and her husband Mad Jack Byron. Jack Byron, father of Byron's half-sister Augusta from his previous marriage, squandered two matrimonial fortunes and died three years after his marriage to Catherine, leaving her a financially embarrassed widow. Mother and child moved to Scotland and then back to England when Byron, at the age of ten, inherited the Gothic master-piece Newstead Abbey. But north or south they were not a happy pair. There were rumours of neglect and of possible abuse by his sinister nanny May Gray. Byron was an almost pathologically shy child and became a seriously overweight adolescent. At Harrow he was cruelly mocked for his limp due to the heavy iron brace he was forced to wear under his trousers. He fought back hard, according to school friend Robert Peel, eventual creator of the Metropolitan Police. Keats, Shelley and Lowell were also playground fighters. Poetry is not for sissies. There were homosexual affairs at school, though in the holidays chaste obsessions with Mary Chaworth and Margaret Parker disturbed his family with their intensity. Dante's belief that such emotional ardour in youth often indicates exceptional artistic gifts would seem to have been true in Byron's case. The lover and fighter were foreshadowed early.

So how did the shy, unhappy boy, the awkward, overweight adolescent, become the legendary Lord Byron? The world, it is said, bends to a committed will. Byron starved himself into physical beauty and became one of the great seducers of his time, of both men and women. Harold Nicolson said of him: 'he was a catalogue of false positions. His brain was male, his character was feminine.' The boy in the iron brace became a legendary swimmer, swimming the Hellespont in under two hours. The boy who cultivated the image of the dilettante and said later, 'I hate a fellow who's all author', in fact read voraciously. Before he went to Trinity, Cambridge, he boasted that he'd read more than 4000 books, including the Old Testament, the classics (particularly Greek tragedy), biography, history and novels and poetry, most particularly Pope, whom he idolised. Then, aged nineteen, catching life and art by the throat, he took his natural narrative gift and his astonishing fluency and dashed into poetry.

'I can never recast anything ... I am like the Tiger, if I miss at first spring / I go back growling to my Jungle again – But if I *do* hit – it is crushing!'

In fact *he* was hit. His first collection, *Hours of Idleness* (1807), was cruelly savaged by the critics. Byron, badly wounded by the reviews, went back to his jungle and then pounced. With his clever satire *English Bards and Scots Reviewers* in 1809 he mocked his enemies. In the same year he took his seat in the House of Lords, where he spoke with eloquence for Liberal causes. In 1812, after two years of extensive and sometimes dangerous travel through Spain, Malta, Armenia and Greece, Byron published the first two cantos of *Childe Harold's Pilgrimage*, and, aged only twenty-four, woke up and found himself famous. He'd invented himself, magnificently. 'It is only the self that he invented that he understood perfectly', according to Eliot. 'Lord Byron,' wrote Stendhal, 'was the unique object of his own attention.' Not quite. Critics and society now showered him with praise. He had no objection. He assiduously polished his image and acquired legions of adoring fans. Amongst them, infamously, was Lady Caroline Lamb, who, when she first saw him, turned and walked away. Alas not for long – though she wrote in her journal that evening that Lord Byron was 'mad – bad – and dangerous to know'. According to Ruskin, Byron was without mercy, perhaps because he believed that 'the great object in life is Sensation', to fill the 'craving void'. Other than his half-sister Augusta, whom he certainly loved deeply and with whom he probably had a child, and Countess Teresa Guiccioli, whom Iris Origo called 'The Last Attachment', few were left unwounded by an encounter with Byron. His wife, the cool, brilliant mathematician Annabelle Milbanke, left him within a year of marriage, taking their child (who as Ada Lovelace would, with Charles Babbage, collaborate on the early computer) amid rumours of sexual abuse within a marriage that was on occasion a bizarre *ménage à trois* with Augusta. Caroline Lamb added to the scandal when in a fit of jealous rage she implied homosexuality. The charge was serious – in 1806 there'd been six hangings; in Byron's time imprisonment was common. He was now hounded out of England. Like Shelley, he was bitter. Like Shelley, he wrote on. His output was prodigious: plays, among them *Manfred*, *The Two Foscari*, *Werner* (translated by Goethe), an Armenian dictionary – a notoriously difficult language to master – and of course the poetry. Of Byron's final masterpiece, *Don Juan*, Eliot said it contained a satire on English society for which he could find no parallel in English literature. 'Society,' Byron wrote, 'is now one polished horde, / Formed of two mighty tribes, the Bores and the Bored.' Though it is the most savagely witty poem in this or any language, it also warns us that 'If I laugh at any mortal thing / 'Tis that I may not weep.'

Byron's death plunged all of Greece and much of Europe into mourning. However, because of his scandalous past, he was refused burial at both Westminster Abbey and St Paul's, and was finally interred in the family vaults near Newstead Abbey. The cortège slowly made its way through towns and villages thronged with those who wished to pay tribute. As he was a peer many aristocrats sent their carriages. He was buried as a nobleman and not as a poet. He knew his country well.

The Poems

'Mr Dallas has placed in your hands a manuscript poem which he tells me you do not object to publishing.' Oh the insouciance, the sheer thrilling confidence of it! The hands were those of Mr John Murray, who with the astonishingly successful publication of *Childe Harold's Pilgrimage* embarked on one of the most turbulent literary and personal relationships between publisher and published. It would not end well. Few relationships with Byron did, and the tears were rarely his. Canto III however opens with a heartbroken lament for his daughter Ada, from whom he was parted for ever when he left England in disgrace in April 1816, 'the wandering outlaw of his own dark mind', and continues into a lament for Napoleon, 'Conqueror and captive of the earth', defeated at Waterloo on 18 June 1815. Verses thirty-six to forty-five present an unforgettable portrait of the ambition which spurs on 'the madmen who have made men mad'.

'The Destruction of Sennacherib' has a ferocious energy, the opening verse irresistible in its rhythmic power. 'Darkness', written earlier, is a surprise to those who like Byron-lite, of whom we shall drink deeply in *Don Juan*. 'Darkness' paints an almost Dantesque nightmare vision of the future. Night of course can sparkle, as did the mourning dress, decorated with spangles, of Lady Anne Wilmot. The dress and its wearer dazzled Byron when he saw her at a party. 'She Walks in Beauty' is a morning-after poem with a difference – it's chaste. It's also a lyrical masterpiece. 'When We Two Parted' is one of the great songs of lost love. It makes one weep. Alas, it's too cruel to speak the last verse, long suppressed to protect the reputation of Lady Frances (Fanny) Webster. Here it is *sotto voce*. 'Then fare thee well, Fanny / Now doubly undone / To prove false unto many / As faithless to one

/ Thou art past all recalling / Even would I recall / For the woman once falling / Forever must fall.' Byron, a feminist – in his fashion! He believed, and was loathed for it, that women were as sexually voracious as men. 'I'd like to know who's been ravished,' he once cried when accused again of promiscuity. 'I've been more ravished myself than anybody since the Trojan War.' Eliot noted a certain passivity in Byron, whose letters imply that, in sexual matters, he often considered himself under obligation! He was aware however that the price for women was higher – as his lines in Julia's letter make clear: 'Man's love is of his life a thing apart, / 'Tis woman's whole existence.' *Don Juan*, his masterpiece, is full of emotion; 'The emotion is hatred. Hatred of hypocrisy,' wrote Eliot. Since, however, Byron had discovered that in the *ottava rima* he could 'without straining hard to versify rattle on exactly as I talk / With anybody in a ride or walk', the delight we feel in listening to or reading *Don Juan* momentarily numbs us to its stinging truthfulness. In Canto I, a deliciously vicious marriage from hell – that of Don Juan's parents Don Jóse and Donna Inez, who wished 'each other, not divorced, but dead' – is followed later, much later, by the initially slow efforts at seduction by the adolescent Don Juan of the very pretty Julia, twenty-three and married to Don Jóse, fifty. It's so unfair that, as Byron notes, 'At *fifty* love for love is rare.' Of the poem, translated by Goethe (a fact which gave Byron considerable satisfaction), the poet declared, 'It may be profligate ... but is it not life? Is it not the thing?' It is indeed. 'Sorrow is knowledge' he wrote in *Manfred*, and few have written a gentler, sweeter poem about the inevitable than Byron's 'So, we'll go no more a roving'.

Childe Harold's Pilgrimage

Canto the Third
[excerpt]

XXXVI

> There sunk the greatest, nor the worst of men,
> Whose spirit antithetically mixt
> One moment of the mightiest, and again
> On little objects with like firmness fixt,
> Extreme in all things! hadst thou been betwixt,
> Thy throne had still been thine, or never been;
> For daring made thy rise as fall: thou seek'st
> Even now to re-assume the imperial mien,
> And shake again the world, the Thunderer of the scene!

XXXVII

> Conqueror and captive of the earth art thou!
> She trembles at thee still, and thy wild name
> Was ne'er more bruited in men's minds than now
> That thou art nothing, save the jest of Fame,
> Who woo'd thee once, thy vassal, and became
> The flatterer of thy fierceness, till thou wert
> A god unto thyself; nor less the same
> To the astounded kingdoms all inert,
> Who deem'd thee for a time whate'er thou didst assert.

XXXVIII

> Oh, more or less than man – in high or low,
> Battling with nations, flying from the field;

Now making monarchs' necks thy footstool, now
More than thy meanest soldier taught to yield;
An empire thou couldst crush, command, rebuild,
But govern not thy pettiest passion, nor,
However deeply in men's spirits skill'd,
Look through thine own, nor curb the lust of war,
Nor learn that tempted Fate will leave the loftiest star.

XXXIX

Yet well thy soul hath brook'd the turning tide
With that untaught innate philosophy,
Which, be it wisdom, coldness, or deep pride,
Is gall and wormwood to an enemy.
When the whole host of hatred stood hard by,
To watch and mock thee shrinking, thou hast smiled
With a sedate and all-enduring eye; –
When Fortune fled her spoil'd and favourite child,
He stood unbow'd beneath the ills upon him piled.

XL

Sager than in thy fortunes; for in them
Ambition steel'd thee on too far to show
That just habitual scorn, which could contemn
Men and their thoughts; 'twas wise to feel, not so
To wear it ever on thy lip and brow,
And spurn the instruments thou wert to use
Till they were turn'd unto thine overthrow;
'Tis but a worthless world to win or lose;
So hath it proved to thee, and all such lot who choose.

XLI

If, like a tower upon a headlong rock,
Thou hadst been made to stand or fall alone,

Such scorn of man had help'd to brave the shock;
But men's thoughts were the steps which paved thy throne,
Their admiration thy best weapon shone;
The part of Philip's son was thine, not then
(Unless aside thy purple had been thrown)
Like stern Diogenes to mock at men;
For sceptred cynics earth were far too wide a den.

XLII

But quiet to quick bosoms is a hell,
And *there* hath been thy bane; there is a fire
And motion of the soul which will not dwell
In its own narrow being, but aspire
Beyond the fitting medium of desire;
And, but once kindled, quenchless evermore,
Preys upon high adventure, nor can tire
Of aught but rest; a fever at the core,
Fatal to him who bears, to all who ever bore.

XLIII

This makes the madmen who have made men mad
By their contagion; Conquerors and Kings,
Founders of sects and systems, to whom add
Sophists, Bards, Statesmen, all unquiet things
Which stir too strongly the soul's secret springs,
And are themselves the fools to those they fool;
Envied, yet how unenviable! what stings
Are theirs! One breast laid open were a school
Which would unteach mankind the lust to shine or rule:

XLIV

Their breath is agitation, and their life
A storm whereon they ride, to sink at last,

And yet so nursed and bigoted to strife,
That should their days, surviving perils past,
Melt to calm twilight, they feel overcast
With sorrow and supineness, and so die;
Even as a flame unfed, which runs to waste
With its own flickering, or a sword laid by,
Which eats into itself, and rusts ingloriously.

XLV

He who ascends to mountain-tops, shall find
The loftiest peaks most wrapt in clouds and snow;
He who surpasses or subdues mankind,
Must look down on the hate of those below.
Though high *above* the sun of glory glow,
And far *beneath* the earth and ocean spread,
Round him are icy rocks, and loudly blow
Contending tempests on his naked head,
And thus reward the toils which to those summits led.

So, we'll go no more a roving

I
So, we'll go no more a roving
    So late into the night,
Though the heart be still as loving,
    And the moon be still as bright.

II
For the sword outwears its sheath,
    And the soul wears out the breast,
And the heart must pause to breathe,
    And love itself have rest.

III
Though the night was made for loving,
    And the day returns too soon,
Yet we'll go no more a roving
    By the light of the moon.

EMILY DICKINSON

Born in Amherst, Massachusetts in 1830, Emily Elizabeth Dickinson, unpublished in her lifetime, has long been recognised as one of America's great nineteenth-century poets. She died in 1886.

EMILY DICKINSON

Heavenly Hurt

When she died in 1886 at the age of fifty-six, Emily Dickinson, the New England spinster daughter of Emily Norcross Dickinson and Edward Dickinson, prominent lawyer and one-time representative to Congress, whose heart, she said, was 'pure and terrible such as I have found in no other', did not have a single book of poetry to her name. Days after her death, her sister Lavinia opened her bureau, in the room that Emily always kept locked, and found, neatly copied and sewn together in groups, over nine hundred poems. The number would eventually total 1775. Emily Dickinson's is the most remarkable story in the history of literature. Eventually, after four years of bitter family disputes, which became known as the Emily Dickinson wars, her first book of poetry was published and became the literary event of 1890. However, it was not until 1955, when the family's oddly touching, artistically disastrous, editorial 'tidying up' process was reversed (they had removed the dashes, dots and capitals that were crucial to her poetic code), that the sheer elemental ferocity of Emily Dickinson's poetry was released.

'Publication – is the Auction / Of the Mind' may be the opening lines of one of her poems, as is 'Fame is a fickle food.' However, during her lifetime she had secretly tried for both, and failed. She tried again and failed again – she knew why 'Success is counted sweetest / By those who ne'er succeed'. On 15 April 1862 – a date that Thomas H. Johnson describes in his introduction to *The Complete Poems* as one of the most significant in American nineteenth-century literature – Emily Dickinson sent four poems to Thomas Wentworth Higginson. She had written to Higginson in response to an article of his for *Atlantic Monthly*. His 'Letter to a Young Contributor' – advice to those who wished to be published – included the admonition, 'Charge your style with life.' Higginson was unaware, as Johnson points out, that Emily Dickinson, then thirty-one, had already written over three hundred poems.

The four he received were shocking enough. Johnson quotes Higginson speaking years later of their impact. 'The impression of a wholly new and original poetic genius was as distinct on my mind at the first reading of these four poems as it is now, after thirty years of further knowledge; and with it came the problem never yet solved, what place ought to be assigned in literature to what is so remarkable, yet so elusive of criticism.' He declined to publish the poems as he thought them 'extreme'. They were: extreme works of genius. 'Strangeness' is, Harold Bloom writes, 'one of the prime requirements for entrance into the Canon'. Emily Dickinson certainly qualified. Bloom declared her 'as individual a thinker as Dante'. She sent three more poems to Higginson. Again, he was confounded. Below is the famous letter that she sent on 7 June 1862 to Higginson, it having taken her less than two months to signal her retreat from the public arena. Note its construction, the dashes, the dots, the capitals.

I smile when you suggest that I delay 'to publish' – that being foreign to my thought, as Firmament to Fin –

If fame belonged to me, I could not escape her – if she did not, the longest day would pass me on the chase – and the approbation of my Dog, would forsake me – then – My Barefoot-Rank is better –

You think my gait 'spasmodic.' I am in danger, Sir.

You think me 'uncontrolled.' – I have no Tribunal. . . .

The Sailor cannot see the North – but knows the Needle can –

It is one of the most elegant exits in literary history. Though she was to continue a correspondence with Higginson, there were to be no more efforts at publication. She withdrew to her genius and lived quietly with it for the rest of her life. 'I don't go from home, unless emergency take me by the hand.' Ecstatics often withdraw. The intensity with which they react to experience often makes its curtailment necessary. St Teresa of Avila – who was 'in the world but not of it' as my mother constantly reminded me: a maternal warning against worldliness – withdrew to a convent. The poet and ecstatic Gerard Manley Hopkins – whose piety was such that in gardens he walked with his head bowed, in order not to be distracted from the worship of God by the beauty of roses (a favourite tale of the nuns) – found solace in a monastery. Emily Dickinson simply stayed at home. Unlike novelist Jane Austen, who in an equally small world looked out at her '3 or 4 families' and created a universe, Dickinson looked inward, and in what Ted Hughes called her 'tranced suspense' came closer than any other writer to the depiction of the sublime. He quotes her reaction to the visit of a circus: 'Friday I tasted life. It was a vast morsel. A Circus passed the house – still I feel the red in my mind.' For such a temperament, her elective, virtual imprisonment in her house was either an act of psychological wisdom or one which made 'the smallest event an immensity' as Ted Hughes believed.

Reclusive, however, is not the same as shy. Emily Dickinson was very popular at school, and later proved an excellent hostess in her father's house (her prizewinning bread was often served). Ted Hughes points out that when in 1870 she finally met the key literary figure in her life, Thomas Wentworth Higginson, he seemed stunned by the 'very wantonness of overstatement' in the conversation of 'his half-cracked poetess', adding: 'I was never with anyone who drained my nerve power so much.' Her description of herself, prior to their meeting, speaks of a considerable self-confidence in her appearance and most especially her colouring. The 'nun of Amherst', as she was eventually called, was not veiled, though she remained hidden. 'I am small like the Wren, and my hair is bold, like the Chestnut bur – and my eyes, like the Sherry in the Glass, that the Guest leaves.' Read it again. Imagine it without the capitals and note that the guest has already drunk his sherry but has left enough in the glass to reflect the colour of her eyes. It is a compelling image, all the more so when one realises that Emily Dickinson suffered from a serious and extremely painful eye condition, possibly rheumatic iritis according to biographer Connie Ann Kirk, who stresses that the poet may have feared the loss of her sight (she shares this awful terror with Joyce and Milton who finally became wholly blind). Emily Dickinson's poetic 'vision' therefore becomes ever more complex; her line, 'Renunciation – is a piercing Virtue', for example, now reads differently. Judith Farr in her introduction to a collection of critical essays makes the intriguing point that, in Emily Dickinson's poetry, wordplay on 'I' and 'eye' occurs in literally hundreds of poems. Whether in her poetry or prose, behind the originality and the glittering brilliance lies something mysterious, shadow-light behind the closed door.

Emily Dickinson is sometimes thought of as a great religious poet. However, she obeyed her own rules, not necessarily those of the Church, which she often refused to visit. Her God was her own. Ted Hughes, whose insight has particular weight in the light of his own marriage to an ecstatic and a poet, Sylvia Plath, notes that 'vision, and the crowded, beloved Creation around her and Death – became her Holy Trinity'. Such passion in real life might well have overwhelmed the object of its affection. Was there an object of affection, of desire? If there was, his identity remains obscure. Harold Bloom says of her work, 'It is a drama of erotic loss.' What is certain is that between 1858 and 1862, she wrote the so-called 'master letters', which continue to puzzle scholars. They are passionate, intimate, full of longing. They were also probably never sent. In what are known as 'the flood years', 1860–66, Emily Dickinson wrote over a thousand poems. They range from 'Given in Marriage unto Thee', and 'Rearrange a "Wife's" affection', passionate poems, full of longing, which give way to poems of loss, such as 'Heart! We will forget him!', shame even, 'Not with a Club, the Heart is broken' resignation, 'After great pain, a formal feeling comes' and the oft-quoted 'My life closed twice'. Perhaps in Hughes' haunting phrase Emily Dickinson realised that her 'unusual endowment of love was not going to be asked for'.

The Poems

Emily Dickinson wrote short. Short does not mean sweet. Short does not mean easy. Just in case you think you can wing it with the nun of Amherst, let me quote Harold Bloom: 'One's mind had better be at its rare best' when reading Dickinson. Approach her with humility and full attention – she has a mind like a laser beam and she can seriously damage your complacency. 'My Life had stood – a Loaded Gun'. So does the poetry. She was an aristocrat of the soul and 'The Soul selects her own Society' is less spiritual hauteur than moral dignity. She also had great strength of character. It is, as Shelley noted, extraordinarily difficult to continue writing with no hope of publication. Her poem 'Success is counted sweetest / By those who ne'er succeed' may in its opening lines speak of that ironic wisdom. However, what follows are not three short verses bewailing her lack of recognition. What we hear is the same 'distant strains of triumph' that the defeated, dying soldier hears and the pain of his cruelly untimely death is 'agonized and clear'. The note, nevertheless, is not political. The poem was written in 1859; the Civil War did not begin until 1861. Though the threat of war and war itself were a constant, and her own poetry is often fiercely violent, Emily Dickinson was possibly the least political poet in nineteenth-century literature. It is perverse wisdom perhaps.

Death, and not only in war, is so close in Dickinson – her elective and constant companion of the imagination – that every sense is sickle-sharpened, most particularly the sense of sound in 'I heard a Fly buzz'. As in the three following poems the note is one of great stillness, indeed of resignation. They disconcert with strange, cryptic power. 'A certain Slant of Light / ... oppresses, like the Heft / Of

Cathedral Tunes / When it comes . . . / Shadows – hold their breath.' Impossible, almost, not to hold one's own. 'Because I could not stop for Death – / He kindly stopped for me –' is a shocking and unforgettable opening. 'After great pain, a formal feeling comes' (the selection of the word 'formal' is a mark of great emotional insight) and 'My life closed twice before its close –' bring death and the maiden ever closer. The 'death' in the last poem freezes us in the icy waters of lost love – a parting no less terrible than the second, indeed, almost secondary, final death. Philip Larkin, whose own obsession with death was as extreme as that of Dickinson, found her poetry 'odd', which in itself is odd. 'Poetry,' he said, is 'an affair of sanity' and he went on to list the 'big sane boys Chaucer, Shakespeare, Wordsworth and Hardy . . . the object of writing is to show life as it is, and if you don't see it like that you're in trouble, not life'. We're all in trouble, as he well knew, and that's the trouble with life'. This unlikely juxtaposition of Dickinson and Larkin proves only John Bayley's point that 'Poetry wanders through the mysterious implications of its own exactness.' Exactly.

My *Life had stood – a Loaded Gun –*

My Life had stood – a Loaded Gun –
In Corners – till a Day
The Owner passed – identified –
And carried Me away –

And now We roam in Sovereign Woods –
And now We hunt the Doe –
And every time I speak for Him –
The Mountains straight reply –

And do I smile, such cordial light
Upon the Valley glow –
It is as a Vesuvian face
Had let its pleasure through –

And when at Night – Our good Day done –
I guard My Master's Head –
'Tis better than the Eider-Duck's
Deep Pillow – to have shared –

To foe of His – I'm deadly foe –
None stir the second time –
On whom I lay a Yellow Eye –
Or an emphatic Thumb –

Though I than He – may longer live
He longer must – than I –
For I have but the power to kill,
Without – the power to die –

Because I could not stop for Death –

Because I could not stop for Death –
He kindly stopped for me –
The Carriage held but just Ourselves –
And Immortality.

We slowly drove – He knew no haste
And I had put away
My labor and my leisure too,
For His Civility –

We passed the School, where Children strove
At Recess – in the Ring –
We passed the Fields of Gazing Grain –
We passed the Setting Sun –

Or rather – He passed Us –
The Dews drew quivering and chill –
For only Gossamer, my Gown –
My Tippet – only Tulle –

We paused before a House that seemed
A Swelling of the Ground –
The Roof was scarcely visible –
The Cornice – in the Ground –

Since then – 'tis Centuries – and yet
Feels shorter than the Day
I first surmised the Horses' Heads
Were toward Eternity –

T. S. ELIOT

Thomas Stearns Eliot, born in St Louis, Missouri in 1888, was a poet, playwright and critic. His *Prufrock and Other Observations*, *The Waste Land* and *Four Quartets* are masterpieces of the twentieth century. He won the Nobel Prize in 1948 and died in 1965.

T. S. ELIOT

I Gotta Use Words When I Talk to You

Virginia Woolf to T. S. Eliot: 'We're not as good as Keats.' T. S. Eliot
to Virginia Woolf: 'Oh yes, we are. We're trying something harder.'
Checkmate! It's a delightful vignette, one of many, in Peter
Ackroyd's brilliant biography. T. S. Eliot was indeed trying something
harder and he succeeded. With the publication of *The Waste Land*,
Eliot broke the mould in poetry, in the same way that Joyce's
Ulysses – published the same year, 1922 – broke the mould in the
novel. In the history of poetry there is before and after Thomas
Stearns Eliot.

Who was he, this man who created a new movement in literature,
virtually a new poetic language that has 'the capacity to cut into our
consciousness with the sharpness of a diamond' (Anders Österling,
Permanent Secretary to The Swedish Academy 1948)? What was he
like, this man about whom Ted Hughes said, 'There is a direct line
which can be traced from Virgil to Dante, from Dante to Milton and
from Milton to Eliot, the greatest poet for over three hundred years'?

Well, the greatest poet for over three hundred years was described
by John Betjeman as 'a quiet, remote figure'. At Lloyd's Bank, where
he worked as a clerk, he cut a figure of great elegance but he was in
fact very good at his job. After the bank years, he became editor, and
then director, at publishers Faber and Gwyer (later Faber and Faber),
where he was known as 'the Pope of Russell Square'. Even after he'd
begun to make a name for himself as a poet, Ackroyd notes that Eliot

did not exactly dazzle those who met him. The society hostess Lady
Ottoline Morrell found him 'dull, dull, dull'. Aldous Huxley said
Eliot was 'just another Europeanised American talking about French
literature in the most uninspiring fashion'. 'The dull, dull man', 'the
boring Europeanised American', who even described himself, in less
than thrilling terms, as 'Classical in literature, Royalist in politics and
Anglo-Catholic in religion', was born in St Louis, Missouri, in
September 1888, a late son to older parents who already had four
daughters and a son. They were, Ackroyd writes, successful, practi-
cal Unitarians, part of the intellectual aristocracy of America. 'They
never did less than was expected of them and Eliot too did what was
expected of him.' He went to the right schools, the right clubs and
the right university, Harvard, where, in the library one day, he came
across Arthur Symons' *The Symbolist Movement in Literature*. Its main
practitioners were French – Mallarmé, Verlaine, Rimbaud and
Laforgue. The discovery of this book was, Eliot himself said, life-
changing. The importance he attached from then on to the *symbol*
of reality, and its associations and affinities, is key to 'experiencing'
Eliot. Mood, subtle connections, strange conjunctions, in language
and image – rather than realism of time and place and incident – all
work together in an Eliot poem with almost hypnotic power. This
Eliot effect I noted again and again at readings, even during his most
demanding work. The hour-long *Four Quartets*, for example, is listened to in a concentrated silence even during long, often daunting
passages.

After Harvard his path was deemed to be clear: academe. He
rebelled and left for Paris in the autumn of 1910. It would not be his
last determined departure and from Harvard to Paris is not only a
question of geography. Through his friendship with a fellow lodger,
Jean Verdenal, Eliot quickly became part of the heady literary life of
Paris. By 1911, Eliot was scribbling in a notebook the poem that Ezra
Pound would call the first American masterpiece of the twentieth
century, 'The Love Song of J. Alfred Prufrock' (later dedicated to

Verdenal, who was killed in the war). He was also writing 'Portrait of a Lady'. He was just twenty-two and it is one of literature's more unnerving facts that he had already taken possession of his gift. The writer Conrad Aiken, Eliot's Harvard friend, is quoted by Ackroyd as having been astonished at 'how sharp and complete and sui generis the whole thing was from the outset . . . The *wholeness* is there, from the beginning.' One journey, from Harvard to Paris, had resulted in great intellectual and artistic riches. Another journey, from Paris to Oxford's Merton College, led him to a darker, personal destiny: marriage to Vivien Haigh-Wood. She it was who would shape his life and influence his work for decades to come. The artistic riches in future would be dearly bought.

Eliot was twenty-seven in 1915 when he met Vivien and, he said later, 'very young for his age, very timid, very inexperienced'. They married quickly, Eliot seemingly wholly unaware that Vivien suffered from a severe hormonal disorder. The morphine-based drugs that were used to treat her exacerbated her often hysterical, sometimes dangerous, behaviour. Over the years the huge financial burden of doctors and sanatoria meant that he rarely worked fewer than fifteen hours a day. The stress almost broke his health. If it was hard for Eliot, it destroyed Vivien. It is a terrible tale and biographers – Ackroyd, Lyndall Gordon and others – approach it with compassion. The American critic Cynthia Ozick is rather harsher in her judgement of Eliot's emotional and psychological journey, which she describes as one from compassion to horror. In 1933, after eighteen years of marriage, he left Vivien, ostensibly to give a series of lectures in Harvard. He had no intention of returning to her. She refused to accept the inevitable. Her illness and her distress led to behaviour that was regarded, in those more constrained times, as bordering on insanity. She was confined for the last years of her life to a mental institution, where she died in 1947. Eliot never visited during that time. *Four Quartets*, which he started in 1936, three years after their separation and published in its entirety in 1943, is his mature masterpiece and it led to his being awarded the Nobel Prize for literature in 1948. 'The more perfect the artist,' he once wrote, 'the more completely separate in him will be the man who suffers and the mind which creates.' Maybe. However, only a man who had suffered deeply could write that one of 'the gifts reserved for age' is 'the awareness of things ill done and done to others' harm / Which once you took for exercise of virtue'.

Late in life, he made a kind of dash for the adult happiness that had eluded him. He married Valerie Fletcher, his young assistant at Faber. It was a marriage that transformed him. This most private of poets wrote of his deep joy in 'A dedication to my Wife', a love poem of 'private words addressed to you in public'. He was now an iconic figure, fêted everywhere he went. 'Viva, Viva, Eliot,' they called to him in Rome and Ackroyd tells us he once gave a lecture to 14,000 people in a football stadium in Minnesota on 'The Frontiers of Criticism'. Those were the days! However, although there were plays and essays, there was to be no more poetry. Larkin's 'rare bird' had flown away.

Eliot died in 1965, aged seventy-seven, with his second wife Valerie at his side. After his death she said he felt he had paid too high a price for poetry. 'The dead writers are that which we know,' he once said. The Nobel academy agreed: 'Tradition is not a dead load which we drag along with us ... it is the soil in which the seeds of coming harvests are to be sown, and from which future harvests will be garnered.'

The Waste Land

Where is it? What is it? It's a state of mind. It continues to induce in the reader what Cyril Connolly described as 'the almost drugged and haunted condition' that it induced in undergraduates in 1922 as they gathered together to read it aloud. Peter Ackroyd notes its 'echoic quality which requires the inflection of the voice of the reader to give it shape'. The writer Edmund Wilson called it 'the great knockout up to date'. It still is.

The original title was 'He Do the Police in Different Voices'. It's Betty Higden's phrase from Dickens' *Our Mutual Friend*: 'You mightn't think it, but Sloppy is a beautiful reader of a newspaper. He do the police in different voices.' Eliot 'do' *The Waste Land* in different voices, many different voices – a multiplicity of sound. Soloists, as in a choir, break in and out of the song. The lines of gender are often blurred. They tell of strange visions interposed with fragments of memory, sometimes in different languages, incorporating lines from Dante, Sanskrit texts or the Bible, occasionally using jazz rhythms (Larkin once noted that jazz is the closest to the unconscious that we have). At other times they sing raucous popular songs, followed by a sudden switch of tone to the formality of Elizabethan language or the incantations of a prayer. 'A Game of Chess' (the second movement) opens slowly in the room, which is heavy with 'her strange synthetic perfumes'. Then, suddenly, the jagged voice of the hysterical woman breaks in – 'My nerves are bad to-night. Yes, bad.' – and then 'What are you thinking of? What thinking? What?' The note is both frightening and sad – then it fades away into 'O O O O that Shakespeherian Rag—' after which, unexpectedly, we're transported to a cockney pub where the landlord recounts the tale of 'poor

Albert' who has 'been in the army four years, he wants a good time', and 'Lil' who 'ought to be ashamed', because she looks 'so antique'. As closing time approaches he calls out, repeatedly, 'HURRY UP PLEASE ITS TIME' (the meaning of the line multi-layered) and he fades away with echoing, gentle salutation 'Good night, ladies, good night, sweet ladies, good night, / good night.' The incomparable soaring genius of the piece, with Eliot the composer and the conductor of its five movements, makes reading *The Waste Land* one of the most thrilling experiences in literature. And life.

What was Eliot's own state of mind when he wrote it and does it matter as one listens or reads the poems? The answer is no. But the question is interesting and has some bearing on the second section of *The Waste Land*, 'A Game of Chess'. This is acknowledged to be, in part, a portrait of his marriage to Vivien Haigh-Wood. In the margin of the dialogue of the nervous, harassed woman, Vivien wrote 'wonderful, wonderful'. A letter from Eliot to British novelist Sydney Schiff, dated November 1921, concerning Part Three of *The Waste Land*, may come as a surprise to those who underestimate Vivien's influence. 'I have done a rough draft but do not know whether it will do, and must wait for Vivien's opinion as to whether it is printable.' According to Ackroyd, Vivien once replied to a question concerning Eliot: 'Tom's mind? I am Tom's mind.' The reason for their estrangement, with its terrible consequence, did not lie in creative dissonance. This marriage, which he said later 'brought to her no happiness', brought to him 'the state of mind out of which came *The Waste Land*'. And that, to many, is a shocking admission from the man to whom the theory of 'impersonality' in art was crucial.

Yet, as John Bayley points out, 'The interior of Eliot's poetry is deeply personal, full of secrets and intimacies.' In his own notes to *The Waste Land*, Eliot quotes F. H. Bradley: 'My experience falls within my own circle, a circle closed on the outside.' How could it be otherwise? Within his own 'circle of experience' at that time lay long days at the bank and a home life that increasingly resembled that of a sanatorium. Vivien's suffering was extreme: 'Have you ever been in such incessant pain that you felt your sanity was going ... that's the way she is,' he wrote in a letter in 1921. The 'outside' was post-war depression and exhaustion, as well as the slow grief of Europe and Britain having seen a generation wiped out. The summer of 1921 was a summer of drought and severe influenza. Eliot, Ackroyd points out, was ill and exhausted and found it enormously difficult to write. He quotes Siegfried Sassoon as having heard Eliot declare around that time, 'All great art is based on a condition of fundamental boredom – passionate boredom.' It was Vivien who encouraged *him* to go to a sanatorium in Lausanne and here *The Waste Land* was born.

It was to have as editor one of the great literary midwives in the history of poetry – the amazing Ezra Pound. When he read it for the first time he wrote to Eliot, 'Complimenti, you bitch. I am wracked by the seven jealousies.' What poet wouldn't be? However, in the British Library, Eliot's original copy is marked through with so many red pencil lines that it resembles a piece of modern art. Ezra Pound, the ruthless surgeon and dedicated friend, cut to the music and carved away anything that dulled the note. *The Waste Land* is dedicated, as it should be, to Ezra Pound *il migliore fabbro* – the better craftsman.

'The Love Song of J. Alfred Prufrock'
'Portrait of a Lady'
'The Hollow Men'

'It is an art of the nerves, this art of Laforgue, and it is what all art would tend towards if we followed our nerves on all our journeys.' These lines come from Symons' *The Symbolist Movement in Literature* concerning the poet Jules Laforgue. 'Eliot followed his nerves in Prufrock' is C. K. Stead's brilliant insight in an essay full of brilliant insights. This journey of the nerves was to last a lifetime and at considerable cost to Eliot's health. Though 'The Love Song of J. Alfred Prufrock' is now acknowledged as the first great poem of the twentieth century, Eliot was 'heartlessly indifferent to its fate' according to Conrad Aiken, who, with Ezra Pound, tried everyone they could think of to have it published. It was no easy task as Ackroyd notes. One publisher turned it down on the basis that 'it's completely insane'.

Do not ask 'What is it?' Accept J. Alfred's invitation: 'Let us go then, you and I'. You will never regret accompanying the middle-aged narrator on his visit. C. K. Stead notes however, that Eliot, in a conversation with Hugh Kenner, disputed the term 'middle-aged': 'Prufrock is a young man.' Of whatever age, he is the repressed, inadequate 'attendant lord' whose surname once adorned a hardware shop in Eliot's home town of St Louis. When asked about 'the love life of J. Alfred Prufrock', Eliot replied, 'I'm afraid that J. Alfred Prufrock didn't have much of a love life.'

The lady in 'Portrait of a Lady' may have suffered a similar fate. It is another poem of nervous tension and the constant possibility of explosive anger. The hyper-awareness of the narrator – not only to the actual words but to the undernote in each statement of 'The Lady' – creates a mood of claustrophobic unease in this piece, often described as the shortest one-act play in literature. She was, according to Ackroyd, Miss Adelaide Moffatt whom Eliot used to visit to 'take tea' and he believes that she represented a Boston way of life with which Eliot was becoming increasingly frustrated. Many find amusement in this poem. I've always found it to be one of subtle, polite cruelty. The chasm between the two individuals is unbridgeable and not just because of the age differential. Their conversation is a duet of misunderstanding and misapprehension, and eventually sadness as she becomes increasingly aware that what she'd hoped for is slipping away into the colder actuality of their relationship. 'I have been wondering frequently of late / (But our beginnings never know our ends!) / Why we have not developed into friends.' The unnamed narrator ponders a final, more cruel question: '. . . what if she should die some afternoon . . . / And should I have the right to smile?' Ironic? Yes, brutally so.

'The Hollow Men' was influenced by Brutus' line from *Julius Caesar*, 'Between the acting of a dreadful thing / And the first motion, all the interim is / Like a phantasma, or a hideous dream', which in Eliot becomes 'Between the idea / And the reality / Between the motion / And the act / Falls the Shadow'. The iconic line from Conrad's masterpiece *Heart of Darkness* – 'Mistah Kurtz – he dead' – is epigram to the poem. In Francis Coppola's film *Apocalypse Now* Marlon Brando speaks the lines: 'We are the hollow men / We are the stuffed men / Leaning together / Headpiece filled with straw. Alas!' Heaney calls it, 'Rare music'. It certainly is – down to the last beat: '*This is the way the world ends / Not with a bang but a whimper.*'

The Love Song of J. Alfred Prufrock

S'io credessi che mia risposta fosse
A persona che mai tornasse al mondo,
Questa fiamma staria senza più scosse.
Ma per ciò che giammai di questo fondo
Non tornò viva alcun, s'i'odo il vero,
Senza tema d'infamia ti rispondo.

Let us go then, you and I,
When the evening is spread out against the sky
Like a patient etherised upon a table;
Let us go, through certain half-deserted streets,
The muttering retreats
Of restless nights in one-night cheap hotels
And sawdust restaurants with oyster-shells:
Streets that follow like a tedious argument
Of insidious intent
To lead you to an overwhelming question . . .
Oh, do not ask, 'What is it?'
Let us go and make our visit.

In the room the women come and go
Talking of Michelangelo.

The yellow fog that rubs its back upon the window-panes,
The yellow smoke that rubs its muzzle on the window-panes,
Licked its tongue into the corners of the evening,
Lingered upon the pools that stand in drains,

Let fall upon its back the soot that falls from chimneys,
Slipped by the terrace, made a sudden leap,
And seeing that it was a soft October night,
Curled once about the house, and fell asleep.

And indeed there will be time
For the yellow smoke that slides along the street
Rubbing its back upon the window-panes;
There will be time, there will be time
To prepare a face to meet the faces that you meet;
There will be time to murder and create,
And time for all the works and days of hands
That lift and drop a question on your plate;
Time for you and time for me,
And time yet for a hundred indecisions,
And for a hundred visions and revisions,
Before the taking of a toast and tea.

In the room the women come and go
Talking of Michelangelo.

And indeed there will be time
To wonder, 'Do I dare?' and, 'Do I dare?'
Time to turn back and descend the stair,
With a bald spot in the middle of my hair—
(They will say: 'How his hair is growing thin!')
My morning coat, my collar mounting firmly to the chin
My necktie rich and modest, but asserted by a simple pin—
(They will say: 'But how his arms and legs are thin!')
Do I dare
Disturb the universe?
In a minute there is time
For decisions and revisions which a minute will reverse.

For I have known them all already, known them all—
Have known the evenings, mornings, afternoons,
I have measured out my life with coffee spoons;
I know the voices dying with a dying fall
Beneath the music from a farther room.
So how should I presume?

And I have known the eyes already, known them all—
The eyes that fix you in a formulated phrase,
And when I am formulated, sprawling on a pin,
When I am pinned and wriggling on the wall,
Then how should I begin
To spit out all the butt-ends of my days and ways?
And how should I presume?

And I have known the arms already, known them all—
Arms that are braceleted and white and bare
(But in the lamplight, downed with light brown hair!)
Is it perfume from a dress
That makes me so digress?
Arms that lie along a table, or wrap about a shawl.
And should I then presume?
And how should I begin?

. . .

Shall I say, I have gone at dusk through narrow streets
And watched the smoke that rises from the pipes
Of lonely men in shirt-sleeves, leaning out of windows? . . .

I should have been a pair of ragged claws
Scuttling across the floors of silent seas.

. . .

And the afternoon, the evening, sleeps so peacefully!
Smoothed by long fingers,
Asleep ... tired ... or it malingers,
Stretched on the floor, here beside you and me.
Should I, after tea and cakes and ices,
Have the strength to force the moment to its crisis?
But though I have wept and fasted, wept and prayed,
Though I have seen my head (grown slightly bald) brought in upon a
     platter,
I am no prophet – and here's no great matter;
I have seen the moment of my greatness flicker,
And I have seen the eternal Footman hold my coat, and snicker,
And in short, I was afraid.

And would it have been worth it, after all,
After the cups, the marmalade, the tea,
Among the porcelain, among some talk of you and me,
Would it have been worth while,
To have bitten off the matter with a smile,
To have squeezed the universe into a ball
To roll it toward some overwhelming question,
To say: 'I am Lazarus, come from the dead,
Come back to tell you all, I shall tell you all'—
If one, settling a pillow by her head,
    Should say: 'That is not what I meant at all.
    That is not it, at all.'

And would it have been worth it, after all,
Would it have been worth while,
After the sunsets and the dooryards and the sprinkled streets,
After the novels, after the teacups, after the skirts that trail along the
    floor—
And this, and so much more?—
It is impossible to say just what I mean!

But as if a magic lantern threw the nerves in patterns on a screen:
Would it have been worth while
If one, settling a pillow or throwing off a shawl,
And turning toward the window, should say:
    'That is not it at all,
    That is not what I meant, at all.'

           . . .

    No! I am not Prince Hamlet, nor was meant to be;
Am an attendant lord, one that will do
To swell a progress, start a scene or two,
Advise the prince; no doubt, an easy tool,
Deferential, glad to be of use,
Politic, cautious, and meticulous;
Full of high sentence, but a bit obtuse;
At times, indeed, almost ridiculous –
Almost, at times, the Fool.

    I grow old . . . I grow old . . .
I shall wear the bottoms of my trousers rolled.

    Shall I part my hair behind? Do I dare to eat a peach?
I shall wear white flannel trousers, and walk upon the beach.
I have heard the mermaids singing, each to each.

I do not think that they will sing to me.

    I have seen them riding seaward on the waves
Combing the white hair of the waves blown back
When the wind blows the water white and black.

    We have lingered in the chambers of the sea
By sea-girls wreathed with seaweed red and brown
Till human voices wake us, and we drown.

Portrait of a Lady

Thou hast committed —
Fornication: but that was in another country,
And besides, the wench is dead.

The Jew of Malta

I

    Among the smoke and fog of a December afternoon
You have the scene arrange itself—as it will seem to do—
With 'I have saved this afternoon for you';
And four wax candles in the darkened room,
Four rings of light upon the ceiling overhead,
An atmosphere of Juliet's tomb
Prepared for all the things to be said, or left unsaid.
We have been, let us say, to hear the latest Pole
Transmit the Preludes, through his hair and finger-tips.
'So intimate, this Chopin, that I think his soul
Should be resurrected only among friends
Some two or three, who will not touch the bloom
That is rubbed and questioned in the concert room.'
—And so the conversation slips
Among velleities and carefully caught regrets
Through attenuated tones of violins
Mingled with remote cornets
And begins.
'You do not know how much they mean to me, my friends,
And how, how rare and strange it is, to find
In a life composed so much, so much of odds and ends,

(For indeed I do not love it ... you knew? you are not blind!
How keen you are!)
To find a friend who has these qualities,
Who has, and gives
Those qualities upon which friendship lives.
How much it means that I say this to you—
Without these friendships—life, what *cauchemar*!'

Among the windings of the violins
And the ariettes
Of cracked cornets
Inside my brain a dull tom-tom begins
Absurdly hammering a prelude of its own,
Capricious monotone
That is at least one definite 'false note'.
—Let us take the air, in a tobacco trance,
Admire the monuments,
Discuss the late events,
Correct our watches by the public clocks.
Then sit for half an hour and drink our bocks.

II
Now that lilacs are in bloom
She has a bowl of lilacs in her room
And twists one in her fingers while she talks.
'Ah, my friend, you do not know, you do not know
What life is, you who hold it in your hands';
(Slowly twisting the lilac stalks)
'You let it flow from you, you let it flow,
And youth is cruel, and has no more remorse
And smiles at situations which it cannot see.'
I smile, of course,
And go on drinking tea.

'Yet with these April sunsets, that somehow recall
My buried life, and Paris in the Spring,
I feel immeasurably at peace, and find the world
To be wonderful and youthful, after all.'

The voice returns like the insistent out-of-tune
Of a broken violin on an August afternoon:
'I am always sure that you understand
My feelings, always sure that you feel,
Sure that across the gulf you reach your hand.

You are invulnerable, you have no Achilles' heel.
You will go on, and when you have prevailed
You can say: at this point many a one has failed.
But what have I, but what have I, my friend,
To give you, what can you receive from me?
Only the friendship and the sympathy
Of one about to reach her journey's end.

I shall sit here, serving tea to friends ...'

I take my hat: how can I make a cowardly amends
For what she has said to me?
You will see me any morning in the park
Reading the comics and the sporting page.
Particularly I remark
An English countess goes upon the stage.
A Greek was murdered at a Polish dance,
Another bank defaulter has confessed.
I keep my countenance,
I remain self-possessed
Except when a street-piano, mechanical and tired
Reiterates some worn-out common song

With the smell of hyacinths across the garden
Recalling things that other people have desired.
Are these ideas right or wrong?

III
    The October night comes down; returning as before
Except for a slight sensation of being ill at ease
I mount the stairs and turn the handle of the door
And feel as if I had mounted on my hands and knees.
'And so you are going abroad; and when do you return?
But that's a useless question.
You hardly know when you are coming back,
You will find so much to learn.'
My smile falls heavily among the bric-à-brac.

    'Perhaps you can write to me.'
My self-possession flares up for a second;
This is as I had reckoned.
'I have been wondering frequently of late
(But our beginnings never know our ends!)
Why we have not developed into friends.'
I feel like one who smiles, and turning shall remark
Suddenly, his expression in a glass.
My self-possession gutters; we are really in the dark.

    'For everybody said so, all our friends,
They all were sure our feelings would relate
So closely! I myself can hardly understand.
We must leave it now to fate.
You will write, at any rate.
Perhaps it is not too late.
I shall sit here, serving tea to friends.'

And I must borrow every changing shape
To find expression ... dance, dance
Like a dancing bear,
Cry like a parrot, chatter like an ape.
Let us take the air, in a tobacco trance—

Well! and what if she should die some afternoon,
Afternoon grey and smoky, evening yellow and rose;
Should die and leave me sitting pen in hand
With the smoke coming down above the housetops;
Doubtful, for a while
Not knowing what to feel or if I understand
Or whether wise or foolish, tardy or too soon ...
Would she not have the advantage, after all?
This music is successful with a 'dying fall'
Now that we talk of dying—
And should I have the right to smile?

ROBERT FROST

Robert Lee Frost was born in San Francisco in 1874. In 1912 he moved to England where his first volumes of poems, *A Boy's Will* (1913) and *North of Boston* (1914), were published to great acclaim. Over a long career he published *Mountain Interval* (1916), *New Hampshire* (1923), *Collected Poems* (1930), *A Witness Tree* (1942) and *In the Clearing* (1962). He won four Pulitzer Prizes – a record that still stands. He died in1963.

ROBERT FROST

The Poet of Terror

On 26 March 1959 a dinner was held at the Waldorf Astoria in New York to honour, on his eighty-fifth birthday, Robert Frost. This literary icon, who many believed wrote of old pieties, old virtues, was the winner of four Pulitzer Prizes – a record which still stands. Lionel Trilling the eminent critic rose to speak: 'I have to say that my Frost . . . is not the Frost I seem to perceive in the minds of so many of his admirers. He is not the Frost who reassures us by his affirmation of old virtues, old simplicities and ways of feeling; he is anything but. Frost's best poems represent the terrible actualities of life. In sum, he is a terrifying poet.' Frost was disconcerted. The audience was disconcerted. Trilling left almost immediately – but Trilling was right. For beneath the guise of the avuncular, Robert Frost was indeed the poet of terror. He was also the poet of courage; he needed it – 'I'd rather be taken for brave than anything else.' His was a life that had not only a tough beginning but one in which he later suffered a Job-like series of tragedies that would have felled all but the bravest. A poem, he wrote, 'begins in delight and ends in wisdom' and in his case the wisdom was dearly bought. He was indeed 'acquainted with the night'.

He was born in San Francisco in 1874 to William Frost, a Harvard-educated journalist and aspiring politician from the East Coast who'd gone West to pursue his ambitions. These, alas, came to nothing. He died aged thirty-four, a gambler and an alcoholic. After funeral expenses his wife, Belle, a teacher and a published poet of Scottish descent (whose family history was overshadowed by the mental illness of which Frost had a deep fear) was left with only eight dollars in the bank. She had no alternative but to take her two children, Robbie and Jeanie, back to her parents-in-law in Boston, where she would resume her schoolteaching career. Frost often helped her in class and, when he could, financially, with work on farms and in factories. He wanted more: 'Inflexible ambition trains us best.' It was, in Frost's case, combined with academic brilliance and a passion for poetry inherited from his mother, as well as for the classics. According to John Updike, Frost, who won a scholarship to Dartmouth and eventually went to Harvard, knew more Greek and Latin than either Eliot or Pound. Yet Frost's poetry is almost devoid of overt classical references. However, in his monologues (and he is as great a monologist as Browning, with a similar genius for creating character) it is possible to trace a form of Greek tragedy in his tales of lives broken by arbitrary fate. His disturbing desire and capacity to 'trip the reader head foremost into the boundless ... Forward, you understand, and in the dark' is clear also in the shorter poems, as in 'Bereft' and 'Fire and Ice'. Joseph Brodsky said 'Frost's is a signal from a far-distant station ... the fuel – grief and reason.' The initial signal came in 1894 with the innocently titled 'My Butterfly', the writing of which he said was like 'cutting along a nerve'. It was his first published poem, appearing in the prestigious *Independent* newspaper. The editor noted that 'there is a secret genius between the lines'. Frost now determined on poetry for life. His previously parsimonious grandfather offered to support him for one year. No, said Frost, it will take me twenty. It did. He supported himself by farming, eventually selling his farm in Derry, New Hampshire, and, after moving to Britain, buying one in Buckinghamshire. It was in England that his first collection *A Boy's Will* was published in 1913, followed a year later by *North of Boston*, to great acclaim. Frost returned to America in his forties and from then on there was no stopping him. He would, even in late life, attract audiences numbering in their thousands. The cool Miss Marianne Moore, not given to hyperbole, said he was the best speaker she had ever heard; Allen Ginsberg said Robert Frost literally created the audience for poetry readings. 'I teach myself,' Frost said, 'my own take on the world'; and 'I sit there radiating poetry.'

It was not to be his only stage. Though he was orthodox in politics – a Liberal, he believed, was someone who wouldn't take his own side in an argument – President Kennedy invited him to read at his inauguration. Frost recited from memory a poem he had written twenty years earlier, 'The Gift Outright'. The glare of the sun had made it impossible for him to read his new poem. In 1962, Kennedy, astonishingly, asked Frost to visit Khrushchev in Moscow to plead against the construction of the Berlin Wall. It didn't work. That his intervention had been sought at all is testimony to how far he'd come.

On his deathbed Frost said, 'Love is all. Romantic love – as in stories and poems. I tremble with it.' 'The Figure a Poem Makes' is, according to his famous essay, 'the same as for love'. Love brought him Elinor White, whom he'd pursued with almost overwhelming passion, once becoming so distraught when he sensed rejection that he went missing for days in the dangerous Virginia swamps. Finally, reader, he married her. She was twenty-three and he was twenty-one. Family life brought neither of them any luck. Their son Eliott died when he was four, a daughter in infancy and another, Marjorie, having successfully fought off serious mental illness (a maternal genetic inheritance), succumbed to puerperal fever with her first child. In 1938 his beloved Elinor died. He was literally mad with grief. This is his Lear-like description: 'I can't touch my mind with a memory of any kind. I can't touch my skin.' He was consumed with guilt: 'She was too frail' for the life he'd given her due to his ruthless ambition, too many children. In a shocking line he wrote, 'God damn me when he gets around to it.' His suffering was not over, for two years later his son Carl shot himself. 'I feel,' he said, 'as though

I am laid out upon a cross.' He died on 28 January 1963, aged eighty-eight: 'I would have written of me on my stone: I had a lover's quarrel with the world.' Only a man who'd carved grace out of tragedy could have written a line of such irony and sweetness.

The Poems

'If [when] you read my poem – you heard a voice, that would be to my liking ... the gold in the ore is the sound.' Few poets believed more passionately in the sound of sense; few had a more finely attuned ear to the sense of sound. In Frost's extraordinary 'A Servant to Servants' the woman's voice is weighted, awkwardly heavy with a life of exhausted love and resignation. The line, repeated, 'I don't know' is in perfect contradictory balance with the familiar beat of her daily rhythm of duty. All is set – in an almost throwaway sequence – against the shattering perspective of family madness.

'Out, Out—' shocks on every level. It tells the true story of the death of a neighbour's child in a sawmill, the awful imagery of the boy's arm leaping away towards the saw, 'Neither refused the meeting.' The last line is one of literature's most savage – 'And they, since they / Were not the one dead, turned to their affairs.' Frost wrote, 'Before I built a wall I'd ask to know / What I was walling in or walling out.' It was with considerable cunning that he recited 'Mending Wall' at an official dinner in Moscow. 'Mending Wall' is, on the surface, a poem of simple verities. However Frost, the master of metaphor, was saying something profound concerning boundaries. He had, Heaney noted, 'an appetite for independence [which] was fierce and expressed itself in a reiterated belief in his rights to limits: his defences, his fences, his freedom were all interdependent.' These limits were perhaps essential, and driven by his fear of the abyss. Poetry, Frost once wrote, is a 'momentary stay against confusion'.

Robert Frost fell in love again, after the death of his beloved Elinor, with Kay Morrison, his beautiful, cool, much admired assistant who, alas, was married. Updike notes that it was for Kay

Morrison that Frost wrote and recited in public to her one of the most enchanting love lyrics in the language, 'Never Again Would Birds' Song be the Same', with its glorious last line: 'And to do that to birds was why she came.'

'Two Look at Two' is about lovers twinned by the vision of a deer and stag, certain that the sighting authenticates their human passion. 'Acquainted With the Night' paints a haunting internal landscape. 'The Road Not Taken' was inspired by Edward Thomas's indecision during their walks in Buckinghamshire as to which path to take – a metaphor for life. The iconic last lines of 'Stopping by Woods on a Snowy Evening' were oft quoted by Kennedy in his speeches, who had fewer 'miles to go' than anyone would have believed possible.

Out, Out—

The buzz-saw snarled and rattled in the yard
And made dust and dropped stove-length sticks of wood,
Sweet-scented stuff when the breeze drew across it.
And from there those that lifted eyes could count
Five mountain ranges one behind the other
Under the sunset far into Vermont.
And the saw snarled and rattled, snarled and rattled,
As it ran light, or had to bear a load.
And nothing happened: day was all but done.
Call it a day, I wish they might have said
To please the boy by giving him the half hour
That a boy counts so much when saved from work.
His sister stood beside them in her apron
To tell them 'Supper.' At the word, the saw,
As if to prove saws knew what supper meant,
Leaped out at the boy's hand, or seemed to leap—
He must have given the hand. However it was,
Neither refused the meeting. But the hand!
The boy's first outcry was a rueful laugh,
As he swung toward them holding up the hand
Half in appeal, but half as if to keep
The life from spilling. Then the boy saw all—
Since he was old enough to know, big boy
Doing a man's work, though a child at heart—
He saw all spoiled. 'Don't let him cut my hand off—
The doctor, when he comes. Don't let him, sister!'
So. But the hand was gone already.

The doctor put him in the dark of ether.
He lay and puffed his lips out with his breath.
And then—the watcher at his pulse took fright.
No one believed. They listened at his heart.
Little—less—nothing!—and that ended it.
No more to build on there. And they, since they
Were not the one dead, turned to their affairs.

The Road Not Taken

Two roads diverged in a yellow wood,
And sorry I could not travel both
And be one traveler, long I stood
And looked down one as far as I could
To where it bent in the undergrowth;

Then took the other, as just as fair,
And having perhaps the better claim,
Because it was grassy and wanted wear;
Though as for that the passing there
Had worn them really about the same,

And both that morning equally lay
In leaves no step had trodden black.
Oh, I kept the first for another day!
Yet knowing how way leads on to way,
I doubted if I should ever come back.

I shall be telling this with a sigh
Somewhere ages and ages hence:
Two roads diverged in a wood, and I –
I took the one less traveled by,
And that has made all the difference.

JOHN KEATS

John Keats was born in London in 1795. Among his friends were
other young Romantics such as Leigh Hunt and Percy Bysshe
Shelley. He published his first sonnets in 1816. These were followed
by *Endymion* in 1818, then in 1820 by *Lamia and Other Poems*,
which included his odes 'To a Nightingale', 'To Autumn' and 'On
Melancholy'. He died from consumption in Italy in 1821.

JOHN KEATS

So Kiss'd to Sleep

'I believe in the holiness of the heart's affections.' And it is perhaps because of that belief that John Keats could fashion so much beauty from so much sorrow. His father, owner of the successful livery stables the Swan and Hoop in Moorfields, London, died when he was nine. His mother remarried within weeks. Catastrophically, she then disappeared, forfeiting her rights to her children and to the business, and turning her son into such a savage playground fighter that many believed he would make his name all right, but as a soldier. She returned six years later, was nursed lovingly by him, and died from the family curse, TB. 'That drop of blood is my death warrant,' he cried out when his own turn came.

It was delivered at a time when he was passionately in love with, and loved in return by, Fanny Brawne, a Hampstead belle with many suitors, which made him fearful. He was very small, and very conscious of it. When Fanny's mother described him as 'quite the little poet', he raged, 'One might as well say Napoleon was quite the little soldier!'

Their love was impossible to consummate, due to the risk of infecting her. A newly discovered letter paints the agony of this.

Haunted beauty, death, permeate 'La Belle Dame Sans Merci'. Robert Graves believed her to be both the muse and consumption. 'When I have Fears That I May Cease to Be' is majestic in its despair.

'On First Looking into Chapman's Homer', that wondrous tribute to the power of art, was placed by Keats on the desk of his friend at Clarke's School in Enfield, where he received his outstanding classical education. The morning after, they both sat till the next daybreak reading Chapman's translation of Homer, Keats crying out with delight at particular passages.

Endymion is a vignette from Keats to his friend Stephens who'd studied medicine with him, '"A thing of beauty is a constant joy." What think you of that, Stephens?' 'It has the true ring, but it is wanting in some way.' Later, '"A thing of beauty is a joy for ever." What think you of that, Stephens?' 'That it will last for ever.'

Keats and his friends had high hopes for *Endymion*, published in four books in 1818. It was savaged, particularly by the critic John Gibson Lockhart in *Blackwood's Magazine*, who mocked the Cockney poet and 'the imperturbable drivelling idiocy that is *Endymion*'. Keats was utterly devastated. Though he would write the great odes during this time, and his dramatic experiments, the wound was deep.

He was now seriously ill, and his friends were desperate for him to escape another English winter. He sailed for Italy in September 1821, and died in Rome the following February, aged twenty-five. His gravestone there reads:

This Grave contains all that was Mortal, of a Young English Poet, Who, on his Death Bed, in the Bitterness of his Heart, at the Malicious Power of his Enemies, Desired these Words to be engraven on His Tomb Stone. Here lies One Whose Name was writ in Water.

In this, John Keats was absolutely wrong. He is an immortal.

On First Looking into Chapman's Homer

Much have I travell'd in the realms of gold,
　　And many goodly states and kingdoms seen;
　　Round many western islands have I been
Which bards in fealty to Apollo hold.
Oft of one wide expanse had I been told
　　That deep-brow'd Homer ruled as his demesne;
　　Yet did I never breathe its pure serene
Till I heard Chapman speak out loud and bold:
Then felt I like some watcher of the skies
　　When a new planet swims into his ken;
Or like stout Cortez when with eagle eyes,
　　He star'd at the Pacific – and all his men
Look'd at each other with a wild surmise –
　　Silent, upon a peak in Darien.

When I have Fears That I May Cease to Be

When I have fears that I may cease to be
    Before my pen has gleaned my teeming brain,
Before high-pilèd books, in character,
    Hold like rich garners the full ripened grain;
When I behold, upon the night's starred face,
    Huge cloudy symbols of a high romance,
And think that I may never live to trace
    Their shadows with the magic hand of chance;
And when I feel, fair creature of an hour,
    That I shall never look upon thee more,
Never have relish in the faery power
    Of unreflecting love – then on the shore
Of the wide world I stand alone, and think
Till love and fame to nothingness do sink.

RUDYARD KIPLING

Poet, novelist and short story writer, Rudyard Kipling was born
of English parents in Bombay in 1865. His *Departmental Ditties*
(1886) and *Barrack-Room Ballads* (1892) brought him worldwide
fame. He won the Nobel Prize in 1907, the first Englishman
to be so honoured. He died in 1936.

RUDYARD KIPLING

Word Warrior

The English, he believed, were slow to hate. If they need a master-class, Kipling's their man. Seamus Heaney famously uses his pen 'to dig with'. Kipling used his as a lethal weapon. He was a word warrior and he was well armed. The day of judgement may indeed have been round the corner but Kipling couldn't wait that long. He took aim at what he saw as injustice and incompetence, dishonesty and disloyalty, vanity and villainy, targeting those responsible: criminally negligent generals, venal politicians, corrupt businessmen, brutal authority figures – most particularly those cruel to children – fired and gravely wounded them. If, as Eliot said, Kipling 'is not only serious, he has a vocation', it was that of literary marksman.

Like all good soldiers he was also a lookout scout. He had an uncanny sense of when and where trouble was brewing and the warning note was swiftly sounded. M. M. Kaye's introduction to the collected works quotes Mark Twain: 'Kipling is the only living person not head of state whose voice is heard around the world the moment it drops a remark. The only such voice in existence that does not go by slow ship and rail but always travels first-class by cable.' Americans, Kaye notes, revered Kipling and when, aged thirty-four, he almost died from pneumonia, 'in the street outside his hotel in New York bark was spread to lessen the noise of passing traffic'. Yet he had no official position politically, economically or militarily. He was a passionate child of Empire, a fact as central to his life as Jean-Paul Sartre's

Communism was to his. He believed it quite simply to be a power for good. Unlike other passionate believers in a political world view (M. Sartre again springs to mind) Kipling exposed the fault lines in the system, ruthlessly.

Although 'The White Man's Burden' in a sense became Kipling's own, 'he was *not* a Fascist. He was further from being one than the most humane or the most "progressive" person is able to be,' declared George Orwell, in his otherwise not uncritical essay on Kipling. Of 'Gehazi' (concerning the Marconi scandal of 1912), one of Kipling's most notorious poems, Ian Gilmour states 'that it is neither evil nor anti-semitic'. Kipling was undoubtedly capable of a Larkinesque mockery of national characteristics but he was democratic in his selection of his target. Few nations escaped, except, surprisingly, the French whom he seemed to love. He was always wholly unimpressed by rank, whether military or social. 'English literature has no adequate account of the British soldier, what he thought of the night before battle, what he thought of his officers, between Henry V and Rudyard Kipling': M. M. Kaye, again. Orwell agrees: 'He had far more interest in the common soldier and far more anxiety that he get a fair deal than most liberals.' Kipling also regularly expressed his contempt for 'the flannelled fools at the wickets or the muddied oafs at the goals'.

Rudyard Kipling was a poet whose collected works run to just under seven hundred pages; a novelist – *Kim* is his masterpiece; a short-story writer – his later ones, which Edmund Wilson called 'The Kipling Whom Nobody Read', are sublime, as are the children's books, *The Jungle Book* and *The Just So Stories*. He was also a journalist and a pamphleteer. He was, said Henry James, 'the most complete man of genius I have ever met'. In addition, Kipling was the first Englishman to win a Nobel Prize for Literature and was also its youngest recipient. *Something of Myself* is the apt title of his autobiography because something is all you get. Eliot said of him, he is 'the most inscrutable of authors ... a writer impossible wholly to understand and quite impossible to belittle'.

He was born in 1865 in Bombay. His father, John Lockwood Kipling, a 'serene and tolerant man' according to Kipling, taught at the school of art. His mother, née Alice MacDonald, was, he said, 'all Celt and three parts fire'. Andrew Lycett in his perceptive biography quotes a family member as saying: 'It was impossible to predict how she would react at any given point.' She was also a talented musician from whom Kipling said he inherited no musical talent whatever, except what he described as 'the brute instinct for the beat necessary for the manufacture of verse'. Rather romantically his mother and father named their first-born after Lake Rudyard in Staffordshire, where they had first met at a picnic. Up to the age of five Rudyard Kipling was, it would seem, thoroughly spoiled. If his tantrums were epic – M. M. Kaye tells us of the small boy who, on a visit to Sussex, stamps off to the village warning inhabitants to get out of the way as there was an angry Rudy coming – the cure was savage. The loving parents, in a stunning act of psychological cruelty, left him, aged five, with his sister Trix, aged three, in a boarding house in Bournemouth, the subject of the bitterly sad short story, 'Baa, Baa, Black Sheep'. From this 'House of Desolation' as he called it in his memoirs, he and Trix attended a local school. It was to be five years before they saw their mother again and seven years before they saw their father. If an unhappy childhood is a great gift to a writer, then Kipling was truly blessed.

Eventually he was rescued and sent to boarding school. Although he was hugely clever, on being told that there was no money for university he returned to India and became a journalist in Lahore. He lived happily with his parents, whom he never seemed to have wished to wound, and when Trix returned Kaye points out that he referred contentedly to them as the 'Family Square'. By the time he reached the age of twenty-three, his *Departmental Ditties* and *Plain Tales From the Hills* were sold at every railway station in India – where, incidentally, he actually lived for fewer than ten years of his adult life. With the publication of *Barrack-Room Ballads* in 1892, when he was twenty-seven, he became world famous.

All biographers refer to his genuine modesty. He regarded himself as a craftsman. He was not greedy for honours for himself, turning down a knighthood, the poet laureateship and the Order of Merit. Though he had little time for 'the long-haired literati', he refused to criticise any 'fellow craftsman's output'. He had respect for the work of others from sea captains to civil servants; C. S. Lewis called him 'the poet of work'. 'Writers,' he said, 'must recognise the gulf that separates even the least of those who do things worthy of being written about from even the best of those who have written things worthy of being talked about.' Not a universal attitude.

Few writers have travelled so much or have lived on so many continents. He witnessed national wars, world war and 'the savage wars of peace'. He lived to see his beloved Empire all but disintegrate. In his own life he suffered the tragedy of the death of his children – his daughter Josephine, who died from pneumonia when aged six, and his only son John, who died in the war. Eliot once wrote of Yeats: 'He was capable of experience', and pointed to the late poetic development that ensued. That does not seem to have happened with Kipling. Though as John Bayley points out he became wiser. His extraordinary diversity in form and in subject matter has at its core emotional, moral and philosophical consistency. There is also something else, an elemental force that is as disturbing as it is unforgettable. Eliot wrote of him, 'There is always something alien about Kipling, as of a visitor from another planet ... Kipling knew something of things which are beyond the frontier ... a queer gift of second-sight, of transmitting messages from elsewhere, a gift so disconcerting when we are made aware of it that henceforth we are never quite sure when it is *not* present.' Kipling on every level makes us uneasy, his ferocity often frightens us, his perverse naivety unnerves us, his imperialism embarrasses us, and yet he continues on, an Immortal. The poems in this book are just some of the many reasons why ...

The Poems

First to Kipling and the women, of whom, in his personal life, there were virtually none. He married his wife Carrie, Caroline Starr Ballestier, after an awkward courtship. He was, in fact, liberal in sexual matters and certainly no innocent. His short story, 'Mrs Bathurst', is one of the most sexually shocking in literature. He fought hard for better medical facilities for women in India and was bitterly opposed to the custom of child brides. 'The Female of the Species' is a delightfully provocative poem that often leads to spirited debate between the sexes. The winner is not a surprise.

From one battlefield to another: fathers and sons. 'Never seen Death yet, Dickie? Well, now is your time to learn.' It's not a sentimental education! 'The Mary Gloster' is one of the great dramatic monologues. 'Sir Anthony Gloster, dying, a baronite' places on the shoulders of his despised son, Dickie, a task equal, almost, to that of Hamlet – but kinder in its way.

To real wars and warnings of war. 'Recessional' was published in *The Times* in 1897 to mark Queen Victoria's sixty years on the throne. Its iconic line, 'Lest we forget' is a not jingoistic celebration. The Queen's Trumpeter, as he is here (when he died he was referred to as 'The King's Trumpeter'), sounds a warning note. Though he was much pilloried for the line 'lesser breeds without the Law', which is often interpreted as 'natives', Kipling was in fact referring to the Germans, who were anything but powerless at the time. They became stronger, as they proved in 1914.

'The Gods of the Copybook Headings' was published in October 1919 and, as Andrew Lycett writes in his biography, 'not only was England drained – so was Kipling. He was fifty-three. His son John was dead.' The exhaustion is clear in the poem, which asks how often must we relearn the old lessons. 'Copybooks' (which lasted in Ireland much longer than in England) were, as Lycett describes them, 'little ruled exercise books used to practise one's handwriting by copying – slowly and carefully – usually twenty times the line of a prayer, proverb or quotation'.

To two war poems. Kipling did not regret the war. Jorge Luis Borges writes that Kipling 'saw war as an obligation, but he never sang of victory, only of the peace that victory brings, and of the hardships of battle'. Execution in war is not only reserved for the enemy. 'Danny Deever' is the poem, above all others, that made Kipling as famous in England as he was in India. Professor Mason, an expert on Milton, is said by Kaye to have excitedly waved a copy at his students and cried out, 'Here's Literature! Here's Literature, at last.' He was right. It's a masterpiece of poetic, rhythmic perfection. As Eliot notes, 'in the combination of heavy beat and variation of pace ... in the regular recurrence of same end words' you can hear the marching feet and the 'movement of the men in disciplined formation'. In the end, it is the pity that lingers, 'after hangin' Danny Deever in the mornin''. 'Tommy' is the ordinary soldier thrown out of bars and theatres while on leave, 'But it's "Thin red line of 'eroes" when the drums begin to roll.' It's a poem to make you hang your head in shame. As Orwell wrote, 'A humanitarian is always a hypocrite' and he quoted the line, 'makin' mock o' uniforms that guard you while you sleep'.

'The Children' is dedicated to John Kipling, killed on his first day of active service at the battle of Loos, where '8,246 men out of 10,000 were killed or wounded in 200 minutes'. The title is interesting in using the plural. 'One can't let one's friends' and neighbours' sons be killed in order to save us and our son,' Carrie Kipling said to a neighbour. Many of the greatest anti-war lines were written by a man often regarded as a warmonger. In 'Epitaphs of the War' Kipling gives individual voice to 'Mine angry and defrauded young' who, like his son John, were mown down in their hundreds of thousands, wave after wave of them marching towards the guns. 'If any question why we died, / Tell them, because our fathers lied.' Nothing changes.

The Mary Gloster

I've paid for your sickest fancies; I've humoured your crackedest
    whim—
Dick, it's your daddy, dying; you've got to listen to him!
Good for a fortnight, am I? The doctor told you? He lied.
I shall go under by morning, and—Put that nurse outside.
Never seen death yet, Dickie? Well, now is your time to learn,
And you'll wish you held my record before it comes to your turn.
Not counting the Line and the Foundry, the Yards and the village, too,
I've made myself and a million; but I'm damned if I made you.
Master at two-and-twenty, and married at twenty-three—
Ten thousand men on the pay-roll, and forty freighters at sea!
Fifty years between 'em, and every year of it fight,
And now I'm Sir Anthony Gloster, dying, a baronite:
For I lunched with his Royal 'Ighness—what was it the papers a-had?
'Not least of our merchant-princes.' Dickie, that's me, your dad!
I didn't begin with askings. I took my job and I stuck;
I took the chances they wouldn't, an' now they're calling it luck.
Lord, what boats I've handled—rotten and leaky and old—
Ran 'em, or—opened the bilge-cock, precisely as I was told.
Grub that 'ud bind you crazy, and crews that 'ud turn you grey,
And a big fat lump of insurance to cover the risk on the way.
The others they dursn't do it; they said they valued their life
(They've served me since as skippers). I went, and I took my wife.
Over the world I drove 'em, married at twenty-three,
And your mother saving the money and making a man of me.
I was content to be master, but she said there was better behind;
She took the chances I wouldn't, and I followed your mother blind.

She egged me to borrow the money, an' she helped me to clear the
loan,
When we bought half-shares in a cheap 'un and hoisted a flag of our
own.
Patching and coaling on credit, and living the Lord knew how,
We started the Red Ox freighters—we've eight-and-thirty now.
And those were the days of clippers, and the freights were clipper-
freights,
And we knew we were making our fortune, but she died in Macassar
Straits—
By the Little Paternosters, as you come to the Union Bank—
And we dropped her in fourteen fathom: I pricked it off where she sank.
Owners we were, full owners, and the boat was christened for her,
And she died in the *Mary Gloster*. My heart, how young we were!
So I went on a spree round Java and well-nigh ran ashore,
But your mother came and warned me and I wouldn't liquor no more:
Strict I stuck to my business, afraid to stop or I'd think,
Saving the money (she warned me), and letting the other men drink.
And I met M'Cullough in London (I'd turned five 'undred then),
And 'tween us we started the Foundry—three forges and twenty men.
Cheap repairs for the cheap 'uns. It paid, and the business grew;
For I bought me a steam-lathe patent, and that was a gold mine too.
'Cheaper to build 'em than buy 'em,' I said, but M'Cullough he shied,
And we wasted a year in talking before we moved to the Clyde.
And the Lines were all beginning, and we all of us started fair,
Building our engines like houses and staying the boilers square.
But M'Cullough 'e wanted cabins with marble and maple and all,
And Brussels an' Utrecht velvet, and baths and a Social Hall,
And pipes for closets all over, and cutting the frames too light,
But M'Cullough he died in the Sixties, and—Well, I'm dying to-
night ...
I knew—I knew what was coming, when we bid on the *Byfleet's* keel—
They piddled and piffled with iron. I'd given my orders for steel!

Steel and the fast expansions. It paid, I tell you, it paid,
When we came with our nine-knot freighters and collared the long-
    run trade!
And they asked me how I did it, and I gave 'em the Scripture text,
'You keep your light so shining a little in front o' the next!'
They copied all they could follow, but they couldn't copy my mind,
And I left 'em sweating and stealing a year and a half behind.
Then came the armour-contracts, but that was M'Cullough's side;
He was always best in the Foundry, but better, perhaps, he died.
I went through his private papers; the notes was plainer than print;
And I'm no fool to finish if a man'll give me a hint.
(I remember his widow was angry.) So I saw what his drawings meant,
And I started the six-inch rollers, and it paid me sixty per cent.
Sixty per cent *with* failures, and more than twice we could do,
And a quarter-million to credit, and I saved it all for you!
I thought—it doesn't matter—you seemed to favour your ma,
But you're nearer forty than thirty, and I know the kind you are.
Harrer an' Trinity College! I ought to ha' sent you to sea—
But I stood you an education, an' what have you done for me?
The things I knew was proper you wouldn't thank me to give,
And the things I knew was rotten you said was the way to live.
For you muddled with books and pictures, an' china an' etchin's an'
    fans,
And your rooms at college was beastly—more like a whore's than a
    man's;
Till you married that thin-flanked woman, as white and as stale as a
    bone,
An' she gave you your social nonsense; but where's that kid o' your
    own?
I've seen your carriages blocking the half o' the Cromwell Road,
But never the doctor's brougham to help the missus unload.
(So there isn't even a grandchild, an' the Gloster family's done.)
Not like your mother, she isn't. *She* carried her freight each run.

But they died, the pore little beggars! At sea she had 'em—they died.
Only you, an' you stood it. You haven't stood much beside.
Weak, a liar, and idle, and mean as a collier's whelp
Nosing for scraps in the galley. No help—my son was no help!
So he gets three 'undred thousand, in trust and the interest paid.
I wouldn't give it you, Dickie—you see, I made it in trade.
You're saved from soiling your fingers, and if you have no child,
It all comes back to the business. 'Gad, won't your wife be wild!
'Calls and calls in her carriage, her 'andkerchief up to 'er eye:
'Daddy! dear daddy's dyin'!' and doing her best to cry.
Grateful? Oh, yes, I'm grateful, but keep her away from here.
Your mother 'ud never ha' stood 'er, and, anyhow, women are
     queer . . .
There's women will say I've married a second time! Not quite!
But give pore Aggie a hundred, and tell her your lawyers'll fight.
She was the best o' the boiling—you'll meet her before it ends.
I'm in for a row with the mother—I'll leave you settle my friends.
For a man he must go with a woman, which women don't understand—
Or the sort that say they can see it they aren't the marrying brand.
But I wanted to speak o' your mother that's Lady Gloster still—
I'm going to up and see her, without it's hurting the will.
     Here! Take your hand off the bell-pull. Five thousand's waiting
      for you,
If you'll only listen a minute, and do as I bid you do.
They'll try to prove me crazy, and, if you bungle, they can;
And I've only you to trust to! (O God, why ain't he a man?)
There's some waste money on marbles, the same as M'Cullough tried—
Marbles and mausoleums—but I call that sinful pride.
There's some ship bodies for burial—we've carried 'em, soldered and
     packed;
Down in their wills they wrote it, and nobody called *them* cracked.
But me—I've too much money, and people might . . . All my fault:
It came o' hoping for grandsons and buying that Wokin' vault . . .

I'm sick o' the 'ole dam' business. I'm going back where I came.
Dick, you're the son o' my body, and you'll take charge o' the same!
I want to lie by your mother, ten thousand mile away,
And they'll want to send me to Woking; and that's where you'll earn
      your pay.
I've thought it out on the quiet, the same as it ought to be done—
Quiet, and decent, and proper—an' here's your orders, my son.
You know the Line? You don't, though. You write to the Board, and
      tell
Your father's death has upset you an' you're goin' to cruise for a spell,
An' you'd like the *Mary Gloster*—I've held her ready for this—
They'll put her in working order and you'll take her out as she is.
Yes, it was money idle when I patched her and put her aside
(Thank God, I can pay for my fancies!)—the boat where your mother
      died.
By the Little Paternosters, as you come to the Union Bank,
We dropped her—I think I told you—and I pricked it off where she
      sank,
(Tiny she looked on the grating—that oily, treacly sea—)
'Hundred and Eighteen East, remember, and South just Three.
Easy bearings to carry—Three South—Three to the dot;
But I gave M'Andrew a copy in case of dying—or not.
And so you'll write to M'Andrew, he's Chief of the Maori Line;
They'll give him leave, if you ask 'em and say it's business o' mine.
I built three boats for the Maoris, an' very well pleased they were,
An' I've known Mac since the Fifties, and Mac knew me—and her.
After the first stroke warned me I sent him the money to keep
Against the time you'd claim it, committin' your dad to the deep;
For you are the son o' my body, and Mac was my oldest friend,
I've never asked 'im to dinner, but he'll see it out to the end.
Stiff-necked Glasgow beggar! I've heard he's prayed for my soul,
But he couldn't lie if you paid him, and he'd starve before he stole.
He'll take the *Mary* in ballast—you'll find her a lively ship;

And you'll take Sir Anthony Gloster, that goes on 'is wedding-trip,
Lashed in our old deck-cabin with all three port-holes wide,
The kick o' the screw beneath him and the round blue seas outside!
Sir Anthony Gloster's carriage—our 'ouse-flag flyin' free—
Ten thousand men on the pay-roll and forty freighters at sea!
He made himself and a million, but this world is a fleetin' show,
And he'll go to the wife of 'is bosom the same as he ought to go—
By the heel of the Paternosters—there isn't a chance to mistake—
And Mac'll pay you the money as soon as the bubbles break!
Five thousand for six weeks' cruising, the staunchest freighter afloat,
And Mac he'll give you your bonus the minute I'm out o' the boat!
He'll take you round to Macassar, and you'll come back alone;
He knows what I want o' the *Mary* . . . I'll do what I please with my
    own.
Your mother 'ud call it wasteful, but I've seven-and-thirty more;
I'll come in my private carriage and bid it wait at the door . . .
For my son 'e was never a credit: 'e muddled with books and art,
And 'e lived on Sir Anthony's money and 'e broke Sir Anthony's
    heart.
There isn't even a grandchild, and the Gloster family's done—
The only one you left me—O mother, the only one!
Harrer and Trinity College—me slavin' early an' late—
An' he thinks I'm dying crazy, and you're in Macassar Strait!
Flesh o' my flesh, my dearie, for ever an' ever amen,
That first stroke came for a warning. I ought to ha' gone to you then.
But—cheap repairs for a cheap 'un—the doctors said I'd do.
Mary, why didn't *you* warn me? I've allus heeded to you,
Excep'—I know—about women; but you are a spirit now;
An' wife, they was only women, and I was a man. That's how.
An' a man 'e must go with a woman, as you could not understand;
But I never talked 'em secrets. I paid 'em out o' hand.
Thank Gawd, I can pay for my fancies! Now what's five thousand to
    me,

For a berth off the Paternosters in the haven where I would be?
I believe in the Resurrection, if I read my Bible plain,
But I wouldn't trust 'em at Wokin'; we're safer at sea again.
For the heart it shall go with the treasure—go down to the sea in
    ships.
I'm sick of the hired women. I'll kiss my girl on her lips!
I'll be content with my fountain. I'll drink from my own well,
And the wife of my youth shall charm me—an' the rest can go to Hell!
(Dickie, *he* will, that's certain.) I'll lie in our standin'-bed,
An' Mac'll take her in ballast—an' she trims best by the head.
Down by the head an' sinkin', her fires are drawn and cold,
And the water's splashin' hollow on the skin of the empty hold—
Churning an' choking and chuckling, quiet and scummy and dark—
Full to her lower hatches and risin' steady. Hark!
That was the after-bulkhead ... She's flooded from stem to stern
Never seen death yet, Dickie? ... Well, now is your time to learn!

Tommy

I went into a public-'ouse to get a pint o' beer,
The publican 'e up an' sez, 'We serve no red-coats here.'
The girls be'ind the bar they laughed an' giggled fit to die,
I outs into the street again an' to myself sez I:
    O it's Tommy this, an' Tommy that, an' 'Tommy, go away';
    But it's 'Thank you, Mister Atkins,' when the band begins to
        play—
    The band begins to play, my boys, the band begins to play,
    O it's 'Thank you, Mister Atkins,' when the band begins to play.

I went into a theatre as sober as could be,
They gave a drunk civilian room, but 'adn't none for me;
They sent me to the gallery or round the music-'alls,
    But when it comes to fightin', Lord! they'll shove me in the stalls!
    For it's Tommy this, an' Tommy that, an' 'Tommy, wait outside';
    But it's 'Special train for Atkins' when the trooper's on the tide—
    The troopship's on the tide, my boys, the troopship's on the tide,
    O it's 'Special train for Atkins' when the trooper's on the tide.

Yes, makin' mock o' uniforms that guard you while you sleep
Is cheaper than them uniforms, an' they're starvation cheap;
An' hustlin' drunken soldiers when they're goin' large a bit
Is five times better business than paradin' in full kit.
    Then it's Tommy this an' Tommy that, an' 'Tommy, 'ow's yer soul?'
    But it's 'Thin red line of 'eroes' when the drums begin to roll—
    The drums begin to roll, my boys, the drums begin to roll,
    O it's 'Thin red line of 'eroes' when the drums begin to roll.

We aren't no thin red 'eroes, nor we aren't no blackguards too,
But single men in barricks, most remarkable like you;
An' if sometimes our conduck isn't all your fancy paints,
Why, single men in barricks don't grow into plaster saints;
    While it's Tommy this, an' Tommy that, an' 'Tommy, fall be'ind,'
    But it's 'Please to walk in front, sir,' when there's trouble in the
        wind—
    There's trouble in the wind, my boys, there's trouble in the wind,
    O it's 'Please to walk in front, sir,' when there's trouble in the
        wind.

You talk o' better food for us, an' schools, an' fires, an' all:
We'll wait for extry rations if you treat us rational.
Don't mess about the cook-room slops, but prove it to our face
The Widow's Uniform is not the soldier-man's disgrace.
    For it's Tommy this an' Tommy that, an' 'Chuck him out, the
        brute!'
    But it's 'Saviour of 'is country' when the guns begin to shoot;
    An' it's Tommy this, an' Tommy that, an' anything you please;
    An' Tommy ain't a bloomin' fool—you bet that Tommy sees!

PHILIP LARKIN

Philip Arthur Larkin was born in Coventry in 1922. A poet, novelist and librarian, his publication of *The Whitsun Weddings* (1964) and *High Windows* (1974) secured his reputation. He refused the position of Poet Laureate in 1984 but accepted membership of the Order of the Companions of Honour in 1985, the year of his death.

PHILIP LARKIN

Too Clever to Live?

In 1984 I approached Philip Larkin to request permission to present an evening of his poetry read by Alan Bates. Though warned by his old friend Kingsley Amis, 'Oh dear, no, Josephine, Philip won't like this at all', I persevered. Mr Larkin said yes. I sent him roses after the reading. In his letter of thanks Philip Larkin described the arrival of the bouquet at reception in Hull Library, where he worked as Chief Librarian, its procession from department to department, the tentative smiles of hope that faded as, impervious to silent entreaties of 'Let it be me', the arrangement was eventually handed to him. In subject matter, that letter could easily have been a Larkin poem, illustrating as it did a key motif in his poetry: the significance of small events and their defining pressure on individual psychology, most particularly his own. An invitation to a drinks party, a visit to an empty church, a recently vacated room in a boarding house: such everyday events are transmuted by Larkin into poetry that gives weight to the ordinary dreams and fears of our daily lives, lived out as they are in the shadow of eternity. We recognise ourselves in his poems, as we do in a Chekhov play, and we smile and our smiles are rueful.

'I like to read about people who have done nothing spectacular, aren't beautiful or lucky; who try to behave well in a limited field of activity and who can see in the little autumnal moments of vision that the so-called "big experiences of life" are going to miss them. I like to read about such things presented not with self-pity or despair or romanticism but with realistic firmness and even humour.' This, Larkin wrote, was the 'moral tone' of Barbara Pym's novels. It is also the moral tone of much of Larkin's work. He believed art should help us either to 'enjoy or endure'. Yet he himself seemed to find neither enjoyment nor endurance easy. Though he was an adored child from a secure middle-class background, tensions in his parents' marriage and the hushed atmosphere in his house may have inspired the sad line, 'What was the rock my gliding childhood struck?'

His parents, Sydney Larkin OBE, and his bookish wife, Eva, encouraged his literary interests and were in fact hugely proud of him. His life was crowned with success. He sailed into Oxford and sailed out again, a published poet, and to his delight, with a first-class honours degree. Shortly after Oxford he published two novels, *Jill* and *A Girl in Winter*, became a professional librarian, combining the roles of scholar, curator and administrator in an exemplary career. His *Who's Who* entry states his occupation as Librarian: 'A man *is* what he is paid for.' His four collections of poetry, *The Less Deceived*, *High Windows*, *The North Ship* and *The Whitsun Weddings*, made him one of the most acclaimed English poets of the twentieth century. He won the Gold Medal for Poetry and was offered, but turned down, the poet laureateship; 'Poetry, that rare bird, has flown out of the window.' In his private life he was a much loved man. Andrew Motion in his biography, *Philip Larkin, A Writer's Life*, charts a course with great elegance through not only the development of the poet but also the labyrinthine ways of Larkin and his women. He makes clear that two women – in particular, Monica Jones and Maeve Brennan – loved him for decades and that there were other, serious relationships. It would seem that Larkin inspired in women levels of self-sacrifice that would have done Byron proud. Ironically, one of his most quoted lines is: 'What will survive of us is love.'

Was he, however, just 'too clever to live'? The question is posed by A. L. Rowse, whose library edition of Larkin's *Required Writing* I had the good luck to buy, containing, as it does, challenging, hand-written comments on virtually every page: 'Kindly face, no kidding him', 'perverse psychology, Irish perhaps?' But it wasn't just clever-ness that made Larkin 'miss out on the big experiences of life'. The 'deprivation', which was to him 'what daffodils were to Wordsworth', was, in his case, elective. The 'examined life' led to a life at bay.

Why? For art's sake? It would seem so. His long dialogue with self, 'Self's the Man' (the title of one of his poems), is a battleground between art and life. 'When I think of being in my *twenties* or even my *thirties*, my external surroundings have changed but inside I've been the same, trying to hold everything off in order to write.' It wasn't just Cyril Connolly's enemy of promise, 'the pram in the hall', that Larkin feared; it was the hall, the kitchen, the sitting room, if they contained people with claims on the time in his life. No poet ever feared the end of his time more than Philip Larkin. In the brutal choice for all artists – and not only artists – of 'perfection of the work rather than of the life' (Yeats's haunting phrase), Larkin came down firmly, knowingly, on the side of art. If at the end of her monologue Joyce's Molly Bloom sounds the most emphatic yes in literature (and in plural), Larkin's poems move inexorably to an emphatic no. In Christopher Ricks's brilliant insight, 'Just as a romantic swell of feel-ing rises' it meets 'a counter thrust of classical impersonality', we have the essence of that tension that makes Larkin's poems so thrilling to read.

Larkin sets you down immediately, with almost cinematic exac-titude, in the 'scene', and as Alan Bennett notes, 'He still has you firmly by the hand as you cross the finishing line.' And Larkin's fin-ishing lines are pure gold. Last lines are 'the stamp', as John Donne wrote, that authenticate what great poetry is – in itself 'the beating out of a piece of gold'. With Larkin, the poetic journey may be short, the image fleeting; there may be stops along the way (interrupted journeys are a recurrent theme); but at the point of arrival we know the place. Perhaps we've been there before. Larkin's round-life trips are more challenging than any round-the-world trip. He knows the great adventure is internal. The man whose voice, as Andrew Motion noted, is 'one of the means by which his country recognises itself', did not travel far, even in England. He was born in Coventry in 1922. He died in Hull in 1985. 'I am going to the inevitable.' No Kipling, he. His own divine comedy was not set in the middle of a dark wood 'but in a railway tunnel, half way through England' as Seamus Heaney said as he listened, as we all do, to Larkin's 'unfoolable mind . . . singing the melody of intelligence'.

The Poems

'He is the only sophisticated poet today who requires no sophisticated response from the reader,' John Bayley wrote in 1983.
Twenty-three years later and long after Larkin's death, Bayley's
insight remains true. Larkin once observed that he'd found a way of
'making novels into poems'. Intriguingly, it was a novelist turned
poet, Thomas Hardy, who killed Larkin's early obsession with the
music of Yeats – 'as pervasive as garlic' in Larkin's later description.
As in many novels resolution is sudden. The rejection in 'Poetry of
Departures' to the elemental dream of leaving comes just as the heart
quickens with the exhilaration of '*He chucked up everything / And just
cleared off*' to 'swagger the nut-strewn roads', or 'Crouch in the fo'c'sle
/ Stubbly with goodness'. Then, suddenly, the race is over before it
has started.

In 'I Remember, I Remember' Larkin reminds us that we all start
from home, the memory of which never leaves us. The train stops at
Coventry, the station sign becoming the Proustian 'madeleine' that
inspires memories of 'where my childhood was unspent', of 'The
bracken where I never trembling sat ... where she / Lay back, and "all
became a burning mist"'. The witty truth of most childhoods tumbles
down to one of the great last lines in poetry: 'Nothing, like something, happens anywhere.' Proust, subverted. It's hard to get away
from nothing. Larkin once described the difficulty in escaping from
home as akin to 'writing *Decline and Fall of the Roman Empire*'. In
'This Be The Verse' there is gender equality in the parental blame
game. Nature and nurture fail. Perhaps Beckett is right, 'Never to
have been born is best.' After all, 'They fuck you up, your mum and
dad.' Larkin, in a letter to Kingsley Amis, said of the poem, 'Clearly

my Lake Isle of Innisfree. I fully expect to hear it recited by a 1000 Girl Guides before I die.' What an excellent idea! Also for boy scouts. Parental guilt removed at a stroke. The last lines are an exercise in exuberant nihilism: 'Get out as early as you can / And don't have any kids yourself.'

'Vers de Société' is Larkin's version of Sartre's 'Hell is other people.' He once said, 'I see life more as an affair of solitude diversified by company than an affair of company diversified by solitude.' The reason is deeper than unsociability. Parties to Larkin are the waste of precious time that would be better 'repaid / Under a lamp, hearing the noise of wind / And looking out to see the moon thinned / To an air-sharpened blade'.

'Mr Bleaney' is a dialogue with a ghost. What do we leave behind us in the rooms we have vacated? Or in the life we have vacated which 'measures our own nature'? Was Mr Bleaney satisfied 'at his age having no more to show / Than one hired box'? Perhaps 'He warranted no better, I don't know.' Who knows?

'Church Going' explores reverence without religion, in an empty church actually in Ireland. The 'unignorable silence' into which the accumulated ceremonies of life and death echo in 'A serious house on serious earth' which is 'proper to grow wise in, / If only that so many dead lie round'. Definitely Ireland.

'The Whitsun Weddings' is a Fellini-like vision on station platforms of 'grinning and pomaded, girls / In parodies of fashion, heels and veils / ... The fathers with broad belts under their suits / ... mothers loud and fat' as 'A dozen marriages got under way / ... with all the power / That being changed can give.'

The Dickensian title of 'Dockery and Son' is apt. It's my favourite Larkin poem, a novel of a poem. Larkin always wanted to be a novelist and believed that 'poetry chose me', luckily for us. The poem is about youth and what one does with it. Dockery is remembered by the wifeless, childless, middle-aged narrator as a boy who seized his moment sexually and begot a son, who now attends their old college.

Then, provocatively, Larkin throws down the philosophical gauntlet: 'Why did he [Dockery] think adding meant increase? / ...Where do these / Innate assumptions come from?' One of the great questions. One of the great poems.

Poetry of Departures

Sometimes you hear, fifth-hand,
As epitaph:
He chucked up everything
And just cleared off,
And always the voice will sound
Certain you approve
This audacious, purifying,
Elemental move.

And they are right, I think.
We all hate home
And having to be there:
I detest my room,
Its specially-chosen junk,
The good books, the good bed,
And my life, in perfect order:
So to hear it said

He walked out on the whole crowd
Leaves me flushed and stirred,
Like *Then she undid her dress*
Or *Take that you bastard*;
Surely I can, if he did?
And that helps me stay
Sober and industrious.
But I'd go today,

Yes, swagger the nut-strewn roads,
Crouch in the fo'c'sle
Stubbly with goodness, if
It weren't so artificial,
Such a deliberate step backwards
To create an object:
Books; china; a life
Reprehensibly perfect.

I Remember, I Remember

Coming up England by a different line
For once, early in the cold new year,
We stopped, and, watching men with number-plates
Sprint down the platform to familiar gates,
'Why, Coventry!' I exclaimed. 'I was born here.'

I leant far out, and squinnied for a sign
That this was still the town that had been 'mine'
So long, but found I wasn't even clear
Which side was which. From where those cycle-crates
Were standing, had we annually departed

For all those family hols? . . . A whistle went:
Things moved. I sat back, staring at my boots.
'Was that,' my friend smiled, 'where you "have your roots"?'
No, only where my childhood was unspent,
I wanted to retort, just where I started:

By now I've got the whole place clearly charted.
Our garden, first: where I did not invent
Blinding theologies of flowers and fruits,
And wasn't spoken to by an old hat.
And here we have that splendid family

I never ran to when I got depressed,
The boys all biceps and the girls all chest,
Their comic Ford, their farm where I could be
'Really myself'. I'll show you, come to that,
The bracken where I never trembling sat,

Determined to go through with it; where she
Lay back, and 'all became a burning mist'.
And, in those offices, my doggerel
Was not set up in blunt ten-point, nor read
By a distinguished cousin of the mayor,

Who didn't call and tell my father *There
Before us, had we the gift to see ahead –*
'You look as if you wished the place in Hell,'
My friend said, 'judging from your face.' 'Oh well,
I suppose it's not the place's fault,' I said.

'Nothing, like something, happens anywhere.'

ROBERT LOWELL

Robert Traill Spence Lowell was born into American aristocracy in Boston in 1917. His first collection, *Lord Weary's Castle*, published in 1946, brought him iconic status and won the Pulitzer Prize. His seminal work *Life Studies* was hugely influential and was followed in 1973 by *The Dolphin*, for which he was awarded his second Pulitzer Prize. He died in 1977.

ROBERT LOWELL

My mind's not right . . .

True. It was however right enough to make Robert Lowell one of America's greatest poets. 'Seeing less than others can be a great strain,' he once wrote, hinting at something deeper than myopia. 'Looking back over thirty years of published work my impression is that the thread that strings the work together is autobiography.' He could have added history, that of his family and his country – the one a shadow outline of the other. According to the critic John Bayley, 'The Lowell family itself was a more potent inspiration than any literature.' His masterpiece is *Life Studies* – they are close to home. Few parents or indeed grandparents have been more assiduously studied than those of Robert Lowell and, as in 'Dolphin' and 'Day by Day', few wives have been portrayed with quite such forensic love as those of Robert Lowell. He poses, in poetry, Cocteau's challenge: 'how far one can go too far'. And answers it thus: 'you want the reader to say, this is true' and 'to believe he was getting the *real* Robert Lowell'. It's a line in which self-granted absolution mingles with strange Pirandello-like reverberations concerning self and persona.

Who was the *real* Robert Lowell? In Lowell's case, since he was often mentally ill, the question has a tragic dimension. He was born on 1 March 1917, into American aristocracy. His family included the Cabots, who talked only to the Lowells, and the Lowells, who talked only to God. His father was Robert Traill Spence Lowell Snr, 'who hadn't a mean bone, an original bone or a funny bone in his body' –

a relative's cruel, though it would seem accurate description. His mother, whose family came over on the *Mayflower*, was the formidable Charlotte Winslow, about whom her son would write two fierce poems of love and frustration: 'To Mother' ('Becoming ourselves, / we lose our nerve for children') and the brutally titled 'Unwanted'. Charlotte was a marital manipulator par excellence: 'she saw her husband as a valet sees through a master'. She dominated him and she effectively thwarted his naval career. His father declined smiling from job to job 'until in his forties his soul went underground': Lowell's haunting description in his prose poem '91 Revere Street'. Even as a child – 'always inside me is the child who died' – he wondered, why doesn't father fight back?

Nothing was going to thwart Robert Lowell Jnr. At school he was physically powerful and psychologically manipulative. He was nicknamed Caligula, mercifully shortened to Cal. In adolescence and young manhood his rages and his recklessness were such that help was sought from Dr Merrill Moore, a poet-psychiatrist, and eventually, later, from Carl Jung: 'If your son is as you have described him, / he is an incurable schizophrenic.' Sadly, nothing could save Lowell from severe mental illness and in his thirties he would tumble into the abyss of psychosis, often hospitalised for his own protection. 'I believed I could stop cars and paralyze their forces by merely standing in the middle of the highway; that I was the reincarnation of The Holy Ghost – To have known the glory, violence and banality of such an experience is corrupting.' However, within the kingdom of poetry, perhaps Lowell sensed he would work miracles or perhaps he sensed salvation. Certainly from the moment he started writing poetry aged seventeen, encouraged by the poet-teacher Richard Eberhart, he demonstrated startling intensity and utterly determined will. When told by the initially bewildered poet Allen Tate of New Criticism fame, whom he'd followed from Harvard to Tennessee, 'we really haven't any room – you'd have to pitch a tent on the lawn', Lowell did precisely that. At Kenyon College they would analyse poetry down to its last Empsonian ambiguity. 'It's such a miracle if you get lines that are halfway right' – though miracles are often troubling and they troubled him. His poems were worked and re-worked. 'You didn't write, you *re*-wrote,' his friend Randall Jarrell commented.

In 1946 his collection *Lord Weary's Castle* was published. It was in style and content American heroic, brilliant, allusive, technically dazzling, spiritual (he'd converted to Catholicism with typical intensity) and difficult. 'The Lord survives the rainbow of His will', the famous last line of 'The Quaker Graveyard in Nantucket', challenges the reader, who is best advised to resist and simply surrender to its beauty. The collection won ecstatic reviews and the Pulitzer Prize. He was barely thirty and he'd arrived – a literary star. In fact he'd achieved notoriety some time earlier with a letter to a president. Lowell, who'd volunteered in 1941 and had been turned down due to his eyesight, was drafted in 1943. 'Dear Mr President, I very much regret that I must refuse the opportunity you have afforded me in your communication of August the 6th 1943 for service in the armed forces.' Lowell attached his Declaration of Personal Responsibility. 'We are prepared to wage war without quarter or principles to the permanent destruction of Germany and Japan. I cannot honorably participate in a war whose persecution constitutes the betrayal of my country.' It was headline news. LOWELL SCION REFUSES TO FIGHT! He was sentenced to a year and a day in the Federal Correction Center in Danbury, prior to which he spent a few days in West Street in the cell next to Lepke of Murder, Inc. – who was eventually executed. Lepke to Lowell: 'I'm in for killing. What are you in for?' 'I'm in for refusing to kill.'

Twenty-two years later, in the sixties, Lowell's involvement in anti-Vietnam demonstrations led to another, though calmer letter to a president, Johnson this time, turning down an invitation to the White House Festival of the Arts. It was again front-page news. By then of course he was America's most celebrated and most controversial poet. The publication in 1959 of *Life Studies* was a seminal moment for Lowell and for American literature. Anna Swir, the eminent critic, has written that the first duty of the writer is to create an individual style and the second – more difficult – to destroy it. Lowell did just that. 'I'd been on tour and reading aloud and more and more I was simplifying my poems.' They were indeed simpler, less allusive; they were also infinitely more disturbing. They inspired, among others, Sylvia Plath and Anne Sexton, both of whom he taught at Harvard. They gave rise to the term 'confessional poetry', a term he hated but it has some accuracy. One critic described them as a form of ordered bleeding onto the page. *Life Studies* was followed in 1973 by the Pulitzer Prize-winning *The Dolphin*, which revealed, perhaps too brutally, the private pain of all concerned when Lowell (previously married to the short-story writer Jean Stafford) left his long marriage to the literary icon Elizabeth Hardwick for the stunningly beautiful, Booker Prize-shortlisted novelist Caroline Blackwood, whom he subsequently married.

'But our beginnings never know our ends' is Eliot's chilling warning. Robert Lowell died of a heart attack in a taxi in New York in 1977. He was just sixty years old. He was carrying a brown paper parcel containing Lucian Freud's portrait of his then wife, Caroline Blackwood, which Grey (Lord) Gowrie, one-time chairman of Sotheby's, had procured for Lowell. It's a heartbreaking scene, and Lowell knew himself to be heartbreaking. He was right. He was also a great poet.

The Poems

'It's better to get your emotions out in a Macbeth than in a confession,' Lowell said in 1961, two years after *Life Studies*, which, he implied, would be his last autobiographical collection. And about that he was wrong. He had recreated himself in poetry once, in 1959, and though his life was to change dramatically when he left Elizabeth Hardwick and America (he became a visiting fellow at All Souls, Oxford, and a lecturer at Kent and Sussex) he would continue to carve out of the personal much of his most enduring poetry.

But not all. Lowell wrote two of the greatest political poems of this or any age, 'Waking Early Sunday Morning' and 'For the Union Dead' – title poem of his hugely praised 1964 collection. This last is a haunting tribute to Col. Robert Gould Shaw, white, twenty-five when he bravely led his black 54 Massachusetts Regiment against Fort Wagner in the Civil War ('They relinquish everything to serve the Republic'). A monument to his courage by Augustus Saint-Gaudens stands in stark contrast to what Lowell perceives as a less honourable time. Lowell felt in his public utterances and behaviour the weight of history inherent in his family name. During anti-Vietnam demonstrations he had 'the unwilling haunted saintliness of a man who was repaying the moral debts of tens of generations of ancestors'. Norman Mailer at his most restrained. 'Commander Lowell', the poet's father – 'once / nineteen, the youngest ensign in his class, / he was "the old man" of a gunboat on the Yangtze' – is 'paid out' for his failure, more economic than moral in this brutal, minor masterpiece. In 'Memories of West Street and Lepke', written in the 'tranquilized *Fifties*, / and I am forty . . .', Lowell remembers his 'manic statement, / telling off the state and president' which led him to prison and to Lepke of Murder, Inc., 'the electric chair— / hanging like an oasis in his air / of lost connections . . .'

A perfect last line, and last lines, as Donne reminds us, 'are the stamp' that authenticates great poetry.

Perhaps his most unforgettable line lies just off-centre of one of his best poems, 'Skunk Hour' – his tribute to his great friend, the poet Elizabeth Bishop. It abruptly changes the rhythm of the poem, and stuns with its awful simplicity: 'My mind's not right.' 'Waking in the Blue' is a dazed love poem from McLean (psychiatric) Hospital as alumni of Boston University ponder I. A. Richards's *The Meaning of Meaning* with those who in their *jeunesse dorée* had been members of Harvard's exclusive club, Porcellian '29. Legend has it that if you did not make your first million by the time you were forty the club would give it to you! Now each holds 'a locked razor'.

The very handsome Lowell married three brilliant writers and was exquisitely sensitive to marital manoeuvres – even in the dark. In 'Man and Wife', her back now turned to him, her 'old-fashioned tirade— / loving, rapid, merciless— / breaks like the Atlantic Ocean on my head'. A line to be treasured. The poem is, according to one critic, in balance with the savage sexuality in 'To Speak of Woe That Is in Marriage', as the female narrator bemoans 'the monotonous meanness of his lust'. Lowell said the poem owed a debt to Catullus. The imagery, however, of the woman who each night tapes a ten-dollar note and the man's car keys to her thigh is based on a shared insight from a friend into his clearly less than ecstatic marriage.

'I enjoyed writing about my life more than living it,' Lowell said towards the end. 'Alas, I can only tell my own story.' His last poem, 'Epilogue', tells us again what it is he tried to do and at such cost. 'Yet why not say what happened? / Pray for the grace of accuracy . . . We are poor passing facts, / warned by that to give / each figure in the photograph / his living name.'

For the Union Dead

'Relinquunt Omnia Servare Rem Publicam.'

The old South Boston Aquarium stands
in a Sahara of snow now. Its broken windows are boarded.
The bronze weathervane cod has lost half its scales.
The airy tanks are dry.

Once my nose crawled like a snail on the glass;
my hand tingled
to burst the bubbles
drifting from the noses of the cowed, compliant fish.

My hand draws back. I often sigh still
for the dark downward and vegetating kingdom
of the fish and reptile. One morning last March
I pressed against the new barbed and galvanized

fence on the Boston Common. Behind their cage,
yellow dinosaur steamshovels were grunting
as they cropped up tons of mush and grass
to gouge their underworld garage.

Parking spaces luxuriate like civic
sandpiles in the heart of Boston.
A girdle of orange, Puritan-pumpkin colored girders
braces the tingling Statehouse,

shaking over the excavations, as it faces Colonel Shaw
and his bell-cheeked Negro infantry
on St. Gaudens' shaking Civil War relief,
propped by a plank splint against the garage's earthquake.

Two months after marching through Boston,
half the regiment was dead;
at the dedication,
William James could almost hear the bronze Negroes breathe.

Their monument sticks like a fishbone
in the city's throat.
Its Colonel is as lean
as a compass-needle.

He has an angry wrenlike vigilance,
a greyhound's gentle tautness;
he seems to wince at pleasure,
and suffocate for privacy.

He is out of bounds now. He rejoices in man's lovely,
peculiar power to choose life and die—
when he leads his black soldiers to death,
he cannot bend his back.

On a thousand small town New England greens,
the old white churches hold their air
of sparse, sincere rebellion; frayed flags
quilt the graveyards of the Grand Army of the Republic.

The stone statues of the abstract Union Soldier
grow slimmer and younger each year—
wasp-waisted, they doze over muskets
and muse through their sideburns . . .

Shaw's father wanted no monument
except the ditch,
where his son's body was thrown
and lost with his 'niggers.'

The ditch is nearer.
There are no statues for the last war here;
on Boylston Street, a commercial photograph
shows Hiroshima boiling

over a Mosler Safe, the 'Rock of Ages'
that survived the blast. Space is nearer.
When I crouch to my television set,
the drained faces of Negro school-children rise like balloons.

Colonel Shaw
is riding on his bubble,
he waits
for the blessèd break.

The Aquarium is gone. Everywhere,
giant finned cars nose forward like fish;
a savage servility
slides by on grease.

Commander Lowell

(1887–1950)

There were no undesirables or girls in my set,
when I was a boy at Mattapoisett—
only Mother, still her Father's daughter.
Her voice was still electric
with a hysterical, unmarried panic,
when she read to me from the Napoleon book.
Long-nosed Marie Louise
Hapsburg in the frontispiece
had a downright Boston bashfulness,
where she grovelled to Bonaparte, who scratched his navel,
and bolted his food—just my seven years tall!
And I, bristling and manic,
skulked in the attic,
and got two hundred French generals by name,
from A to V— from Augereau to Vandamme.
I used to dope myself asleep,
naming those unpronounceables like sheep.

Having a naval officer
for my Father was nothing to shout
about to the summer colony at 'Matt.'
He wasn't at all 'serious,'
when he showed up on the golf course,
wearing a blue serge jacket and numbly cut
white ducks he'd bought

at a Pearl Harbor commissariat ...
and took four shots with his putter to sink his putt.
'Bob,' they said, 'golf's a game you really ought to know how to play,
if you play at all.'
They wrote him off as 'naval,'
naturally supposed his sport was sailing.
Poor Father, his training was engineering!
Cheerful and cowed
among the seadogs at the Sunday yacht club,
he was never one of the crowd.

'Anchors aweigh,' Daddy boomed in his bathtub,
'Anchors aweigh,'
when Lever Brothers offered to pay
him double what the Navy paid.
I nagged for his dress sword with gold braid,
and cringed because Mother, new
caps on all her teeth, was born anew
at forty. With seamanlike celerity,
Father left the Navy,
and deeded Mother his property.

He was soon fired. Year after year,
he still hummed 'Anchors aweigh' in the tub—
whenever he left a job,
he bought a smarter car.
Father's last employer
was Scudder, Stevens and Clark, Investment Advisors,
himself his only client.
While Mother dragged to bed alone,
read Menninger,
and grew more and more suspicious,
he grew defiant.

LIFE SAVING

Night after night,
à la clarté déserte de sa lampe,
he slid his ivory Annapolis slide rule
across a pad of graphs—
piker speculations! In three years
he squandered sixty thousand dollars.

Smiling on all,
Father was once successful enough to be lost
in the mob of ruling-class Bostonians.
As early as 1928,
he owned a house converted to oil,
and redecorated by the architect
of St. Mark's School ... Its main effect
was a drawing room, 'longitudinal as Versailles,'
its ceiling, roughened with oatmeal, was blue as the sea.
And once
nineteen, the youngest ensign in his class,
he was 'the old man' of a gunboat on the Yangtze.

JOHN MILTON

John Milton was born in London in 1608. A poet, political philosopher and pamphleteer, his life was dedicated for over twenty years to the cause of republicanism. His masterpiece *Paradise Lost* was not completed until 1663, by which time he was totally blind. It was followed by *Paradise Regained* (1671) and *Samson Agonistes* – possibly in the same year. He is the greatest epic poet in the English language. He died in 1674.

JOHN MILTON

Simply Sublime

A young John Milton, to his schoolfriend Charles Diodati: 'Allow me to use big language with you. You ask what I am thinking of? I am thinking of immortality. What am I doing? Growing my wings and meditating flight. But as yet our Pegasus raises himself on very tender wings. Let us be lowly wise.'

This charming image, the seductive humility of the last lines, cannot disguise the towering nature of the ambition – immortality. *Paradise Lost*, published when Milton was sixty, 'long choosing and beginning late', fulfilled his desire 'to leave something so written to after times as they should not willingly let it die'. We haven't, and 'after times' won't. The poem, over ten thousand words long, bestowed on Milton a form of poetic deity. He is variously described as divine (Wordsworth), sublime (Byron), and, for Coleridge, 'Milton is the deity of prescience.' Ted Hughes believed there is 'a direct line which can be traced from Virgil to Dante, from Dante to Milton'. (It continued, Hughes noted, to Eliot.)

Milton on Mount Parnassus. How did he get there? John Milton was born on 9 December 1608 in Bread Street in London's Cheapside to John Milton Snr, a wealthy scrivener and an excellent composer of music, whose own father, the keeper of the Forest of Shotover and a zealous papist, disinherited his son because he'd forsaken the religion of his ancestors. Disobedience in pursuit of intellectual and spiritual freedom requires courage. Milton learnt early that courage comes at a cost, though in the light of his father's success he may also have deduced it was not necessarily prohibitive. Initially he was educated at home, then at St Paul's School, followed by Christ's College, Cambridge, where, perhaps due to his good looks (he had wonderful hair) he was known as the 'Lady of Christ's'. His 'honest haughtiness' (his phrase) did not endear him either to his fellow students or to teachers and, according to Dr Johnson, Milton, who may have been rusticated, was possibly one of the last students to suffer the indignity of 'corporal correction'. At Cambridge he wrote the oft-anthologised 'Il Penseroso', the contemplative man who praises Melancholy, and its companion piece, 'L'Allegro', in which Melancholy is banished in favour of the delightful invitation to 'come, and trip it as ye go / on the light fantastic toe'. Seduction by argument drives his Mask, the rather strange *Comus*, rarely performed (perhaps advisedly), in which 'The Lady' is implored by Comus to 'be not cosen'd with that same vaunted name Virginity . . . if you let slip time, like a neglected rose / It withers on the stalk with languish'd head . . . Beauty is nature's brag.' In 'Lycidas', his haunting monody (written in memory of Edward King, a college contemporary drowned in the Irish Sea), pastoral beauty is in disturbing contrast to violent images of the drowning young man's futile battle with the sea. The philosopher's instinct to set in balance opposing views is clear in these early poems. They are a powerful harbinger of things to come – later, much later, after decades of political dissent and of little poetry.

Milton initially rejected a life in the Church – 'a clergyman must subscribe slave . . . bought and begun with servitude and forswearing', which was not his style . . . 'Thoughts of Obedience, whether Canonical or Civil, raised his indignation,' said Dr Johnson. Instead he dedicated himself to six years' intense study of Greek, Latin and Hebrew (Milton is perhaps literature's most erudite poet). He then embarked on a tour of Europe, where he visited Galileo – no doubt a perfect meeting of minds – though we have no record of the conversation. In 1639, aged thirty-one, he returned to England to what was about to become the most turbulent period in its history – the Civil War and the execution of a king. The ardent Platonist had found the cause of his life, republicanism; it would cost him dearly. Starting in 1641 Milton's life and his brilliance were to be dedicated to a tireless, personally dangerous series of writings in defence of liberty, be it religious or civil – the philosophical cornerstone of his masterpiece should he live long enough to write it. Macaulay spoke of the 'deadly hatred which he bore to bigots and tyrants' and of 'the faith which he so sternly kept with his country'. From 1641 almost twenty years passed of passionate politics, philosophy, marriages, births and deaths, during which Milton would serve as Secretary for Foreign Tongues under Oliver Cromwell and write, with reckless courage, two months after the execution of Charles I, 'The Tenure of Kings and Magistrates'. An ardent pamphleteer, he published attacks on the episcopacy, particularly Bishops Ussher and Hall: *Of Reformation in England and the Causes that Hitherto Have Hindered It*; and on the Government in the still-stirring *Areopagitica* – his great defence of the liberty of the press and the only work by a poet to have legal stature in American courts. According to Professor Myron Taylor the Bill of Rights owes more to John Milton than to John Locke. His work would be publicly burnt in Europe.

Private life was hardly much calmer. His first wife left him after six weeks of marriage, thus inspiring his pamphlet on divorce, *The Doctrine and Discipline of Divorce*. She returned, perhaps influenced by the pamphlet or, possibly, the fact that he'd courted 'a young lady of great accomplishments', a certain Miss Davis. Milton married three times; death, rather than divorce, was the catalyst. These marriages produced a son, who died, and three daughters. Though Dr Johnson commented rather meanly that on the death of his second wife, Katherine Woodcock (who died after fifteen months of marriage, aged just thirty), 'the poet honoured her memory with a poor sonnet', the poem is very lovely indeed. Milton, dreaming of his dead wife, cries out, 'But O as to embrace me she enclined, / I wak'd, she fled, and day brought back my night.'

There was another, more terrible darkness which would engulf him – blindness. By 1651 Milton, aged only forty-three, was totally blind. 'The most important fact about Milton for my purpose is his blindness . . . it would seem indeed to have helped him concentrate on what he could do best,' wrote Eliot. Stripped of all political involvement by the Restoration in 1660, blind and battered, arrested and released (Marvell was one of those who pleaded for him), Milton, forced to 'stand and wait' – didn't. He was, according to Harold Bloom, 'unsinkable, there may be no larger triumph of the visionary will in western literature'. *Paradise Lost*, published 27 April 1667, was followed in 1671 by *Paradise Regained*.

Milton died on 8 November 1674, a month before his sixty-sixth birthday. One hopes he died 'calm of mind, all passion spent', the last line of his final great poem, *Samson Agonistes*.

Paradise Lost

It's a long poem. 'No man ever wished *Paradise Lost* were longer', according to Dr Johnson. However, to 'justify the ways of God to men' is no mean task. God, as we all know, moves in mysterious ways. In *Paradise Lost*, Milton's God, as William Empson tells us, can be mysteriously repellent: 'God started all the trouble in the first place ... the reason why the poem is so good is that it makes God so bad.' It is also the reason it is so thrilling. God, as Shelley noted, is alleged to have no moral superiority over his adversary, Satan. The sheer moral courage that this required of the 'central Protestant poet' is sublime. Milton's psychological insight into the soul of Satan, tortured by Freudian ambivalence, loving and hating God at the same time, makes Satan one the most enduringly tragic figures in all literature. Rage at rejection and displacement fuels his rebellion and his destruction. God, without warning, announces to all Heaven: 'This day I have begot whom I declare / My onely Son, and on this holy Hill / Him have anointed, whom ye now behold / At my right hand; Your head I him appoint; / And by my Self have sworn to him shall bow / All knees in Heav'n, and shall confess him Lord.' And that's an order! The penalty for disobedience? Severe. 'Him who disobeys' will be 'cast out from God ... into utter darkness ... his place ordained without redemption.' Satan, previously known as Lucifer, bringer of light, fights back magnificently. He has a cause. We will be sacrificed to it. For eternity. The stakes, as they say, are high. Satan works on a grander scale than Iago, to whom he is sometimes compared, 'bringing down all mankind rather than one brave but limited general': Harold Bloom at his most succinct.

Initially, *Paradise Lost* was planned as a drama, a stage tragedy in five acts entitled 'Adam Unparadised'. Why did Milton change his mind? Shakespeare, Bloom suggests, was the catalyst. Milton, who was seven when Shakespeare died, knew the eternal genius of Shakespeare's plays could never be surpassed, and perhaps an example of Bloom's 'anxiety of influence' can be seen at work in Milton, who from youth longed for immortality. So he struck out in another direction, the Epic Poem. However, he would write it in blank verse, previously confined to the drama, 'rhyme being no necessary adjunct or true ornament of poem or good verse'. A decision of genius. Milton is, as Eliot noted, 'outside the theatre our greatest master of freedom within form'. Though Eliot feared the weight of Milton's language had a deadening effect, as did Addison, he also acknowledged in his essay 'Milton II' that 'the full beauty of the line is found in its context – and that is conclusive evidence of his supreme mastery'.

Within the line and form of his epic masterpiece lies literature's most passionate intellectual argument for freedom of will, a passion grounded in a lifetime's courageous dedication to its cause, in language of beauty and logic and wisdom – the triumph of the man blind and ill, and of the poet. In the face of his achievement we stand astonished. How did he do it? In his head. Sometimes, in the middle of the night, Milton, suddenly inspired, called to his daughters to 'secure what came' – and thereby hangs a tale. No doubt he was a difficult man and in extreme difficulty. His gift to us was *Paradise Lost*.

Milton must be read aloud, according to Douglas Bush. The passages we have selected from Book I (lines 105–24; 249–63) are from Satan's speech as he rallies his fallen angels burning in Hell. It is a hymn to courage, to independence: 'The mind is its own place, and in itself / Can make a Heav'n of Hell, a Hell of Heav'n . . . Better to reign in Hell, than serve in Heav'n.' It is little wonder Blake wrote of Milton that 'he was a true Poet and of the Devil's party without knowing it'. In the selection from Book IX Satan, now in the guise of snake in the Garden of Eden, has resolved that 'all good to me is lost; / Evil, be thou my good . . .' and plots the downfall of Adam and Eve, whom he overhears in a (celestial) argument about – what else? – freedom. Eve wishes to be free to wander alone in the garden, Adam the anxious first man is worried but surrenders to Eve – *plus ça change*. Eve encounters Satan, who appeals not only to her vanity but also to something more noble – her desire for Knowledge, which resides in the Tree of Knowledge, the only tree in the Garden of Eden forbidden to Adam and Eve. God at his most perverse. A fearful Eve is reassured by Satan: 'ye shall not die: How should ye? by the fruit? it gives you life / To knowledge.' Eve succumbs, and having eaten of the fruit she muses on the power of Knowledge – and in contemplating the first female lie she wonders whether she really ought to keep the Knowledge, i.e. the power, to herself . . . and be the superior one. On the other hand if the warning is right she will die and comes there another Eve? 'Adam wedded to another Eve, / Shall live with her enjoying, I extinct', a less than pleasing prospect to our first mother. Therefore Adam too must eat of the tree. If she's doomed, he's coming with her – a rather searing insight into female psychology. She now sets out to persuade as she has been persuaded. She understands her man. For Adam, knowing immediately Eve is doomed, sacrifices himself for love: 'flesh of flesh / Bone of my bone thou art, and from thy state / Mine never shall be parted, bliss or woe'. He eats the fruit and is immediately enflamed by carnal desire to which Eve delightedly responds and, as Milton tells us, with considerable erotic power: 'in lust they burn'. Off they go, our first parents, to a shady bank in the garden and to the inevitable. Just as inevitably, the first act of intercourse results in the first post-coital guilt followed, alas, by the first post-coital blame game – If only you had listened to me etc. – and we part from this short excerpt in the midst of a male–female battle which, like *Paradise Lost*, will continue for eternity.

Thousands of glorious lines later our sad banished parents are led by 'the hast'ning Angel' from Paradise. 'Some natural tears they dropp'd, but wip'd them soon.' All, it would seem, is not lost. Milton's strangely healing last lines tell us 'The World was all before them, where to choose / Their place of rest, and Providence their guide: / They hand in hand, with wand'ring steps and slow, / Through *Eden* took their solitary way.'

The End. And the beginning ...

Paradise Lost

[excerpts]

from Book I

What though the field be lost?
All is not lost; the unconquerable will,
And study of revenge, immortal hate,
And courage never to submit or yield:
And what is else not to be overcome?
That glory never shall his wrath or might
Extort from me. To bow and sue for grace
With suppliant knee, and deify his power
Who from the terror of this arm so late
Doubted his empire, that were low indeed,
That were an ignominy and shame beneath
This downfall; since by Fate the strength of gods
And this empyreal substance cannot fail,
Since through experience of this great event
In arms not worse, in foresight much advanced,
We may with more successful hope resolve
To wage by force or guile eternal war
Irreconcilable, to our grand Foe,
Who now triúmphs, and in th' excess of joy
Sole reigning holds the tyranny of Heav'n.

. . .

Farewell happy fields
Where joy for ever dwells: hail horrors, hail
Infernal world, and thou profoundest Hell
Receive thy new possessor: one who brings
A mind not to be changed by place or time.
The mind is its own place, and in itself
Can make a Heav'n of Hell, a Hell of Heav'n.
What matter where, if I be still the same,
And what I should be, all but less than he
Whom thunder hath made greater? Here at least
We shall be free; th' Almighty hath not built
Here for his envy, will not drive us hence:
Here we may reign secure, and in my choice
To reign is worth ambition though in Hell:
Better to reign in Hell, than serve in Heav'n.

from Book IV [Satan is in soliloquy]
Ah gentle pair, ye little think how nigh
Your change approaches, when all these delights
Will vanish and deliver ye to woe,
More woe, the more your taste is now of joy;
Happy, but for so happy ill secured
Long to continue, and this high seat your Heav'n
Ill fenced for Heav'n to keep out such a foe
As now is entered; yet no purposed foe
To you whom I could pity thus forlorn
Though I unpitied: league with you I seek,
And mutual amity so strait, so close,
That I with you must dwell, or you with me
Henceforth.

from Book IX [Adam and Eve are in dialogue]
Daughter of God and man, immortal Eve,
For such thou art, from sin and blame entire:
Not diffident of thee do I dissuade
Thy absence from my sight, but to avoid
Th' attempt itself, intended by our Foe.
For he who tempts, though in vain, at least asperses
The tempted with dishonour foul, supposed
Not incorruptible of faith, not proof
Against temptation: thou thyself with scorn
And anger wouldst resent the offered wrong,
Though ineffectual found: misdeem not then,
If such affront I labour to avert
From thee alone, which on us both at once
The Enemy, though bold, will hardly dare,
Or daring, first on me th' assault shall light.
Nor thou his malice and false guile contemn;
Subtle he needs must be, who could seduce
Angels, nor think superfluous others' aid.
I from the influence of thy looks receive
Accéss in every virtue, in thy sight
More wise, more watchful, stronger, if need were
Of outward strength; while shame, thou looking on,
Shame to be overcome or overreached
Would utmost vigour raise, and raised unite.
Why shouldst not thou like sense within thee feel
When I am present, and thy trial choose
With me, best witness of thy virtue tried.
So spake domestic Adam in his care
And matrimonial love; but Eve, who thought
Less attributed to her faith sincere,
Thus her reply with accent sweet renewed.
If this be our condition, thus to dwell

In narrow circuit straitened by a Foe,
Subtle or violent, we not endued
Single with like defence, wherever met,
How are we happy, still in fear of harm?
But harm precedes not sin: only our Foe
Tempting affronts us with his foul esteem
Of our integrity: his foul esteem
Sticks no dishonour on our front, but turns
Foul on himself; then wherefore shunned or feared
By us? Who rather double honour gain
From his surmise proved false, find peace within,
Favour from Heav'n, our witness from th' event.
And what is faith, love, virtue unassayed
Alone, without exterior help sustained?
Let us not then suspect our happy state
Left so imperfect by the Maker wise,
As not secure to single or combined.
Frail is our happiness, if this be so,
And Eden were no Eden thus exposed.
To whom thus Adam fervently replied.
O woman, best are all things as the will
Of God ordained them; his creating hand
Nothing imperfect or deficient left
Of all that he created, much less man,
Or aught that might his happy state secure,
Secure from outward force; within himself
The danger lies, yet lies within his power:
Against his will he can receive no harm.
But God left free the will, for what obeys
Reason, is free, and reason he made right,
But bid her well beware, and still erect,
Lest by some fair appearing good surprised
She dictate false, and misinform the will

To do what God expressly hath forbid.
Not then mistrust, but tender love enjoins,
That I should mind thee oft, and mind thou me.
Firm we subsist, yet possible to swerve,
Since reason not impossibly may meet
Some specious object by the Foe suborned,
And fall into deception unaware,
Not keeping strictest watch, as she was warned.
Seek not temptation then, which to avoid
Were better, and most likely if from me
Thou sever not: trial will come unsought.
Wouldst thou approve thy constancy, approve
First thy obedience; th' other who can know,
Not seeing thee attempted, who attest?
But if thou think, trial unsought may find
Us both securer than thus warned thou seem'st,
Go; for thy stay, not free, absents thee more;
Go in thy native innocence, rely
On what thou hast of virtue, summon all,
For God towards thee hath done his part, do thine.

. . .

[Eve] from her husband's hand her hand
Soft she withdrew

. . .

O much deceived, much failing, hapless Eve,
Of thy presumed return! event perverse!
Thou never from that hour in Paradise
Found'st either sweet repast, or sound repose;
Such ambush hid among sweet flow'rs and shades

177

Waited with Hellish rancour imminent
To intercept thy way, or send thee back
Despoiled of innocence, of faith, of bliss.
For now, and since first break of dawn the Fiend,
Mere serpent in appearance, forth was come,
And on his quest, where likeliest he might find
The only two of mankind, but in them
The whole included race, his purposed prey.
In bow'r and field he sought, where any tuft
Of grove or garden-plot more pleasant lay,
Their tendance or plantation for delight;
By fountain or by shady rivulet
He sought them both, but wished his hap might find
Eve separate; he wished, but not with hope
Of what so seldom chanced, when to his wish,
Beyond his hope, Eve separate he spies

. . .

Thoughts, whither have ye led me, with what sweet
Compulsion thus transported to forget
What hither brought us, hate, not love, nor hope
Of Paradise for Hell, hope here to taste
Of pleasure, but all pleasure to destroy,
Save what is in destroying; other joy
To me is lost. Then let me not let pass
Occasion which now smiles; behold alone
The woman, opportune to all attempts,
Her husband, for I view far round, not nigh,
Whose higher intellectual more I shun,
And strength, of courage haughty, and of limb
Heroic built, though of terrestrial mould,
Foe not informidable, exempt from wound,

I not; so much hath Hell debased, and pain
Enfeebled me, to what I was in Heav'n.
She fair, divinely fair, fit love for gods,
Not terrible, though terror be in love
And beauty, not approached by stronger hate,
Hate stronger, under show of love well-feigned,
The way which to her ruin now I tend.

. . .

Into the heart of Eve his words made way

. . .

Empress, the way is ready, and not long,
Beyond a row of myrtles, on a flat,
Fast by a fountain, one small thicket past
Of blowing myrrh and balm; if thou accept
My conduct, I can bring thee thither soon.
     Lead then, said Eve. He leading swiftly rolled
In tangles, and made intricate seem straight,
To mischief swift.

. . .

So glistered the dire snake, and into fraud
Led Eve our credulous mother, to the tree
Of prohibition, root of all our woe;
which when she saw, thus to her guide she spake.
Serpent, we might have spared our coming hither,
Fruitless to me, though fruit be here to excess,
The credit of whose virtue rest with thee,
Wondrous indeed, if cause of such effects.

But of this tree we may not taste nor touch;
God so commanded, and left that command
Sole daughter of his voice; the rest, we live
Law to ourselves, our reason is our law.
To whom the Tempter guilefully replied.
Indeed? hath God then said that of the fruit
Of all these garden trees ye shall not eat,
Yet lords declared of all in earth or air?
To whom thus Eve yet sinless. Of the fruit
Of each tree in the garden we may eat,
But of the fruit of this fair tree amidst
The garden, God hath said, Ye shall not eat
Thereof, nor shall ye touch it, lest ye die.

. . .

Queen of this universe, do not believe
Those rigid threats of death; ye shall not die:
How should ye? by the fruit? it gives you life
To knowledge. By the Threat'ner? look on me,
Me who have touched and tasted, yet both live,
And life more perfect have attained than Fate
Meant me, by vent'ring higher than my lot.
Shall that be shut to man, which to the beast
Is open? or will God incense his ire
For such a petty trespass, and not praise
Rather your dauntless virtue, whom the pain
Of death denounced, whatever thing death be,
Deterred not from achieving what might lead
To happier life, knowledge of good and evil;

. . .

And what are gods that man may not become
As they, participating god-like food?
The gods are first, and that advantage use
On our belief, that all from them proceeds;
I question it, for this fair earth I see,
Warmed by the sun, producing every kind,
Them nothing: if they all things, who enclosed
Knowledge of good and evil in this tree,
That whoso eats thereof, forthwith attains
Wisdom without their leave? and wherein lies
Th' offence, that man should thus attain to know?
What can your knowledge hurt him, or this tree
Impart against his will if all be his?
Or is it envy, and can envy dwell
In Heav'nly breasts? these, these and many more
Causes import your need of this fair fruit.
Goddess humane, reach then, and freely taste.

. . .

[Eve is in soliloquy]
Here grows the cure of all, this fruit divine,
Fair to the eye, inviting to the taste,
Of virtue to make wise: what hinders then
To reach, and feed at once both body and mind?

So saying, her rash hand in evil hour
Forth reaching to the fruit, she plucked, she ate:
Earth felt the wound, and Nature from her seat
Sighing through all her works gave signs of woe,
That all was lost. Back to the thicket slunk
The guilty serpent, and well might, for Eve
Intent now wholly on her taste, naught else
Regarded, such delight till then, as seemed,

LIFE SAVING

In fruit she never tasted, whether true
Or fancied so, through expectation high
Of knowledge, nor was Godhead from her thought.
Greedily she engorged without restraint,
And knew not eating death: satiate at length,
And heightened as with wine, jocund and boon,
Thus to herself she pleasingly began.

. . .

I grow mature
In knowledge, as the gods who all things know;
Though others envy what they cannot give;

. . .

But to Adam in what sort
Shall I appear? shall I to him make known
As yet my change, and give him to partake
Full happiness with me, or rather not,
But keep the odds of knowledge in my power
Without copartner? so to add what wants
In female sex, the more to draw his love,
And render me more equal, and perhaps,
A thing not undesirable, sometime
Superior; for inferior who is free?
This may be well: but what if God have seen,
And death ensue? then I shall be no more,
And Adam wedded to another Eve,
Shall live with her enjoying, I extinct;
A death to think. Confirmed then I resolve,
Adam shall share with me in bliss or woe:
So dear I love him, that with him all deaths
I could endure, without him live no life.

. . .

Eve, now I see thou art exact of taste,
And elegant, of sapience no small part,
Since to each meaning savour we apply,
And palate call judicious; I the praise
Yield thee, so well this day thou hast purveyed.
Much pleasure we have lost, while we abstained
From this delightful fruit, nor known till now
True relish, tasting; if such pleasure be
In things to us forbidden, it might be wished,
For this one tree had been forbidden ten.
But come, so well refreshed, now let us play,
As meet is, after such delicious fare;
For never did thy beauty since the day
I saw thee first and wedded thee, adorned
With all perfections, so inflame my sense
With ardour to enjoy thee, fairer now
Than ever, bounty of this virtuous tree.

So said he, and forbore not glance or toy
Of amorous intent, well understood
Of Eve, whose eye darted contagious fire.
Her hand he seized, and to a shady bank,
Thick overhead with verdant roof embow'red
He led her nothing loath; flow'rs were the couch,
Pansies, and violets, and asphodel,
And hyacinth, earth's freshest softest lap.
There they their fill of love and love's disport
Took largely, of their mutual guilt the seal,
The solace of their sin, till dewy sleep
Oppressed them, wearied with their amorous play.
Soon as the force of that fallacious fruit,
That with exhilarating vapour bland
About their spirits had played, and inmost powers

Made err, was now exhaled, and grosser sleep
Bred of unkindly fumes, with conscious dreams
Encumbered, now had left them, up they rose
As from unrest, and each the other viewing,
Soon found their eyes how opened, and their minds
How darkened; innocence, that as a veil
Had shadowed them from knowing ill, was gone;
Just confidence, and native righteousness
And honour from about them, naked left
To guilty Shame: he covered, but his robe
Uncovered more. So rose the Danite strong
Hercúlean Samson from the harlot-lap
Of Phílistéan Dálila, and waked
Shorn of his strength, they destitute and bare
Of all their virtue: silent, and in face
Confounded long they sat, as strucken mute,
Till Adam, though not less than Eve abashed,
At length gave utterance to these words constrained.

　　O Eve, in evil hour thou didst give ear
To that false worm, of whomsoever taught
To counterfeit man's voice, true in our Fall,
False in our promised rising; since our eyes
Opened we find indeed, and find we know
Both good and evil, good lost, and evil got,
Bad fruit of knowledge, if this be to know,
Which leaves us naked thus, of honour void,
Of innocence, of faith, of purity,
Our wonted ornaments now soiled and stained,
And in our faces evident the signs
Of foul concupiscence; whence evil store;
Even shame, the last of evils; of the first
Be sure then. How shall I behold the face
Henceforth of God or angel, erst with joy

And rapture so oft beheld? those Heav'nly shapes
Will dazzle now this earthly, with their blaze
Insufferably bright. O might I here
In solitude live savage, in some glade
Obscured, where highest woods impenetrable
To star or sunlight, spread their umbrage broad
And brown as evening: cover me ye pines,
Ye cedars, with innumerable boughs
Hide me, where I may never see them more.
But let us now, as in bad plight, devise
What best may for the present serve to hide
The parts of each from other, that seem most
To shame obnoxious, and unseemliest seen
Some tree whose broad smooth leaves together sewed,
And girded on our loins, may cover round
Those middle parts, that this new comer, Shame,
There sit not, and reproach us as unclean.
    So counselled he, and both together went
Into the thickest wood, there soon they chose
The fig tree . . .
They gathered, broad as Amazonian targe,
And with what skill they had, together sewed,
To gird their waist, vain covering if to hide
Their guilt and dreaded shame; O how unlike
To that first naked glory. Such of late
Columbus found th' American so girt
With feathered cincture, naked else and wild
Among the trees on isles and woody shores.
Thus fenced, and as they thought, their shame in part
Covered, but not at rest or ease of mind,
They sat them down to weep, nor only tears
Rained at their eyes, but high winds worse within
Began to rise, high passions, anger, hate,

Mistrust, suspicion, discord, and shook sore
Their inward state of mind, calm region once
And full of peace, now tossed and turbulent:
For understanding ruled not, and the will
Heard not her lore, both in subjection now
To sensual appetite, who from beneath
Usurping over sov'reign reason claimed
Superior sway: from thus distempered breast,
Adam, estranged in look and altered style,
Speech intermitted thus to Eve renewed.

    Would thou hadst hearkened to my words, and stayed
With me, as I besought thee, when that strange
Desire of wand'ring this unhappy morn,
I know not whence possessed thee; we had then
Remained still happy, not as now, despoiled
Of all our good, shamed, naked, miserable.
Let none henceforth seek needless cause to approve
The faith they owe; when earnestly they seek
Such proof, conclude, they then begin to fail.

    To whom soon moved with touch of blame thus Eve.
What words have passed thy lips, Adam severe,
Imput'st thou that to my default, or will
Of wand'ring, as thou call'st it, which who knows
But might as ill have happened thou being by,
Or to thyself perhaps: hadst thou been there,
Or here th' attempt, thou couldst not have discerned
Fraud in the serpent, speaking as he spake;
No ground of enmity between us known,
Why he should mean me ill, or seek to harm.
Was I to have never parted from thy side?
As good have grown there still a lifeless rib.
Being as I am, why didst not thou the head
Command me absolutely not to go,

Going into such danger as thou saidst?
Too facile then thou didst not much gainsay,
Nay, didst permit, approve, and fair dismiss.
Hadst thou been firm and fixed in thy dissent,
Neither had I transgressed, nor thou with me.
　　To whom then first incensed Adam replied.
Is this the love, is this the recompense
Of mine to thee, ingrateful Eve, expressed
Immutable when thou wert lost, not I,
Who might have lived and joyed immortal bliss,
Yet willingly chose rather death with thee:
And am I now upbraided, as the cause
Of thy transgressing? not enough severe,
It seems, in thy restraint: what could I more?
I warned thee, I admonished thee, foretold
The danger, and the lurking Enemy
That lay in wait; beyond this had been force,
And force upon free will hath here no place.
But confidence then bore thee on, secure
Either to meet no danger, or to find
Matter of glorious trial, and perhaps
I also erred in overmuch admiring
What seemed in thee so perfect, that I thought
No evil durst attempt thee, but I rue
That error now, which is become my crime,
And thou th' accuser. Thus it shall befall
Him who to worth in women overtrusting
Lets her will rule; restraint she will not brook,
And left to herself, if evil thence ensue,
She first his weak indulgence will accuse.
　　Thus they in mutual accusation spent
The fruitless hours, but neither self-condemning,
And of their vain contést appeared no end.

MARIANNE MOORE

Born in 1887 in Kirkwood, Missouri, Marianne Craig Moore was a poet, essayist and translator. Her *Selected Poems* (1935) was published with an introduction by T. S. Eliot. She won both the Gold Medal for Poetry from the American Academy of Arts and Letters and the Pulitzer Prize. She died in 1972.

MARIANNE MOORE

Poetry . . . I, Too, Dislike It

'I like country fairs, roller-coasters, merry-go-rounds, dog shows, museums, avenues of trees, old elms, vehicles' (on being asked to name the new Ford she suggested 'the utopian turtle top' or 'the intelligent whale'), 'experiments in timing, like our ex-Museum of Science and Invention's two roller-bearings in a gravity chute, synchronized with a ring-bearing, revolving vertically. I am fond of animals and take inordinate interest in mongooses, squirrels, crows, elephants.' This is Marianne Moore on Marianne Moore, one of the 'Authors of 1951 Speaking for Themselves' in the *New York Herald Tribune*. She also listed as among the few great artists of her time Casals, Soledad, Alec Guinness and the Lipizzaner horsemen. She adored gardenias, beautiful clothes, Beatrix Potter and baseball, which she compared to writing. She told *Esquire* in 1962 that she regarded the statement by a famous player that 'Marianne Moore speaks to our condition as ballplayers' as one of the great compliments of her life. She wrote the liner notes to Muhammad Ali's TV series, 'I Am the Greatest'.

Though she never married, lived quietly at home and was an inveterate letter writer, Emily Dickinson she is not.

Neither love ('My Senses Do Not Deceive Me') nor death are primarily her subjects, nor does time feature greatly. Art gets more attention, as does war, the pangolin, roses, monkeys, snails, steamrollers and that most fascinating subject, human behaviour. She is

cool. She is thrilling. Despite the fact that Hilda Doolittle first published Moore (without her permission); that she became a mentor to
Elizabeth Bishop; that Grace Schulman edited the current Faber collection, nevertheless she may have found her precursors were men
rather than women, according to Cynthia Hogan. And the men
found her. 'Miss Moore's poetry forms part of the small body of
durable poetry written in our time ... in which an original sensibility and alert intelligence and deep feeling have been engaged in
maintaining the life of the English language': T. S. Eliot in his preface to *Selected Writings by Marianne Moore*. W. H. Auden said of her,
'Marianne Moore is one of the very few modern-day poets I can read
any day, or in any mood.' She numbered fellow poets William Carlos
Williams and Randall Jarrell among her admirers. She won the
Bollingen Prize, the National Book Award, the Pulitzer Prize and, for
her translation of the fables of La Fontaine – a work that took her
over ten years to complete – the coveted Croix de Chevalier de
l'Ordre des Arts et Lettres.

'The Mind Is an Enchanting Thing,' she wrote. Marianne Moore's
mind enchants us with its truthfulness, its clarity, its wit. For once,
the word 'rapier-like' is legitimate. 'If Miss Moore is laughing at us,
it is laughter that catches us ... and half-paralyses us, as light flashed
from a very fine steel blade, wielded playfully, ironically ... Yet with
all that craftsmanship ... her art resides only in that serene palace of
her own world of inspiration – frail, yet as all beautiful things are,
absolutely hard': Hilda Doolittle in her essay on Moore for *The
Egoist* – the short-lived but immensely influential literary journal.
Her art is also direct. There is with other poets, and particularly
Dickinson, the delight in the thing seen 'slant'. That is not where
delight is found in Marianne Moore. Though she is intellectually
complex, the fresh-washed quality of her work comes from the
'straight on' vision. She sees 'the rock crystal thing to see'. She is, as
Randall Jarrell said of her in his essay 'Her Shield', 'the poet of the
particular'. The particular, and the demand that it be described

accurately, was key to the aesthetic philosophy with which she is associated: imagism. 'The natural object is always the adequate symbol' was Ezra Pound's mantra. (Pound was, it seems, everywhere.) Grace Schulman points out that her laboratory studies affected Moore's poetry profoundly. 'Art is exact perception' is the opening line of one of her poems 'And no man who's done his part / Need apologize for art.'

She did not write poetry 'for money or fame. To earn a living is needful, but it can be done in routine ways. One writes because one has a burning desire to objectify what it is indispensable to one's happiness to express.' 'Objectify' is the operative word in that sentence. In her poetry, which she once referred to as Escher compositions, each word is precisely positioned on the page, though not necessarily in the precise position one might expect! Moore was, as Grace Schulman notes, often irritated by those who commented upon the strict syllabic method from which she did not deviate. However, its accommodation – which necessitated the regular splitting of words from line to line – is fundamental to the structure of her work and its Pound-like visual effect on the page. Later in life, however, she was to say to Schulman that the sound of her poetry was more important to her than its visual effect on the page.

The visual effect is nevertheless powerful – but always to a purpose, for example, her generous use of inverted commas around every borrowed or stolen line, even from dinner-party guests. When asked why, she said, 'When a thing has been said so well that it could not be said better, why paraphrase it? Hence my writing is, if not a cabinet of fossils, a kind of collection of flies in amber.' Thus one learns to trust her. It is strange how compelling that reaction becomes, as one begins to see clearly what Auden saw: 'with what unfreckled integrity it has all been done'.

The seeds of that integrity were sown early. Until she was seven Marianne Moore lived in the home of her grandfather, a Presbyterian pastor. Her father, over whose mental health there seems to have been a shadow, disappeared shortly before her birth – she was never to meet him. She attended Bryn Mawr. In her introduction to *Selected Letters*, and there were thousands from which one could select, Bonnie Costello quotes a line of rather daunting self-knowledge from a letter to a friend: 'My experience [at Bryn Mawr] gave me security in my determination to have what I want.' Commercial college in Carlisle, Pennsylvania, followed, where she studied typing and business, which she then taught, evidently extremely well. In 1918 when she was thirty-one Marianne Moore moved to New York – 'the savage's romance' that gave her 'accessibility to experience'. Since she worked for the New York Public Library and later edited the prestigious *The Dial*, a literary journal, which counted Yeats, Eliot and Pound among its contributors, it also gave her accessibility to virtually every major literary figure in America. Marianne Moore's was a long and brilliant life in literature, in which the black-caped, three-corner-hatted, white-haired woman became an icon of American letters.

Her very 'properness' gives a surprising salt and dash to her work. She was never for sale – to anyone. Her disciplined artist's eye looked on her own work and cut it ruthlessly. Patricia C. Willis notes in her introduction to *Marianne Moore, Woman and Poet* that the poem titled 'Poetry' once shrank from five stanzas to thirteen lines, and eventually to three lines! Luckily she relented, though as she said, 'Omissions are not accidents.' She died in 1972, aged eighty-five. Grace Schulman tells us that Ezra Pound came out of his long seclusion to recite her poem 'What are Years?' at her memorial service. The last line of the poem is appropriate to a woman who looked unflinchingly at life and its inevitable end: 'This is mortality / this is eternity.' She may have written of poetry, 'I, too, dislike it: there are things that are important beyond all this fiddle.' The poem, however, continues, 'Reading it, however, with a perfect contempt for it, one discovers in it, after all, a place for the genuine.'

The Poems

'Making, Knowing, Judging', Auden's trinity, 'an insight of casual genius' according to Heaney, seems particularly applicable to the work of Marianne Moore. And of these three virtues, with Marianne Moore, the greatest, I think, is knowing. 'The Mind Is an Enchanting Thing', one of her most brilliant poems, emblematic of her particular respect for the intellect, ends with the famous 'it's / not a Herod's oath that cannot change'. She did not, in fact, change her mind about much philosophically. She did, however, like Lowell, constantly refine and redefine her own work. Lines were often erased – silenced. 'We All Know It': 'That silence is best.' Do we? 'A strange idea that one must say what one thinks in order to be understood.'

'Silence', the title this time, opens with the conversational 'My father used say, / "Superior people never make long visits."' A remark made by a visiting professor is juxtaposed with Edmund Burke's eighteenth-century invitation to someone he'd met in a bookshop: to 'Make my house your inn'. Add Moore's coolly subversive last line – 'Inns are not residences' – and we glimpse the subtle art of being either guest or host. I would visit Miss Moore with some trepidation and would certainly try to curb the intensity with which I speak.

'To Be Liked by You Would Be a Calamity' is possibly the best put-down in poetry. Moore, evidently a brilliant conversationalist, enjoyed the elegant thrust and parry of intellectual debate. The blunt instrument of aggression, however, which aims to put 'My flesh beneath your feet', leads to a contemptuous withdrawal. She stood up *to* – that most difficult act of honour – as well as *for* her friends. Perhaps this quality was key to the great respect in which she was held by her contemporaries. It's also, perhaps, a slightly thorny quality. In 'Roses Only' the thorn garners exquisite attention – 'compelling audience to / the remark that it is better to be forgotten than to be remembered too violently, / your thorns are the best part of you'.

The clever 'I Like A Horse but I Have a Fellow Feeling for A Mule' should be treasured, and not only for its title. I would guess that Moore had a stubborn streak. Guessing would no doubt meet with disapproval; she had an admirable respect for facts. Moore expresses her gratitude to the mule in measured, careful beats – like him, never going too far; 'he skirts the treeless precipice'. Moore had a 'fellow feeling' for most animals and gave each of them their due. Her masterpiece, 'The Pangolin', deserves an essay in itself. Alas!

'Spenser's Ireland' cuts to the soul of Auden's 'mad Ireland' and Yeats's country of the 'fanatic heart'. She once said, 'I am of Irish descent – wholly Celt.' Despite the genetic inheritance – elective to some extent – her poetic restraint is not necessarily in the Irish tradition. Pound believed her poetry to be distinctively American. He's right, of course. Spenser, author of *The Faerie Queene*, was burned out of his home, Castle Kilcolman, during the insurrection of 1598 and though there is no reference to this event in the poem certain lines have a resonance. 'The Irish say your trouble is their / trouble and your / joy their joy? I wish / I could believe it. I'm dissatisfied, I'm Irish.' Enough said!

In 'We Call Them the Brave' there are no heroics. It's not her style. 'Better not euphemize the grave.' She knows how death plays out in the 'fashionable town'. Even now, the warning resounds: what will happen 'when no one will fight for anything / and there's nothing of worth to save'?

To Be Liked by You Would Be a Calamity

'Attack is more piquant than concord,' but when
    You tell me frankly that you would like to feel
        My flesh beneath your feet,
            I'm all abroad; I can but put my weapon up, and
                Bow you out.
Gesticulation—it is half the language.
    Let unsheathed gesticulation be the steel
        Your courtesy must meet,
            Since in your hearing words are mute, which to my senses
                Are a shout.

Roses Only

You do not seem to realize that beauty is a liability rather than
        an asset—that in view of the fact that spirit creates form we are
            justified in supposing
                that you must have brains. For you, a symbol of the unit, stiff
                and sharp,
            conscious of surpassing by dint of native superiority and liking
                for everything
self-dependent, anything an

ambitious civilization might produce: for you, unaided, to attempt
        through sheer
            reserve to confute presumptions resulting from observation is
                idle. You cannot make us think
                you a delightful happen-so. But rose, if you are brilliant, it
            is not because your petals are the without-which-nothing of
                pre-eminence. You would look, minus
thorns—like a what-is-this, a mere

peculiarity. They are not proof against a storm, the elements, or
        mildew
            but what about the predatory hand? What is brilliance without
                coordination? Guarding the
                infinitesimal pieces of your mind, compelling audience to
            the remark that it is better to be forgotten than to be
                remembered too violently,
your thorns are the best part of you.

SYLVIA PLATH

Poet and novelist, Sylvia Plath was born in Boston, Massachusetts in 1932. *Ariel*, her famous collection published posthumously in 1965, edited by her husband, the poet Ted Hughes, established her iconic reputation. She died in 1963.

SYLVIA PLATH

The Woman is Perfected

At the time of her death in 1963, aged thirty, Sylvia Plath had published just one collection of poetry, to muted response, and one novel. Yet she is now, and has been for decades, recognised as a major poet whose life and work challenge us artistically, psychologically and morally. How did this come about, this quite extraordinary posthumous fame?

The catalyst was the *Ariel* poems, discovered by her husband, the poet Ted Hughes, after her suicide in 1963, edited by him and published by Faber and Faber in 1965. Many were written in the autumn of 1962, after their separation, and the final poems in January 1963 when she was living with their two children in a flat once occupied by W. B. Yeats – a source of pleasure to her. These poems, as Erica Wagner points out in *Ariel's Gift*, were originally arranged in manuscript form by Plath to begin with the word 'Love' and end with 'Spring'. Wagner also traces with poise the interconnectedness between the two poets and their poetry. Plath's last poems are a concentrated rush to greatness. And she knew it. 'When my sleeping pill wears off, I am up at about five, in my study, writing like mad.' She woke, Heaney writes, already composed in Yeats's terms into 'something intended, complete' feeling 'like a very efficient tool or weapon used and in demand from moment to moment'. She had become herself – her persona – sounding out the poems, which, as she wrote to her mother, 'will make my name my name'. They did. 'With these poems,' said Robert Lowell, she became 'something newly, wildly and subtly created, hardly a person at all or a woman but one of those super-real hypnotic great classical heroines.' Intense selfhood ('le moi profond'), as Lowell knew better than most, can be hazardous, particularly if you believe as Plath did, 'the blood jet is poetry, / There is no stopping it.' Philip Larkin said of her poems, 'They exist in a prolonged, high-pitched ecstasy, like nothing else in Literature.' He wondered, had her own talent overwhelmed her? Larkin, to whom life seemed dangerous to art, seems to pose the question: is art dangerous to life? Perhaps.

Sylvia Plath was born on 27 October 1932, in Jamaica Plain, Boston, Massachusetts, to Emil Plath, a Prussian immigrant and Professor of German at Boston University, and Aurelia Schober, a high-school teacher of Austrian extraction who was twenty years his junior. When Sylvia was eight her father, a diabetic, died as a result of surgery to remove a gangrenous leg. Everything about this death is shocking, the appalling imagery, the loss of home as well as father, the necessity for Aurelia to return to work to support her children. It left Sylvia Plath with a fierce sense of angry desolation. Childhood was over. Later, in 'Ocean 1212-W' she wrote, 'Those first nine years of my life sealed themselves off like a ship in a bottle, beautiful, obsolete, a fine, white flying myth.'

The family survived. Sylvia survived. Indeed, it would seem, she blossomed. She was a brilliant student who wrote poetry and understood her vocation early. She wrote, at sixteen, 'You ask me why I spend my life writing / do I find entertainment? / Is it worthwhile? / Above all does it pay? I write only because there is a voice within me which will not be stilled.' She eventually attended Smith College supported by a scholarship. She was a social success, extremely pretty and popular; was on the board of the college; was shortlisted for poetry prizes; and was guest editor for the fashion magazine *Mademoiselle*. On the surface, a *jeunesse dorée*. This surface impression of intelligent, attractive gaiety was to last well into her twenties.

'What was she like?' Eileen Atkins asked Charles Osborne, after a poetry reading I'd organised years ago. 'Well,' said Charles, who knew Sylvia Plath during her years in London, 'initially, she struck me as a very pretty, very vivacious American cheerleader.' That same evening a man came up to me and said, 'This is the first time I've ever been frightened by poetry.'

From her teenage years onwards Sylvia Plath suffered from severe depression and Aurelia, aware that the illness was endemic in Otto's family, sought help, including electroconvulsive treatment. In 1953 when she was twenty-one she attempted suicide and began the intensive therapy that she would continue throughout her short life. Considerable strength of character was required for her to hold hard to her dreams of academic excellence and artistic fulfilment, and to return to Smith. Her brilliance and her perseverance won her a Fulbright Scholarship to study at Newnham College, Cambridge, and in the autumn of 1955 she set sail for England.

Nine months later, after a serious *coup de foudre*, Sylvia Plath, aged twenty-three, married the poet Ted Hughes, aged twenty-five, on 16 June 1956, Bloomsday for Joyce fans. Of her first meeting with him she wrote to her mother, 'I shall tell you something most miraculous and thundering and terrifying. It is this man I have never known anything like it ... The more he writes poems the more he writes poems ... daily I too am full of poems ... my joy whirls in tongues of words ... I shall be a woman beyond women.' These are the words of an ecstatic, and ecstatics are born, not made. 'Marriage, Iris Murdoch believed, 'is a very private place.' Because of its tragic aftermath few marriages have been subjected to more analysis than that of the young poets Sylvia Plath and Ted Hughes. Possibly because their story weaves together art and passion with the intensity of Greek tragedy, Janet Malcolm, Diane Middlebrook, Jacqueline Rose, Anne Stevenson and Erica Wagner are among the many who with honour have approached this modern tale of abiding sadness. At the end of his life, having not 'spoken' before (the protection of children often demands silence), Ted Hughes wrote the haunting *Birthday Letters*.

Suffice to say here that their seven years together were drenched in passion and pain, as the two hugely ambitious, mutually supportive poets set up home, had children – Frieda in 1960, Nicholas in January 1962 – all the while trying to make a living and striving daily, hourly, endlessly, to create great poetry. It was a full life, perhaps overwhelmingly so. Her early poetry did not come easily to Plath, who during their marriage, Ted Hughes said, 'composed very slowly, consulting her Thesaurus and dictionary for almost every word, putting a slow strong line of ink under each word that attracted her'. She herself once said she'd rather live with her thesaurus than a bible on a desert island. She had a 'vision' of the kind of poems she would like to write but '[I] do not. When will they come?' They were waiting. The marriage, already under strain, was broken by Ted Hughes' affair with Assia Wevill and they separated in August 1962. In the autumn of the same year Plath wrote most of the poems that made her immortal.

On 10 February 1963, having had flu, as had her children, during one of the coldest Januarys on record, Sylvia Plath took her own life. Her mother wrote, 'Her physical energies having been depleted by illness, anxiety and overwork and although she had for so long managed to be gallant and equal to the life experience, some darker day than usual had temporarily made it seem impossible to pursue.' Seamus Heaney took, as the title of his essay on Plath, a line from one of her last poems, 'The indefatigable hoof-taps'. They continue to reverberate.

The Poems

'Because I could not stop for Death – / He kindly stopped for me,' wrote Emily Dickinson. Well, Plath stopped for him. And as an artist, at a most particular moment – one of secret fulfilment. Even in an early Plath poem, 'Mushrooms', one can hear an underground note of advancement – determined, almost military, as the usually benign mushroom warns us, 'Our foot's in the door.' Plath's feeling for syllable and rhythm, which Eliot marked as one of the key components in the auditory imagination, is already apparent.

'The Colossus' is her father, writ large. 'Thirty years now I have labored / To dredge the silt from your throat. / I am none the wiser.' It's an old story. 'The Colossus' was the title poem of her first collection, which itself went through endless permutations, including, as Hughes points out, the telling 'Full Fathom Five', also, and just as compelling and provocative, 'The Bull of Bendylaw'.

Philip Larkin wrote of the opening lines of 'Two Views of a Cadaver Room', 'the shock is sudden'. He'd read the poems chronologically and, though impressed, this is the poem of which he said, 'The possibility that she is simply trying on another style is dispelled' and, he continues, 'she has found her subject matter'. It is a line that tolls like a bell. The painting referred to in the poem is Pieter Bruegel's *Triumph of Death* and there are echoes also, I believe, of the poet Gottfried Benn's 'Morgue'.

Plath died young and virtually unknown. So I quote her where possible on her own work. Of the speaker in 'The Applicant', she said, He 'is an executive . . . [who] wants to be sure the applicant for his marvelous product . . . will treat it right'. The question 'Will you marry it, marry it, marry it' strikes a sinister, Pinteresque note. She was much criticised for her almost obsessive use of repetition, as Tim Kendall points out in *Sylvia Plath: A Critical Study*. However, in her inner ear that is how Plath heard the beat. Like Lear's 'never', repeated five times, to sound his despair at Cordelia's death, the human voice releases the power of repetition from the page. Of 'Death & Co.' she said, it 'is about the double or schizophrenic nature of death – the marmoreal coldness of Blake's death mask, say, hand in glove with the fearful softness of worms ... I imagine these two aspects of death as two men ... who have come to call.' There is nothing to add.

The wild rhythms and the terrifying energy of 'Daddy' are controlled, just, by the artist. She herself said of it, 'Here is a poem spoken by a girl with an Electra complex. Her father died while she thought he was God.' Camille Paglia described it as 'garish, sarcastic and profane and one of the strongest poems ever written by a woman'. It would take a strong woman to disagree.

At a BBC reading (and few writers loved the BBC more than Plath), she introduced the dramatic monologue of 'Lady Lazarus' thus: 'The speaker is a woman who has the great and terrible gift of being reborn. The only trouble is, she has to die first.' The lines 'I rise with my red hair / And I eat men like air' are terrifying. In 'Edge', 'The woman is perfected'.

Daddy

You do not do, you do not do
Any more, black shoe
In which I have lived like a foot
For thirty years, poor and white,
Barely daring to breathe or Achoo.

Daddy, I have had to kill you.
You died before I had time—
Marble-heavy, a bag full of God,
Ghastly statue with one gray toe
Big as a Frisco seal

And a head in the freakish Atlantic
Where it pours bean green over blue
In the waters off beautiful Nauset.
I used to pray to recover you.
Ach, du.

In the German tongue, in the Polish town
Scraped flat by the roller
Of wars, wars, wars.
But the name of the town is common.
My Polack friend

Says there are a dozen or two.
So I never could tell where you
Put your foot, your root,
I never could talk to you.
The tongue stuck in my jaw.

It stuck in a barb wire snare.
Ich, ich, ich, ich,
I could hardly speak.
I thought every German was you.
And the language obscene

An engine, an engine
Chuffing me off like a Jew.
A Jew to Dachau, Auschwitz, Belsen.
I began to talk like a Jew.
I think I may well be a Jew.

The snows of the Tyrol, the clear beer of Vienna
Are not very pure or true.
With my gypsy ancestress and my weird luck
And my Taroc pack and my Taroc pack
I may be a bit of a Jew.

I have always been scared of *you*,
With your Luftwaffe, your gobbledygoo.
And your neat mustache
And your Aryan eye, bright blue.
Panzer-man, panzer-man, O You—

Not God but a swastika
So black no sky could squeak through.
Every woman adores a Fascist,
The boot in the face, the brute
Brute heart of a brute like you.

You stand at the blackboard, daddy,
In the picture I have of you,
A cleft in your chin instead of your foot

But no less a devil for that, no not
Any less the black man who

Bit my pretty red heart in two.
I was ten when they buried you.
At twenty I tried to die
And get back, back, back to you.
I thought even the bones would do.

But they pulled me out of the sack,
And they stuck me together with glue.
And then I knew what to do.
I made a model of you,
A man in black with a Meinkampf look

And a love of the rack and the screw.
And I said I do, I do.
So daddy, I'm finally through.
The black telephone's off at the root,
The voices just can't worm through.

If I've killed one man, I've killed two—
The vampire who said he was you
And drank my blood for a year,
Seven years, if you want to know.
Daddy, you can lie back now.

There's a stake in your fat black heart
And the villagers never liked you.
They are dancing and stamping on you.
They always *knew* it was you.
Daddy, daddy, you bastard, I'm through.

Lady Lazarus

I have done it again.
One year in every ten
I manage it—

A sort of walking miracle, my skin
Bright as a Nazi lampshade,
My right foot

A paperweight,
My face a featureless, fine
Jew linen.

Peel off the napkin
O my enemy,
Do I terrify?—

The nose, the eye pits, the full set of teeth?
The sour breath
Will vanish in a day.

Soon, soon the flesh
The grave cave ate will be
At home on me

And I a smiling woman.
I am only thirty.
And like the cat I have nine times to die.

This is Number Three.
What a trash
To annihilate each decade.

What a million filaments.
The peanut-crunching crowd
Shoves in to see

Them unwrap me hand and foot—
The big strip tease.
Gentlemen, ladies

These are my hands
My knees.
I may be skin and bone,

Nevertheless, I am the same, identical woman.
The first time it happened I was ten.
It was an accident.

The second time I meant
To last it out and not come back at all.
I rocked shut

As a seashell.
They had to call and call
And pick the worms off me like sticky pearls.

Dying
Is an art, like everything else.
I do it exceptionally well.

LIFE SAVING

I do it so it feels like hell.
I do it so it feels real.
I guess you could say I've a call.

It's easy enough to do it in a cell.
It's easy enough to do it and stay put.
It's the theatrical

Comeback in broad day
To the same place, the same face, the same brute
Amused shout:

'A miracle!'
That knocks me out.
There is a charge

For the eyeing of my scars, there is a charge
For the hearing of my heart—
It really goes.

And there is a charge, a very large charge
For a word or a touch
Or a bit of blood

Or a piece of my hair or my clothes.
So, so, Herr Doktor.
So, Herr Enemy.

I am your opus,
I am your valuable,
The pure gold baby

That melts to a shriek.
I turn and burn.
Do not think I underestimate your great concern.

Ash, ash—
You poke and stir.
Flesh, bone, there is nothing there—

A cake of soap,
A wedding ring,
A gold filling.

Herr God, Herr Lucifer
Beware
Beware.

Out of the ash
I rise with my red hair
And I eat men like air.

CHRISTINA ROSSETTI

Christina Georgina Rossetti was born in London in 1830. Her masterpiece collection *Goblin Market and Other Poems* appeared in 1862 and won her instant acclaim. *The Prince's Progress and Other Poems* followed in 1866 and *Sing-Song: A Nursery Rhyme Book* in 1872. Her many religious poems, 'Devotional Pieces', added to her huge popularity. She died in 1894.

CHRISTINA ROSSETTI

Upstairs, Downstairs . . .

'Downstairs I laugh, I sport and jest with all; / But in my solitary room above / I turn my face in silence to the wall; / My heart is breaking for a little love.' Upstairs, broken-hearted or not, 'in the fireless top back bedroom on the corner of the cracked washstand, on the backs of old letters Christina sat writing', according to Ford Madox Ford. Downstairs, a constant and copious stream of old friends from Naples and Rome, and new, English friends, among them Coventry Patmore, William Morris, John Ruskin, came to visit her expatriate father, Professor of Italian at King's College, London, and her adored Mamma, who presided with immense pride over her brilliant brood: Maria Francesca, who would write an acclaimed study of Dante; painter and poet Gabriel Charles Dante (who would, in a further tribute to the great poet, eventually call himself Dante Gabriel Rossetti); and William Michael, co-founder of the Pre-Raphaelite Brotherhood. It was in necessary isolation that Christina 'shut the door to face the naked truth' and carved out of the drama of her soul a poetry in which an intensity of feelings and emotions is captured with exquisite, painful precision. 'My heart dies inch by inch, the time grows old': the heart laid bare with a verbal scalpel. 'Nearly every one of her poems was an instance . . . of an emotion.' Her emotional power is not, however, for sentimentalists, as Philip Larkin makes clear. Rossetti's work, he writes, is 'unequalled for its objective expression of happiness denied and a certain unfamiliar steely stoicism'. The steely stoicism may have been due less to the bowing of her head in resignation than to the fact that the 'hope deferred' was deferred by the spiritually wilful Christina Georgina Rossetti (she very much liked her middle name), who turned away from love. Twice. Why? God, who requires a fine fidelity, would seem to have been responsible. 'I love, as you would have me, God the most; Would not lose Him, but you, must one be lost ... / This say I, having counted up the cost': one of the sonnets from *Monna Innominata*, which, though written in the voice of Dante's Beatrice, clearly echoes Rossetti's own choice.

She settled early on her life's priority, one of deeply religious observance and passionate love of God. Men came second. Within that dialogue with self, in the battleground between soul and body, Rossetti, a girl of extreme temperament (she suffered a mental breakdown in early teenage years) and temper – her tantrums when young were formidable – found her poetic inspiration. God, and what Rossetti interpreted as His demands, inspired much of her poetry – both the love poetry and the devotional pieces, which number in the hundreds. Her first love, James Collinson, RA, whom she met when she was eighteen and who painted a darkly forbidding portrait of his young beloved (unlike Dante Gabriel's light-filled portrait of his sister as Mary at the Annunciation: *Ecce Ancilla Domini*), was rather unreliable spiritually. This was a fatal flaw in the eyes of the deeply religious Christina. Collinson changed his religion from that of committed Catholic to Protestant and then back again to Catholic. He was not perhaps a man for the long haul of the soul. Her second, perhaps deeper, affection was for Charles Bagot Cayley, from whom, aged thirty, she eventually received a proposal. Cayley was, alas, untroubled by any belief at all – which, of course, was the trouble. Virginia Woolf commented that if she were 'bringing a case against God', Christina Rossetti would be her first witness. Certainly there is something of Francis Thompson's 'The Hound of Heaven' in what Rossetti saw as God's unending pursuit: 'But all night long that voice spake urgently: / "Open to Me / . . . Rise, let Me in."' (From the poem 'Despised and Rejected'.)

Another poem, 'Dost Thou Not Care?', ends with Christ's reminder of His sacrifice, *'Did I not die for thee? / Do I not live for thee? leave Me tomorrow.'* A line which allows for no escape. Spiritual battles can be profoundly exhausting. In 'Weary in Well-Doing' resignation is a touch resentful. 'He broke my will from day to day, / He read my yearnings unexpressed / And said them nay . . . But, Christ my God, when will it be / That I may let alone my toil / And rest with Thee?'

Before she rested anywhere and despite her perpetual internal war Rossetti set about the publication of her work with a pragmatic professionalism, indeed worldliness, which may surprise many who link her with the nun of Amherst, Emily Dickinson. After the initial rejection of her poems Dickinson, the more fiercely intellectual of the two, declined with disdainful elegance to pursue publication, while neatly collating one poetic masterwork after another to be discovered after her death. Rossetti, on the other hand, aged only seventeen had two poems, 'Death's Chill Between' and 'Heart's Chill Between' (the titles clear indicators of what was to come), published in the prestigious literary weekly the *Athenaeum*. She was declared the poet in the family, continued to write, upstairs, and was published in various magazines including the bizarrely named *The Germ*, a short-lived literary publication started by her brothers. Then in April 1862, when she was thirty-two, her debut collection *Goblin Market and Other Poems* was published by Macmillan and thus she entered literary history. The acclaim was immediate and deeply satisfying to its author, who, though she would follow it four years later with *The Prince's Progress and Other Poems*, which includes the beautiful hymn, 'A Christmas Carol' ('In the bleak mid-winter'), would never again in her many later collections stun her readers in quite the same way. Almost one hundred and fifty years after publication it stuns us still. It contains one of the most bewildering poems in literature, 'Goblin

Market', which Edith Sitwell regarded as one of the most perfect poems written by a woman in the English language. Yet the poem which guaranteed its author immortality cannot be read, as she insisted to her less than convinced brother, William Michael, as simply a fairy tale. She was not a prude. Nor was she a nun. Her tragic sibling Dante Gabriel, with whom she shared a house, lived a not so secret life of debauchery. Recent biographies have pointed out that in the years 1859–60, and immediately prior to its publication, Christina Rossetti worked in a house for fallen women in Highgate – and worked so successfully that she was offered and declined the post of Principal. Though she was to live another thirty-two years and see 'Goblin Market' republished she never gave us any further guidance. Why should she? She knew what she'd done.

Christina Rossetti died from breast cancer in December 1894, aged sixty-four. Margaret Reynolds in *The Culture of Christina Rossetti* sounds a warning bell to all who claim definitive insight into this mysterious poet: 'Once upon a time Christina Rossetti was simple.' However, as we have discovered, that was 'Long ago and long ago', the last line of her aptly titled 'Maiden-Song'.

The Poems

Sisterhood, whether Pre-Raphaelite or not, is a challenging state, one which is quite different from that of brotherhood. It is never more challenging than in 'Goblin Market', the tale of two sisters, Lizzie and Laura. Laura, recklessly, 'with a golden curl', succumbs to the tones 'as smooth as honey' of the goblins' incessant cry to 'Come buy our orchard fruits, / Come buy, come buy' and, having 'sucked and sucked and sucked the more ... until her lips were sore', finds that yet her 'mouth waters still', and she wishes to 'Buy more'. Alas, the goblins seem to have disappeared and Lizzie, fearful that her sister will die from longing for the juice which has so entranced her, bravely sets out to find them. It is a dangerous endeavour, for when she does they 'Kicked and knocked her, / Mauled and mocked her'. Lizzie, 'white and golden' though dripping in their juice, never allows their poison to pass her lips. She rushes back to Laura and commands her to 'Eat me, drink me, love me; / Laura, make much of me: / For your sake I have braved the glen / and had to do with goblin merchant men.' Years later this tale of sisterly love ('there is no friend like a sister / In calm or stormy weather') is recounted by the repentant Laura, when both 'were wives / With children of their own'. It is a masterpiece of broken yet insistent rhythms so compelling as to seem as irresistible as the goblins' fruit, with their implied images of the Eucharist that mingle with nursery imagery and impossible-to-ignore luscious sexual innuendo. It is a Miltonian tale of temptation and triumph over evil – his *Comus* was widely believed to have been an inspiration. 'Goblin Market' itself is meant to have inspired *Alice's Adventures Under Ground*, whose author Charles Dodgson (Lewis Carroll) regarded Rossetti's tale as a work of genius. It is a telling compliment from the author of another surrealist masterpiece that also lends itself to a multitude of interpretations. The debate concerning Rossetti's poem has continued since publication. Is it, as the *Spectator* believed in 1862, a genuine childhood poem, as Arthur Rackham's enchanting 1933 illustrations would tend to confirm? Or, are the rather sinister later illustrations by George Gershinowitz and Martin Ware more truthful representations? Finally, and most controversially of all, do Kinuko Craft's 1973 illustrations for *Playboy* have a validity beyond George Bataille's concept of the phallic eye? The critic and poet Tom Paulin has ranked 'Goblin Market' alongside 'The Wreck of the *Deutschland*' as one of the greatest achievements of Victorian poetry. He is right.

Sisterhood is the subject of another disturbing poem from Rossetti, 'Sister Maude', who 'lurked to spy and peer' and who, through jealousy, brings about the death of her sister's lover and is then cursed in a brutal last line: 'But sister Maude, oh sister Maude, / Bide *you* with death and sin.'

The poem '"No, Thank You, John"' shows Rossetti in a rare, very rare, cool and witty mood. There was, evidently, an unfortunate John, a marine painter, who was dispatched with some contempt: 'Here's friendship for you if you like; but love, – / No, thank you, John.'

I have, alas, for decades misconstrued one of her best-known and best-loved poems: 'When I am dead, my dearest, / Sing no sad songs for me ... I shall not see the shadows, I shall not feel the rain; ... Haply I may remember, / And haply may forget' does not denote 'happily' – it means by chance, which rather alters the mood!

The mood in 'Dost Thou Not Care?' is not open to misinterpretation of any kind. It is a despairing love song to Christ, an anguished cry: 'Dost Thou not love me, Lord, or care / For this mine ill?' 'Memory' is one of the poems which most merits Larkin's 'steely stoicism' insight. 'I faced the truth alone ... None know the choice I made and broke my heart ... I have braced my will / Once, chosen for once my part ... I broke it at a blow ... laid it cold ...'. Will is perhaps the operative word in this remarkable poem of emotional self-destruction in the cause of the soul. The first stanza of 'Up-Hill' was, as Betty S. Flowers tells us, spoken in a sermon by the then lay-preacher in London, Vincent Van Gogh. Its last lines might have comforted that sad genius more: 'Will there be beds for me and all who seek? / Yea, beds for all who come.'

Goblin Market

Morning and evening
Maids heard the goblins cry:
'Come buy our orchard fruits,
Come buy, come buy:
Apples and quinces,
Lemons and oranges,
Plump unpecked cherries,
Melons and raspberries,
Bloom-down-cheeked peaches,
Swart-headed mulberries,
Wild free-born cranberries,
Crab-apples, dewberries,
Pine-apples, blackberries,
Apricots, strawberries; –
All ripe together
In summer weather, –
Morns that pass by,
Fair eves that fly;
Come buy, come buy:
Our grapes fresh from the vine,
Pomegranates full and fine,
Dates and sharp bullaces,
Rare pears and greengages,
Damsons and bilberries,
Taste them and try:
Currants and gooseberries,
Bright-fire-like barberries,

Figs to fill your mouth,
Citrons from the South,
Sweet to tongue and sound to eye;
Come buy, come buy.'

Evening by evening
Among the brookside rushes,
Laura bowed her head to hear,
Lizzie veiled her blushes:
Crouching close together
In the cooling weather,
With clasping arms and cautioning lips,
With tingling cheeks and finger tips.
'Lie close,' Laura said,
Pricking up her golden head:
'We must not look at goblin men,
We must not buy their fruits:
Who knows upon what soil they fed
Their hungry thirsty roots?'
'Come buy,' call the goblins
Hobbling down the glen.
'Oh,' cried Lizzie, 'Laura, Laura,
You should not peep at goblin men.'
Lizzie covered up her eyes,
Covered close lest they should look;
Laura reared her glossy head,
And whispered like the restless brook:
'Look, Lizzie, look, Lizzie,
Down the glen tramp little men.
One hauls a basket,
One bears a plate,
One lugs a golden dish
Of many pounds weight.

How fair the vine must grow
Whose grapes are so luscious;
How warm the wind must blow
Thro' those fruit bushes.'
'No,' said Lizzie: 'No, no, no;
Their offers should not charm us,
Their evil gifts would harm us.'
She thrust a dimpled finger
In each ear, shut eyes and ran:
Curious Laura chose to linger
Wondering at each merchant man.
One had a cat's face,
One whisked a tail,
One tramped at a rat's pace,
One crawled like a snail,
One like a wombat prowled obtuse and furry,
One like a ratel tumbled hurry skurry.
She heard a voice like voice of doves
Cooing all together:
They sounded kind and full of loves
In the pleasant weather.

Laura stretched her gleaming neck
Like a rush-imbedded swan,
Like a lily from the beck,
Like a moonlit poplar branch,
Like a vessel at the launch
When its last restraint is gone.

Backwards up the mossy glen
Turned and trooped the goblin men,
With their shrill repeated cry,
'Come buy, come buy.'

When they reached where Laura was
They stood stock still upon the moss,
Leering at each other,
Brother with queer brother;
Signalling each other,
Brother with sly brother.
One set his basket down,
One reared his plate;
One began to weave a crown
Of tendrils, leaves and rough nuts brown
(Men sell not such in any town);
One heaved the golden weight
Of dish and fruit to offer her:
'Come buy, come buy,' was still their cry.
Laura stared but did not stir,
Longed but had no money:
The whisk-tailed merchant bade her taste
In tones as smooth as honey,
The cat-faced purr'd,
The rat-paced spoke a word
Of welcome, and the snail-paced even was heard;
One parrot-voiced and jolly
Cried 'Pretty Goblin' still for 'Pretty polly;' –
One whistled like a bird.

But sweet-tooth Laura spoke in haste:
'Good folk, I have no coin;
To take were to purloin:
I have no copper in my purse,
I have no silver either,
And all my gold is on the furze
That shakes in windy weather
Above the rusty heather.'

'You have much gold upon your head,'
They answered all together:
'Buy from us with a golden curl.'
She clipped a precious golden lock,
She dropped a tear more rare than pearl,
Then sucked their fruit globes fair or red:
Sweeter than honey from the rock,
Stronger than man-rejoicing wine,
Clearer than water flowed that juice;
She never tasted such before,
How should it cloy with length of use?
She sucked and sucked and sucked the more
Fruits which that unknown orchard bore;
She sucked until her lips were sore;
Then flung the emptied rinds away
But gathered up one kernel-stone,
And knew not was it night or day
As she turned home alone.

Lizzie met her at the gate
Full of wise upbraidings:
'Dear, you should not stay so late,
Twilight is not good for maidens;
Should not loiter in the glen
In the haunts of goblin men.
Do you not remember Jeanie,
How she met them in the moonlight,
Took their gifts both choice and many,
Ate their fruits and wore their flowers
Plucked from bowers
Where summer ripens at all hours?
But ever in the noonlight
She pined and pined away;

Sought them by night and day,
Found them no more but dwindled and grew grey;
Then fell with the first snow,
While to this day no grass will grow
Where she lies low:
I planted daisies there a year ago
That never blow.
You should not loiter so.'
'Nay, hush,' said Laura:
'Nay, hush, my sister:
I ate and ate my fill,
Yet my mouth waters still;
Tomorrow night I will
Buy more:' and kissed her:
'Have done with sorrow;
I'll bring you plums tomorrow
Fresh on their mother twigs,
Cherries worth getting;
You cannot think what figs
My teeth have met in,
What melons icy-cold
Piled on a dish of gold
Too huge for me to hold,
What peaches with a velvet nap,
Pellucid grapes without one seed:
Odorous indeed must be the mead
Whereon they grow, and pure the wave they drink
With lilies at the brink,
And sugar-sweet their sap.'

Golden head by golden head,
Like two pigeons in one nest
Folded in each other's wings,

They lay down in their curtained bed:
Like two blossoms on one stem,
Like two flakes of new-fall'n snow,
Like two wands of ivory
Tipped with gold for awful kings.
Moon and stars gazed in at them,
Wind sang to them lullaby,
Lumbering owls forbore to fly,
Not a bat flapped to and fro
Round their rest:
Cheek to cheek and breast to breast
Locked together in one nest.

Early in the morning
When the first cock crowed his warning,
Neat like bees, as sweet and busy,
Laura rose with Lizzie:
Fetched in honey, milked the cows,
Aired and set to rights the house,
Kneaded cakes of whitest wheat,
Cakes for dainty mouths to eat,
Next churned butter, whipped up cream,
Fed their poultry, sat and sewed;
Talked as modest maidens should:
Lizzie with an open heart,
Laura in an absent dream,
One content, one sick in part;
One warbling for the mere bright day's delight,
One longing for the night.

At length slow evening came:
They went with pitchers to the reedy brook;
Lizzie most placid in her look,

Laura most like a leaping flame.
They drew the gurgling water from its deep;
Lizzie plucked purple and rich golden flags,
Then turning homewards said: 'The sunset flushes
Those furthest loftiest crags;
Come, Laura, not another maiden lags,
No wilful squirrel wags,
The beasts and birds are fast asleep.'
But Laura loitered still among the rushes
And said the bank was steep.
And said the hour was early still
The dew not fall'n, the wind not chill:
Listening ever, but not catching
The customary cry,
'Come buy, come buy,'
With its iterated jingle
Of sugar-baited words:
Not for all her watching
Once discerning even one goblin
Racing, whisking, tumbling, hobbling;
Let alone the herds
That used to tramp along the glen,
In groups or single,
Of brisk fruit-merchant men.
Till Lizzie urged, 'O Laura, come;
I hear the fruit-call but I dare not look:
You should not loiter longer at this brook:
Come with me home.
The stars rise, the moon bends her arc,
Each glowworm winks her spark,
Let us get home before the night grows dark:
For clouds may gather
Tho' this is summer weather,

Put out the lights and drench us thro';
Then if we lost our way what should we do?'

Laura turned cold as stone
To find her sister heard that cry alone,
That goblin cry,
'Come buy our fruits, come buy.'
Must she then buy no more such dainty fruit?
Must she no more such succous pasture find,
Gone deaf and blind?
Her tree of life drooped from the root:
She said not one word in her heart's sore ache;
But peering thro' the dimness, nought discerning,
Trudged home, her pitcher dripping all the way;
So crept to bed, and lay
Silent till Lizzie slept;
Then sat up in a passionate yearning,
And gnashed her teeth for baulked desire, and wept
As if her heart would break.

Day after day, night after night,
Laura kept watch in vain
In sullen silence of exceeding pain.
She never caught again the goblin cry:
'Come buy, come buy;' –
She never spied the goblin men
Hawking their fruits along the glen:
But when the noon waxed bright
Her hair grew thin and gray;
She dwindled, as the fair full moon doth turn
To swift decay and burn
Her fire away.

One day remembering her kernel-stone
She set it by a wall that faced the south;
Dewed it with tears, hoped for a root,
Watched for a waxing shoot,
But there came none;
It never saw the sun,
It never felt the trickling moisture run:
While with sunk eyes and faded mouth
She dreamed of melons, as a traveller sees
False waves in desert drouth
With shade of leaf-crowned trees
And burns the thirstier in the sandful breeze.
She no more swept the house
Tended the fowls or cows,
Fetched honey, kneaded cakes of wheat,
Brought water from the brook:
But sat down listless in the chimney-nook
And would not eat.

Tender Lizzie could not bear
To watch her sister's cankerous care
Yet not to share.
She night and morning
Caught the goblins' cry:
'Come buy our orchard fruits,
Come buy, come buy:' –
Beside the brook, along the glen,
She heard the tramp of goblin men,
The voice and stir
Poor Laura could not hear;
Longed to buy fruit to comfort her,
But feared to pay too dear.
She thought of Jeanie in her grave,

LIFE SAVING

Who should have been a bride;
But who for joys brides hope to have
Fell sick and died
In her gay prime,
In earliest Winter time,
With the first glazing rime,
With the first snow-fall of crisp Winter time.

Till Laura dwindling
Seemed knocking at Death's door:
Then Lizzie weighed no more
Better and worse;
But put a silver penny in her purse,
Kissed Laura, crossed the heath with clumps of furze
At twilight, halted by the brook:
And for the first time in her life
Began to listen and look.

Laughed every goblin
When they spied her peeping:
Came towards her hobbling,
Flying, running, leaping,
Puffing and blowing,
Chuckling, clapping, crowing,
Clucking and gobbling,
Mopping and mowing,
Full of airs and graces,
Pulling wry faces,
Demure grimaces,
Cat-like and rat-like,
Ratel- and wombat-like,
Snail-paced in a hurry,
Parrot-voiced and whistler,

Helter skelter, hurry skurry,
Chattering like magpies,
Fluttering like pigeons,
Gliding like fishes, –
Hugged her and kissed her,
Squeezed and caressed her:
Stretched up their dishes,
Panniers, and plates:
'Look at our apples
Russet and dun,
Bob at our cherries,
Bite at our peaches,
Citrons and dates,
Grapes for the asking,
Pears red with basking
Out in the sun,
Plums on their twigs;
Pluck them and suck them,
Pomegranates, figs.' –

'Good folk,' said Lizzie,
Mindful of Jeanie:
'Give me much and many:' –
Held out her apron,
Tossed them her penny.
'Nay, take a seat with us,
Honour and eat with us,'
They answered grinning:
'Our feast is but beginning.
Night yet is early,
Warm and dew-pearly,
Wakeful and starry:
Such fruits as these

No man can carry;
Half their bloom would fly,
Half their dew would dry,
Half their flavour would pass by.
Sit down and feast with us,
Be welcome guest with us,
Cheer you and rest with us.' –
'Thank you,' said Lizzie: 'But one waits
At home alone for me:
So without further parleying,
If you will not sell me any
Of your fruits tho' much and many,
Give me back my silver penny
I tossed you for a fee.' –
They began to scratch their pates,
No longer wagging, purring,
But visibly demurring,
Grunting and snarling.
One called her proud,
Cross-grained, uncivil;
Their tones waxed loud,
Their looks were evil.
Lashing their tails
They trod and hustled her,
Elbowed and jostled her,
Clawed with their nails,
Barking, mewing, hissing, mocking,
Tore her gown and soiled her stocking,
Twitched her hair out by the roots,
Stamped upon her tender feet,
Held her hands and squeezed their fruits
Against her mouth to make her eat.
White and golden Lizzie stood,

Like a lily in a flood, –
Like a rock of blue-veined stone
Lashed by tides obstreperously, –
Like a beacon left alone
In a hoary roaring sea
Sending up a golden fire, –
Like a fruit-crowned orange tree
White with blossoms honey-sweet
Sore beset by wasp and bee, –
Like a royal virgin town
Topped with gilded dome and spire
Close beleaguered by a fleet
Mad to tug her standard down.

One may lead a horse to water,
Twenty cannot make him drink.
Tho' the goblins cuffed and caught her,
Coaxed and fought her,
Bullied and besought her,
Scratched her, pinched her black as ink,
Kicked and knocked her,
Mauled and mocked her,
Lizzie uttered not a word;
Would not open lip from lip
Lest they should cram a mouthful in:
But laughed in heart to feel the drip
Of juice that syrupped all her face,
And lodged in dimples of her chin,
And streaked her neck which quaked like curd.
At last the evil people
Worn out by her resistance
Flung back her penny, kicked their fruit
Along whichever road they took,

LIFE SAVING

Not leaving root or stone or shoot;
Some writhed into the ground,
Some dived into the brook
With ring and ripple,
Some scudded on the gale without a sound,
Some vanished in the distance.
In a smart, ache, tingle,
Lizzie went her way;
Knew not was it night or day;
Sprang up the bank, tore thro' the furze,
Threaded copse and dingle,
And heard her penny jingle
Bouncing in her purse,
Its bounce was music to her ear.
She ran and ran
As if she feared some goblin man
Dogged her with gibe or curse
Or something worse:
But not one goblin skurried after,
Nor was she pricked by fear;
The kind heart made her windy-paced
That urged her home quite out of breath with haste
And inward laughter.

She cried 'Laura,' up the garden,
'Did you miss me?
Come and kiss me.
Never mind the bruises,
Hug me, kiss me, suck my juices
Squeezed from goblin fruits for you,
Goblin pulp and goblin dew.
Eat me, drink me, love me;
Laura, make much of me:

For your sake I have braved the glen
And had to do with goblin merchant men.'

Laura started from her chair,
Flung her arms up in the air,
Clutched her hair:
'Lizzie, Lizzie, have you tasted
For my sake the fruit forbidden?
Must your light like mine be hidden,
Your young life like mine be wasted,
Undone in mine undoing
And ruined in my ruin,
Thirsty, cankered, goblin-ridden?' –
She clung about her sister,
Kissed and kissed and kissed her:
Tears once again
Refreshed her shrunken eyes,
Dropping like rain
After long sultry drouth;
Shaking with aguish fear, and pain,
She kissed and kissed her with a hungry mouth.
Her lips began to scorch,
That juice was wormwood to her tongue,
She loathed the feast:
Writhing as one possessed she leaped and sung,
Rent all her robe, and wrung
Her hands in lamentable haste,
And beat her breast.
Her locks streamed like the torch
Borne by a racer at full speed,
Or like the mane of horses in their flight,
Or like an eagle when she stems the light
Straight toward the sun,

Or like a caged thing freed,
Or like a flying flag when armies run.

Swift fire spread thro' her veins, knocked at her heart,
Met the fire smouldering there
And overbore its lesser flame;
She gorged on bitterness without a name:
Ah! fool, to choose such part
Of soul-consuming care!
Sense failed in the mortal strife:
Like the watch-tower of a town
Which an earthquake shatters down,
Like a lightning-stricken mast,
Like a wind-uprooted tree
Spun about,
Like a foam-topped waterspout
Cast down headlong in the sea,
She fell at last;
Pleasure past and anguish past,
Is it death or is it life?

Life out of death.
That night long Lizzie watched by her,
Counted her pulse's flagging stir,
Felt for her breath,
Held water to her lips, and cooled her face
With tears and fanning leaves:
But when the first birds chirped about their eaves,
And early reapers plodded to the place
Of golden sheaves,
And dew-wet grass
Bowed in the morning winds so brisk to pass,
And new buds with new day

Opened of cup-like lilies on the stream,
Laura awoke as from a dream,
Laughed in the innocent old way,
Hugged Lizzie but not twice or thrice;
Her gleaming locks showed not one thread of grey,
Her breath was sweet as May
And light danced in her eyes.

Days, weeks, months, years
Afterwards, when both were wives
With children of their own;
Their mother-hearts beset with fears,
Their lives bound up in tender lives;
Laura would call the little ones
And tell them of her early prime,
Those pleasant days long gone
Of not-returning time:
Would talk about the haunted glen,
The wicked, quaint fruit-merchant men,
Their fruits like honey to the throat
But poison in the blood;
(Men sell not such in any town·)
Would tell them how her sister stood
In deadly peril to do her good,
And win the fiery antidote:
Then joining hands to little hands
Would bid them cling together,
'For there is no friend like a sister
In calm or stormy weather;
To cheer one on the tedious way,
To fetch one if one goes astray,
To lift one if one totters down,
To strengthen whilst one stands.'

Memory

I

    I nursed it in my bosom while it lived,
I hid it in my heart when it was dead;
In joy I sat alone, even so I grieved
      Alone and nothing said.

I shut the door to face the naked truth,
    I stood alone—I faced the truth alone,
Stripped bare of self-regard or forms or ruth
      Till first and last were shown.

I took the perfect balances and weighed;
    No shaking of my hand disturbed the poise;
Weighed, found it wanting: not a word I said,
      But silent made my choice.

None know the choice I made; I make it still.
    None know the choice I made and broke my heart,
Breaking mine idol: I have braced my will
      Once, chosen for once my part.

I broke it at a blow, I laid it cold,
    Crushed in my deep heart where it used to live.
My heart dies inch by inch; the time grows old,
      Grows old in which I grieve.

II

I have a room whereinto no one enters
    Save I myself alone:
    There sits a blessed memory on a throne
There my life centres;

While winter comes and goes—oh tedious comer!—
    And while its nip-wind blows;
    While bloom the bloodless lily and warm rose
Of lavish summer.

If any should force entrance he might see there
    One buried yet not dead,
    Before whose face I no more bow my head
Or bend my knee there;

But often in my worn life's autumn weather
    I watch there with clear eyes,
    And think how it will be in Paradise
When we're together.

PERCY BYSSHE SHELLEY

Percy Bysshe Shelley was born into an aristocratic family in Sussex
in 1792. Poet, playwright and courageous pamphleteer, his long
poem *Queen Mab*, published in 1813 when he was twenty, was
regarded as one of the most revolutionary poems in the language.
The Revolt of Islam (1818), *The Mask of Anarchy* (1819),
Prometheus Unbound (1820), his haunting odes and his final work
The Triumph of Life (published posthumously in 1824) testify to his
intellectual and lyric genius. He drowned in the
Bay of Lerici in 1822.

PERCY BYSSHE SHELLEY

What Stopped Him?

Only death. 'I always go on until I am stopped,' he once wrote, 'and I am never stopped.' Youth! It was not wasted on young Percy Bysshe Shelley. He lived his short life in an ecstasy of being and creating – one and the same thing to Shelley. He was born on 4 August 1792 to Sir Timothy Shelley, MP for Horsham, Sussex, Whig aristocrat and a deeply religious man. He had high hopes for his brilliant and beautiful boy. Like many of his class he saw his son's future as a chronicle of a life foretold. Shelley, however, intended to write his own. Sir Timothy had bred an immortal – never a comfortable position for a father. His son believed poetry to be 'a fountain flowing with the waters of wisdom and delight', 'a sword of lightning, forever unsheathed'. He pursued the extreme not only in poetry and prose but also in his most emphatically unordinary life. If his father was abashed, so are we. The incandescence of his nature, his febrile sensitivity, the sometimes reckless intensity of his political and philosophical idealism, his fantastical dreams, his sublime intelligence – sharp as a blade – all astonish us and sometimes hint at the edge of madness. He began as he meant to go on.

In the nursery he was the thrilling brother of adoring sisters, whose chilblains he would eventually promise to cure by means of electrification. The family cat was perhaps a less willing victim. At Syon House, his preparatory school, where he was mercilessly bullied, he 'surprised' his school friends when, with gunpowder, he blew off the lid of his desk. At Eton, where he was again bullied, 'Mad' Shelley's rages were themselves electrifying (though he gained respect as a published novelist with the violent, passionate *Zastrozzi* – fee £40). At Oxford he horrified everyone by writing 'The Necessity of Atheism', its provocative conclusion: 'Every reflecting mind must allow that there is no proof of the existence of a Deity. QED.' He could perhaps have put it more subtly. He was sent down – atheism was dangerous, treacherous, blasphemous and therefore possibly criminal. Sir Timothy, horrified and himself fearful of legal proceedings, sent his communications to his son through legal channels. A furious Shelley disinherited himself by surrendering his claim on the family estate, Field Place, for an annuity of £2000, thus wounding himself and his father.

He found consolation with the Westbrook family, well-off coffee merchants. The daughters of the house, Eliza and Harriet, were enchanting and, after consideration of each, he ran away with Harriet, aged sixteen. They married and had two children, Ianthe and Eliza. Shelley seemed initially happy with Harriet: 'Love seems inclined to stay in the prison.' Alas, it would escape. For Shelley fell madly in love with another, the phrase, in this case, forensically accurate. Mary Godwin was the brilliant, beautiful daughter of philosopher William Godwin and Mary Wollstonecraft, author of *A Vindication of the Rights of Woman*, who had died shortly after her daughter's birth. Distraught by the possibility their love might be thwarted Shelley held out laudanum to the ashen-faced Mary. 'They wish to separate us, my beloved; but Death shall unite us.' Happily for us Mary resisted the laudanum and thus left us her strange masterpiece *Frankenstein*. She did not, however, resist Shelley. What sixteen-year-old could? She left home, as had Harriet. She didn't leave alone; fathers Beware! In case the couple might get lonely Shelley took her fifteen-year-old half-sister, Jane, with them. She, finding the name less than alluring, changed it to Claire – allurement being the *raison d'être* of Claire Clairmont. (She would practise it ruthlessly on Lord Byron, succeed briefly and be equally ruthlessly rejected. She would also become pregnant from her ten minutes of 'happy passion' with Lord Byron.) William Godwin was, understandably, initially enraged. It is one thing to believe in free love, another matter altogether to have it practised on one's daughter. He soothed himself eventually. Aristocratic connections have a charm all their own. Free love came, as it always does, at a high price. Shelley was no lust-filled predator. He loathed grossness of any kind. However, his high romanticism about sexual love made him more dangerous and indeed more cruel than Byron – with whom you at least knew what you were getting. Consumed by his obsession with Mary, Shelley endeavoured to persuade Harriet, whom he did not wish to divorce (though their marriage was, as he cruelly explained to her, not one of passion), of the philosophical and moral rightness of his true passion for Mary. He failed, and in 1816 Harriet drowned herself. The heartbroken Westbrook family applied for custody of the children, as did Shelley. They both lost, and the children were fostered. The tragedy cast a long shadow. Few were well disposed to a declared atheist whose young wife and mother of his children had committed suicide, her heart broken by cruel infidelity. The reviews in 1818 of his long poem The Revolt of Islam, inspired by the French Revolution, were savage. Previously titled 'Laon and Cythna', it had been suppressed due to its perceived theme of incest. Though he declared in the preface, 'I have written fearlessly ... I believe that Homer, Shakespeare, and Milton wrote with an utter disregard of anonymous censure', he was aware that his future in England, like his past, was bleak. In a sense he allowed himself to be hounded out of England, although not before writing one of the greatest lyrics in the language, 'Ozymandias', king of kings: 'Look on my works, ye Mighty, and despair!' The five years remaining to him were years of exile in Italy and of unbearable tragedy. His daughter with Mary, Clara, died in 1818 aged one; the following year his son William, aged three, died. He wrote on in virtual literary obscurity, with much of his work being published posthumously. In his last years he bequeathed us *Julian and Maddalo*, a precursor to Browning's dramatic monologues; the great metaphysical poem, 'The Cloud' ('I change, but I cannot die'); *The Mask of Anarchy* ('I met Murder on the way – / He had a mask like Castlereagh'); odes 'To the West Wind' ('tameless, and swift, and proud'), 'To a Skylark' ('Our sweetest songs are those that / tell of saddest thought'); *Adonaïs*, his passionate defence of Keats; and *Epipsychidion*; the plays *The Cenci* and *Prometheus Unbound* (a sacred text to Yeats); and *A Defence of Poetry*, in which poets are declared to be 'the unacknowledged legislators of the world'.

He was in the midst of writing *The Triumph of Life* when his own ended. He drowned on 8 July 1822, aged twenty-nine, in a storm in the Bay of Lerici, having refused an offer of assistance from another boat. He'd designed his own, the *Don Juan* in honour of Byron. It had a built-in fault. When his body was recovered (a copy of Keats's *Hyperion* in his pocket) he was cremated on the sands. His heart wouldn't burn. And that's the essence of Shelley. His heart was indestructible. *Cor Cordium*, heart of hearts, reads his gravestone. Probably literature's most truthful epitaph.

The Poems

'The poet and the man are two different natures.' Shelley, like Eliot, believed in that distance. Yet emotional self-expression is a prime characteristic of the Romantics, and Shelley was, as Harold Bloom notes, the greatest 'High Romantic' of them all. *Queen Mab*, printed but not published for fear of prosecution (the notes are as notorious as the poem), throws down the gauntlet: atheism, vegetarianism and free love are all praised. *Queen Mab* tells us, sadly, that 'Even love is sold'. 'Ozymandias', his finest sonnet according to Richard Holmes, is the result of a challenge. Shelley and a friend had visited the British Museum's Egyptian exhibition and each agreed to write a sonnet. Only one is remembered; such is genius. 'Hymn to Intellectual Beauty' honours Byron, who enjoyed the recognition and success that eluded Shelley in his lifetime. 'I have lived too long near Lord Byron,' he said, 'and the sun has extinguished the glow worm.' Not quite, as time would prove.

Julian [Shelley] *and Maddalo* [Byron] is a conversation between the two poets – 'the child' is believed to be Allegra, Byron's daughter by Claire Clairmont. Love's terrible cost is told by 'the madman' who loved 'the lady who had left him', and though she returned had been destroyed by her. *The Mask of Anarchy* is not only a response to the Peterloo Massacre, in which a number of unarmed protesters were killed and over five hundred injured, it is also a Miltonian hymn to liberty and burns with a hatred of authority. 'Love's Philosophy', supposedly written to Sophia Stacey, a ward of Shelley's uncle who shared a house with them in Florence, is mischievous and sweet. It is also disconcerting, as Shelley was at the time in the midst of tragedy. More was to come. Shelley, Keats and Byron, a poetic constellation, were wiped out within a few years of each other. Keats, who did not much care for Shelley, was the first to die, aged twenty-five. *Adonaïs*, Shelley's tribute to him, is also a fierce attack on the critics who had caused Keats despair such that he would wish for an unmarked grave. 'Here lies one whose name was writ in water.' It was water that claimed Shelley who, strangely, as a schoolboy often quoted Southey's *The Curse of Kehama*: 'And water shall see thee / And fear thee, and fly thee / The waves shall not touch thee / As they pass by thee!' They did not flee him. He left unfinished, mid-sentence, 'Then, what is Life? / ... Happy those for whom the fold' / Of', the poem which, according to Harold Bloom, persuades us is how Dante would sound, had he composed in English. The 550-line fragment, *The Triumph of Life*, is, according to Bloom, 'the most despairing poem, of true eminence, in the language ... It would bewilder and depress us were it not for its augmented poetic power.' Shelley is buried beside Keats, in the Protestant Cemetery in Rome. 'Nothing of him that doth fade / But doth suffer a sea-change / Into something rich and strange.'

Ozymandias

I met a traveller from an antique land
Who said: Two vast and trunkless legs of stone
Stand in the desert ... Near them, on the sand,
Half sunk, a shattered visage lies, whose frown,
And wrinkled lip, and sneer of cold command,
Tell that its sculptor well those passions read
Which yet survive, stamped on these lifeless things,
The hand that mocked them, and the heart that fed:
And on the pedestal these words appear:
'My name is Ozymandias, king of kings:
Look on my works, ye Mighty, and despair!'
Nothing beside remains. Round the decay
Of that colossal wreck, boundless and bare
The lone and level sands stretch far away.

The Mask of Anarchy

Written on the occasion of the massacre at Manchester

I
As I lay asleep in Italy
There came a voice from over the Sea
And with great power it forth led me
To walk in the visions of Poesy.

II
I met Murder on the way—
He had a mask like Castlereagh—
Very smooth he looked, yet grim;
Seven blood-hounds followed him:

III
All were fat; and well they might
Be in admirable plight,
For one by one, and two by two,
He tossed them human hearts to chew
Which from his wide cloak he drew.

IV
Next came Fraud, and he had on,
Like Eldon, an ermined gown;
His big tears, for he wept well,
Turned to mill-stones as they fell.

V

And the little children, who
Round his feet played to and fro,
Thinking every tear a gem,
Had their brains knocked out by them.

VI

Clothed with the Bible, as with light,
And the shadows of the night,
Like Sidmouth, next, Hypocrisy
On a crocodile rode by.

VII

And many more Destructions played
In this ghastly masquerade,
All disguised, even to the eyes,
Like Bishops, lawyers, peers, or spies.

VIII

Last came Anarchy: he rode
On a white horse, splashed with blood;
He was pale even to the lips,
Like Death in the Apocalypse.

IX

And he wore a kingly crown;
And in his grasp a sceptre shone;
On his brow this mark I saw—
'I AM GOD, AND KING, AND LAW!'

X

With a pace stately and fast,
Over English land he passed,
Trampling to a mire of blood
The adoring multitude,

XI

And a mighty troop around,
With their trampling shook the ground,
Waving each a bloody sword,
For the service of their Lord.

XII

And with glorious triumph, they
Rode through England proud and gay,
Drunk as with intoxication
Of the wine of desolation.

XIII

O'er fields and towns, from sea to sea,
Passed the Pageant swift and free,
Tearing up, and trampling down;
Till they came to London town.

XIV

And each dweller, panic-stricken,
Felt his heart with terror sicken
Hearing the tempestuous cry
Of the triumph of Anarchy.

XV

For with pomp to meet him came,
Clothed in arms like blood and flame,
The hired murderers, who did sing
'Thou art God, and Law, and King.

XVI

'We have waited, weak and lone
For thy coming, Mighty One!
Our purses are empty, our swords are cold,
Give us glory, and blood, and gold.'

XVII

Lawyers and priests, a motley crowd,
To the earth their pale brows bowed;
Like a bad prayer not over loud
Whispering—'Thou art Law and God.'—

XVIII

Then all cried with one accord,
'Thou art King, and God, and Lord;
Anarchy, to thee we bow,
Be thy name made holy now!'

XIX

And Anarchy, the Skeleton,
Bowed and grinned to every one,
As well as if his education
Had cost ten millions to the nation.

XX

For he knew the Palaces
Of our Kings were rightly his;
His the sceptre, crown, and globe,
And the gold-inwoven robe.

XXI

So he sent his slaves before
To seize upon the Bank and Tower,
And was proceeding with intent
To meet his pensioned Parliament

XXII

When one fled past, a maniac maid,
And her name was Hope, she said:
But she looked more like Despair,
And she cried out in the air:

XXIII

'My father Time is weak and gray
With waiting for a better day;
See how idiot-like he stands,
Fumbling with his palsied hands!

XXIV

'He has had child after child,
And the dust of death is piled
Over every one but me—
Misery, oh, Misery!'

XXV

Then she lay down in the street,
Right before the horses' feet,
Expecting, with a patient eye,
Murder, Fraud, and Anarchy.

XXVI

When between her and her foes
A mist, a light, an image rose,
Small at first, and weak and frail
Like the vapour of a vale:

XXVII

Till as clouds grow on the blast,
Like tower-crowned giants striding fast,
And glare with lightnings as they fly,
And speak in thunder to the sky,

XXVIII

It grew—a Shape arrayed in mail
Brighter than the viper's scale,
And upborne on wings whose grain
Was as the light of sunny rain.

XXIX

On its helm, seen far away,
A planet, like the Morning's, lay;
And those plumes its light rained through
Like a shower of crimson dew.

XXX
With step as soft as wind it passed,
O'er the heads of men—so fast
That they knew the presence there,
And looked,—but all was empty air.

XXXI
As flowers beneath May's footstep waken,
As stars from Night's loose hair are shaken,
As waves arise when loud winds call,
Thoughts sprung where'er that step did fall.

XXXII
And the prostrate multitude
Looked—and ankle-deep in blood,
Hope, that maiden most serene,
Was walking with a quiet mien:

XXXIII
And Anarchy, the ghastly birth,
Lay dead earth upon the earth;
The Horse of Death tameless as wind
Fled, and with his hoofs did grind
To dust the murderers thronged behind.

XXXIV
A rushing light of clouds and splendour,
A sense awakening and yet tender
Was heard and felt—and at its close
These words of joy and fear arose

XXXV

As if their own indignant Earth
Which gave the sons of England birth
Had felt their blood upon her brow,
And shuddering with a mother's throe

XXXVI

Had turnèd every drop of blood
By which her face had been bedewed
To an accent unwithstood,—
As if her heart had cried aloud:

XXXVII

'Men of England, heirs of Glory,
Heroes of unwritten story,
Nurslings of one mighty Mother,
Hopes of her, and one another;

XXXVIII

'Rise like Lions after slumber
In unvanquishable number,
Shake your chains to earth like dew
Which in sleep had fallen on you—
Ye are many—they are few.'

WALT WHITMAN

Walt Whitman was born in 1819, the son of a carpenter, in New York. He worked as a teacher and journalist, then in 1855 published the first edition of *Leaves of Grass*, immediately acclaimed by Ralph Waldo Emerson as 'a most extraordinary piece of wit and wisdom'. The collection, which expanded in the following eight editions into over four hundred poems, is regarded as an American classic. Whitman died in 1892.

WALT WHITMAN

Defiant Passions

Few poets ever caught life in language with as much defiant passion as did Walt Whitman in *Leaves of Grass*, of which Robert Louis Stevenson wrote that it 'tumbled the world upside down for me, blew into space a thousand cobwebs of genteel and ethical illusion, and, having thus shaken my tabernacle of lies, set me back again on a strong foundation.' This was not the initial response. Thomas Wentworth Higginson wrote: 'It is no discredit to Walt Whitman that he wrote *Leaves of Grass*, only that he did not burn it afterwards.' Its egotism – 'I celebrate myself . . . One's-self I sing' – and its exultation of the body, particularly sexually, as equal to the soul 'I Sing the Body Electric', horrified many.

Indeed he was sacked by his shocked employer. However, Walt Whitman persevered, and over thirty-three years added four hundred poems to the original twelve first published in 1855 (though published at his own expense) in response to Emerson's famous challenge to America to produce its own new, unique voice. Though Emerson praised the work in a private letter, which Walt, without permission published, sales were for many years abysmal. Whitman, however, believed *Leaves of Grass* to be 'unkillable'.

And he was right. The last line of the incandescent 'Song of Myself', from which we have taken excerpts, is sublimely confident: 'I stop somewhere waiting for you.' Indeed he does. We follow with the only poem anthologised in his lifetime, 'O Captain! My

Captain!', mourning the death of Lincoln who had steered the ship of state in stormy waters.

Song of Myself

[excerpts]

VI

A child said What is the grass? fetching it to me with full hands,
How could I answer the child? I do not know what it is any more
    than he.
I guess it must be the flag of my disposition, out of hopeful green
    stuff woven.

Or I guess it is the handkerchief of the Lord,
A scented gift and remembrancer designedly dropped,
Bearing the owner's name someway in the corners, that we may see
    and remark, and say Whose?

Or I guess the grass is itself a child, the produced babe of the vegetation.

Or I guess it is a uniform hieroglyphic,
And it means, Sprouting alike in broad zones and narrow zones,
Growing among black folks as among white,
Canuck, Tuckahoe, Congressman, Cuff, I give them the same, I receive
    them the same.

And now it seems to me the beautiful uncut hair of graves.

Tenderly will I use you curling grass,
It may be you transpire from the breasts of you men,
It may be if I had known them I would have loved them,
It may be you are from old people, or from offspring taken soon out of
    their mothers' laps,
And here you are the mothers' laps.

This grass is very dark to be from the white heads of old mothers,
Darker than the colorless beards of old men,
Dark to come from under the faint red roof of mouths.

O I perceive after all so many uttering tongues,
And I perceive they do not come from the roofs of mouths for
    nothing.

I wish I could translate the hints about the dead young men and
    women,
And the hints about old men and mothers, and the offspring taken
    soon out of their laps.
What do you think has become of the young and old men?
And what do you think has become of the women and children?

They are alive and well somewhere,
The smallest sprout shows there is really no death,
And if ever there was it led forward life, and does not wait at the end
    to arrest it,
And ceased the moment life appeared.

All goes onward and outward, nothing collapses,
And to die is different from what anyone supposed, and luckier.

VII
The spotted hawk swoops by and accuses me, he complains of my gab
    and my loitering.

I too am not a bit tamed, I too am untranslatable,
I sound my barbaric yawp over the roofs of the world.

The last scud of day holds back for me,
It flings my likeness after the rest and true as any on the shadow'd
    wilds,

It coaxes me to the vapor and the dusk.

I depart as air, I shake my white locks at the runaway sun,
I effuse my flesh in eddies, and drift it in lacy jags.

I bequeath myself to the dirt to grow from the grass I love,
If you want me again look for me under your boot-soles.

You will hardly know who I am or what I mean,
But I shall be good health to you nevertheless,
And filter and fibre your blood.

Failing to fetch me at first keep encouraged,
Missing me one place search another,
I stop somewhere waiting for you.

O Captain! My Captain!

O Captain! my Captain! our fearful trip is done,
The ship has weather'd every rack, the prize we sought is won,
The port is near, the bells I hear, the people all exulting,
While follow eyes the steady keel, the vessel grim and daring;
  But O heart! heart! heart!
   O the bleeding drops of red,
    Where on the deck my Captain lies,
     Fallen cold and dead.

O Captain! my Captain! rise up and hear the bells;
Rise up—for you the flag is flung—for you the bugle trills,
For you bouquets and ribbon'd wreaths—for you the shores a-crowding,
For you they call, the swaying mass, their eager faces turning;
  Here Captain! dear father!
   The arm beneath your head!
    It is some dream that on the deck,
     You've fallen cold and dead.

My Captain does not answer, his lips are pale and still,
My father does not feel my arm, he has no pulse nor will,
The ship is anchor'd safe and sound, its voyage closed and done,
From fearful trip the victor ship comes in with object won;
  Exult O shores, and ring O bells!
   But I with mournful tread,
    Walk the deck my Captain lies,
     Fallen cold and dead.

OSCAR WILDE

Oscar Wilde was born in Dublin in 1854. His first collection
of poetry was published in 1881. He is also remembered for his
short stories and his only novel, *The Picture of Dorian Gray* (1890),
and for his plays including *Lady Windermere's Fan* and *The
Importance of Being Earnest* (1895). *The Ballad of Reading Gaol*
was inspired by the prison term he served on conviction of
homosexuality. He died in Paris in 1900.

OSCAR WILDE

Each Man Kills The Thing He Loves

Please let us hear no more of the tragedy of Oscar Wilde ... Oscar was no tragedian. He was the superb comedian of the century, one to whom misfortune, disgrace and imprisonment were external yet traumatic.

His gaiety of soul was invulnerable; it shines through the blackest pages of *De Profundis* as clearly as in his wittiest epigrams. Even on his deathbed he found in himself no pity, 'playing for a laugh with his last breath, and getting it with as sure a stroke as in his balmiest days', according to George Bernard Shaw.

He belongs to our world. Now beyond the reach of scandal, he comes before us still, a towering figure, laughing and weeping with parables and paradoxes, 'so generous, so amusing and so right' — the last lines of Richard Ellmann's essential biography.

Wilde was born in October 1854, in Dublin, to Sir William Wilde, a noted eye surgeon and prolific writer (not only of articles for scientific journals, but also of literary criticism), and Jane Francesca Elgee, who believed she could trace her family back to Dante. She was a published poet, an expert on Celtic myths, a passionate republican, a kind of maternal Maud Gonne who penned such inflammatory political satire under the magnificent pseudonym of Speranza that she twice came close to being tried for sedition.

It must not be forgotten, wrote Shaw, that though by culture Wilde was a citizen of all civilised capitals, he was a very Irish Irishman and, as such, a foreigner everywhere but Ireland.

Well, the Irish foreigner would write the greatest English drawing-room comedy, an indisputable masterpiece, aged forty-one. *The Importance of Being Earnest*, written in three weeks, opened in triumph on Valentine's Day in 1895.

A hugely celebrated playwright, Wilde was one of the greatest of the Victorian era. *Lady Windermere's Fan* in 1892, *A Woman of No Importance* in 1893, *An Ideal Husband* in 1895, the first night attended by the Prince of Wales. As Wilde said of himself on that glorious first night of *An Ideal Husband*, he was 'The King of Life'.

A recognised scholar, winner at Trinity College Dublin of the Berkeley Gold Medal for Greek, he won a scholarship to Oxford. The Irish scholar John Mahaffy was meant to have said: 'Off you go, off to Oxford, Oscar – you're not clever enough for us here.' He was clever enough to get a double first.

In 1878, he won the Newdigate Prize for poetry at Oxford for his long poem 'Ravenna'.

Leader of the aesthetic movement, lampooned in Gilbert and Sullivan's *Patience*, one must remember the dandy in velvet breeches was well over six foot and very strong ...

He was editor, for a time, of *The Woman's World*, published by Cassell's. When asked by a fellow editor, 'How often do you go to the office?' he replied, Three times a week for an hour a day. But I have since struck off one of those days – and I never answer their letters. I have known men come to London with bright prospects and seen them complete wrecks in a few months through a habit of answering letters.'

Wilde was an essayist. 'The Decay of Lying', 'The Soul of Man Under Socialism'. A novelist, whose *Picture of Dorian Gray*, though attacked by the critics as 'vile' and 'leprous', was surreptitiously read and admired all over Europe. A short-story writer: 'The Happy Prince', 'Lord Arthur Savile's Crime'.

'The greatest conversationalist I have ever heard', according to Max Beerbohm. 'The best of his writing is only a pale reflection of his conversation,' said André Gide.

This genius became clear on his hugely successful lecture tour of America, where at one stage he lectured the miners in Leadville in the Rocky Mountains on Florentine art. They were, he said, the best-dressed men in America. When asked later had his audience not been rather rough, he said: 'Ready, but not rough. The revolver is their book of etiquette – it teaches lessons that are not forgotten.'

A man respectably married, to Constance Lloyd, lovely daughter of a Dublin solicitor. They had two sons, Cyril and Vyvyan.

On 18 February 1895 the Marquess of Queensberry, whose eldest son Viscount Drumlanrig had four months earlier been killed by the discharge of his gun at a shooting party (which many believed was due to the threatened emergence of a previously repressed homosexual scandal), left at the Albemarle Club a card bearing the words: 'To Oscar Wilde, posing as a Sodomite'. In fact, he'd misspelt the word. Queensberry was enraged that his youngest son Lord Alfred Douglas, known as Bosie, twenty-four, incredibly handsome, talented and vicious, was undoubtedly the subject of gossip about his relationship with Oscar Wilde. The hall porter put the card in an envelope. Ten days later it was found by Wilde.

Why did Wilde not throw the card away?

'The question,' he once wrote, 'arises a long time after the answer.'

Wilde immediately sent to his great friend Robbie Ross, possibly the greatest friend in literary history, a note which ended with these words: 'The tower of ivory is assailed by the foul thing. On the sands is my life spilt.' No it wasn't. Not then ...

These are the words of a man who not only seems to sense ruin but has already accepted it. Later he wrote, in an insight of the artist into his own work: 'It was foreshadowed in my plays.' In each play someone has a secret, the truth of which may destroy them or someone close to them. In each play catastrophe is averted, but as we know, not in life.

Though advised not to, Wilde sued for libel. And while the Marquess of Queensberry and his legal team worked feverishly with private detectives to investigate more fully the dangerous double life of Oscar Wilde, he, in an act of arrogant folly, went with Bosie to Monte Carlo, spending money with reckless abandon. It was madness bordering on self-destruction.

It is as wrong to canonise him as it was to demonise him.

On a visit to André Gide, who advised him not to return to England, Wilde protested: 'I must go on. Something must happen, something else, and I have no interest in happiness, pleasure. One must always seek the most tragic.' Gide would write later: 'Nietzsche was no shock to me. After all, I'd listened to Oscar Wilde.'

On 3 April Oscar Wilde appeared before Mr Justice Henn-Collins – 'Despite the stunning brilliance with which Wilde gave vent to his polished paradoxes with careless nonchalance,' reported one newspaper, he lost the libel case. He was arrested the same day, and held at Holloway.

The trial opened on 26 April, he was found not guilty on some counts, and was then recharged. He took refuge for a time in his mother's house, where she and his brother Willie urged him to behave like an Irish hero and face the music. This had proved an effective tactic in their family history – his father had survived a court case concerning the alleged seduction under chloroform of a female patient. 'Wildes don't run' seemed to be the message.

Though begged by friends to leave, it was Bosie who urged Wilde to fight it and Bosie's hated father the Marquess, all the way. This he did. 'I have never doubted he was right to do so,' said Yeats.

In *Irish Peacock & Scarlet Marquess*, based on the transcript of the trial which, with many other fascinating items, are in the British Library archive, Merlin Holland, Wilde's grandson, makes clear that Oscar now saw himself as defender of the freedom of the artist and eloquent defender of the affection the artist can feel for a wonderful and beautiful person – or mind. Wilde was emphatic at his trial that accusations of homosexuality against him were false.

He lied. 'The love that dare not speak its name' – not Wilde's line, but that of Bosie, from his very good 'Two Loves' – came at a high price.

Oscar Wilde was sentenced to two years' imprisonment, with hard labour. He almost collapsed when the sentence was handed down. His life was now indeed spilt upon the ground; it had taken precisely twelve weeks to destroy him.

After a short time in Wandsworth Prison Wilde was taken to Reading Gaol – where he did not write *The Ballad*, but where, day after day, sheet by sheet (he was allowed one page per day), he wrote *De Profundis*, an essential precursor to *The Ballad*. It is mostly – though there are some passages of self-pity – a ferocious examination of conscience.

He found himself guilty of having become 'the spendthrift of my own genius ... What the paradox was to me in the sphere of thought, perversity became to me in the sphere of passion. Desire at the end, was a malady, or a madness, or both. I grew careless of the lives of others. I took pleasure where it pleased me and passed on.'

He knowingly feasted with panthers 'The danger,' he said, 'was half the excitement.'

De Profundis ends with these lines to Bosie: 'Perhaps I am chosen to teach you something much more wonderful, the meaning of Sorrow and its beauty.'

Sorrow courses through *The Ballad of Reading Gaol*. That, and pity. It is Pity to a Purpose – it was written over a period of ten days when Wilde was living in France under the name of Sebastian Melmoth, the satanic hero of Charles Maturin's hugely influential *Melmoth the Wanderer*. Maturin was related to him on his mother's side.

Wilde, the man who believed in 'Art for Art's sake' and wished to burn as Walter Pater admonished, 'with a hard, gem-like flame', had now written a poem of humility and compassion. It is 'a nearly great poem' said Yeats ... for Yeats believed Wilde had identified too much with his subject. Of the line 'Yet each man kills the thing he loves', Wilde once said 'treachery is inseparable from faith. I often betray myself with a kiss.' And when editing *The Oxford Book of Modern Poetry*, Yeats excised those famous lines.

Now Yeats, in fact, is right that *The Ballad* is finally amongst the great, and Oscar the artist was of course aware of the artistic price of this identification. Seamus Heaney in his brilliant, provocatively titled 'Speranza in Reading Gaol' believed that in this poem Wilde became the kind of propagandist poet Speranza had been, and Wilde had always admired her nobility of purpose. Indeed, Heaney's essay opens with the famous aphorism 'All women become like their mothers. That is their tragedy. No man does. That is his.'

The reason the poem will last, and the reason for its power, is because, as Heaney argues: 'In the gathering force of its lamentation there lies a plea which is uniquely disturbing.' It is poetry as a means of redress, and Oscar Wilde was well aware, as Ellmann points out, of the elements of propaganda.

As to the prison conditions of the time, there was much to redress. Oscar Wilde spent six hours a day on the treadmill. His hands were torn to shreds by the picking of oakum. The sanitary conditions were so appalling that prisoners continually suffered the humiliation of diarrhoea. Books were forbidden. The one-hour walk per day had to be undertaken in silence – the punishment for breaking this rule was solitary confinement; double for the man who spoke first – a Kafkaesque note.

However, the poem is not about Wilde's suffering; it is about the terror, love and pity he and every other inmate felt for the man who's got to swing. His name was Charles Thomas Wooldridge. 'The man's face,' he said, 'will haunt me till I die.' And in that horror lies the moral force of the poem – against capital punishment.

The poem, whose title was suggested by Robbie Ross, was

published on 9 February 1898 by 'the most learned erotomaniac in Europe', Leonard Smithers, who published it when no one would touch anything by Wilde. Indeed no one would touch Wilde. Period.

So savage had been the reaction of society, that his wife Constance (poor kind Constance who'd travelled to Reading Gaol from Italy to tell Oscar personally of Speranza's death) had been forced to change her name and that of the children to Holland, an old family name. From the day of his arrest Oscar Wilde never saw his children again.

The poem was published as written by C 3.3, Wilde's cell number, Cell 3 on the third landing. The print run of four thousand was sold out in days – so at last a little good news for Oscar. It was reprinted, and sold brilliantly. The last edition in his lifetime bore his name – his publisher Smithers saying to him, 'I think the time has now come when you should own "The Ballad", Oscar.'

It was about all he did own. He had little money. He'd of course been declared bankrupt. His house was ransacked after the trial. Constance offered a small allowance, conditional on his not seeing Bosie. This, Wilde refused to do. It was, as Ellmann says, 'a berserk passion'.

Within a short period of time his family was decimated. His brother, Willie, died. Constance died. When he visited her grave in Genoa, he said: 'Life is a very terrible thing.'

His own life ended a year later in Paris. He died from meningitis on 30 November 1900, having become a Catholic the day before. 'Catholicism is the only religion to die in.'

The Marquess of Queensberry had died the same year, and in *The Times* his obituary was longer than that of Oscar Wilde's – though much, much shorter than Bosie's, 'a Poet of Distinction' – who amazingly went to prison for libel. While in prison, he wrote a poem – his answer to *De Profundis* – *In Excelsis*. Wilde whose 'gaiety of soul', as Shaw noted, was 'invulnerable', would have smiled.

Few men have ever known such dizzying heights; few have fallen so far, so fast.

None in the depths of humiliation and grief have found such

sweetness, such generosity and pity for the human condition as are found in this poem. That is why, perhaps, there are always fresh flowers on Wilde's grave in the Père Lachaise cemetery in Paris, where his body lies under Jacob Epstein's beautiful monument bearing the words:

And alien tears will fill for him
Pity's long-broken urn.

The Ballad of Reading Gaol

[excerpts]

He did not wear his scarlet coat,
    For blood and wine are red,
And blood and wine were on his hands
    When they found him with the dead,
The poor dead woman whom he loved,
    And murdered in her bed.

He walked amongst the Trial Men
    In a suit of shabby grey,
A cricket cap was on his head,
    And his step seemed light and gay;
But I never saw a man who looked
    So wistfully at the day.

I never saw a man who looked
    With such a wistful eye
Upon that little tent of blue
    Which prisoners call the sky,
And at every drifting cloud that went
    With sails of silver by.

I walked, with other souls in pain,
    Within another ring,
And was wondering if the man had done
    A great or little thing,
When a voice behind me whispered low,
    'That fellow's got to swing.'

LIFE SAVING

Dear Christ! the very prison walls
    Suddenly seemed to reel,
And the sky above my head became
    Like a casque of scorching steel;
And, though I was a soul in pain,
    My pain I could not feel.

I only knew what hunted thought
    Quickened his step, and why
He looked upon the garish day
    With such a wistful eye;
The man had killed the thing he loved
    And so he had to die.

Yet each man kills the thing he loves
    By each let this be heard,
Some do it with a bitter look,
    Some with a flattering word,
The coward does it with a kiss,
    The brave man with a sword!

Some kill their love when they are young,
    And some when they are old;
Some strangle with the hands of Lust,
    Some with the hands of Gold:
The kindest use a knife, because
    The dead so soon grow cold.

Some love too little, some too long,
    Some sell, and others buy;
Some do the deed with many tears,
    And some without a sigh:
For each man kills the thing he loves,
    Yet each man does not die.

. . .

Six weeks our guardsman walked the yard,
    In a suit of shabby grey:
His cricket cap was on his head,
    And his step seemed light and gay,
But I never saw a man who looked
    So wistfully at the day.

I never saw a man who looked
    With such a wistful eye
Upon that little tent of blue
    Which prisoners call the sky,
And at every wandering cloud that trailed
    Its raveled fleeces by.

He did not wring his hands, as do
    Those witless men who dare
To try to rear the changeling Hope
    In the cave of black Despair:
He only looked upon the sun,
    And drank the morning air.

He did not wring his hands nor weep,
    Nor did he peek or pine,
But he drank the air as though it held
    Some healthful anodyne;
With open mouth he drank the sun
    As though it had been wine!

And I and all the souls in pain,
    Who tramped the other ring,
Forgot if we ourselves had done
    A great or little thing,
And watched with gaze of dull amaze
    The man who had to swing.

And strange it was to see him pass
    With a step so light and gay,
And strange it was to see him look
    So wistfully at the day,
And strange it was to think that he
    Had such a debt to pay.

That night the empty corridors
    Were full of forms of Fear,
And up and down the iron town
    Stole feet we could not hear,
And through the bars that hide the stars
    White faces seemed to peer.

He lay as one who lies and dreams
    In a pleasant meadow-land,
The watcher watched him as he slept,
    And could not understand
How one could sleep so sweet a sleep
    With a hangman close at hand?

But there is no sleep when men must weep
    Who never yet have wept:
So we – the fool, the fraud, the knave –
    That endless vigil kept,
And through each brain on hands of pain
    Another's terror crept.

They hanged him as a beast is hanged:
    They did not even toll
A requiem that might have brought
    Rest to his startled soul,
But hurriedly they took him out,
    And hid him in a hole.

They stripped him of his canvas clothes,
    And gave him to the flies;
They mocked the swollen purple throat
    And the stark and staring eyes:
And with laughter loud they heaped the shroud
    In which their convict lies.

The Chaplain would not kneel to pray
    By his dishonoured grave:
Nor mark it with that blessed Cross
    That Christ for sinners gave,
Because the man was one of those
    Whom Christ came down to save.

Yet all is well; he has but passed
    To Life's appointed bourne:
And alien tears will fill for him
    Pity's long-broken urn,
For his mourner will be outcast men,
    And outcasts always mourn.

V

I know not whether Laws be right,
    Or whether Laws be wrong;
All that we know who lie in goal
    Is that the wall is strong;
And that each day is like a year,
    A year whose days are long.

But this I know, that every Law
    That men have made for Man,
Since first Man took his brother's life,
    And the sad world began,
But straws the wheat and saves the chaff
    With a most evil fan.

This too I know – and wise it were
    If each could know the same –
That every prison that men build
    Is built with bricks of shame,
And bound with bars lest Christ should see
    How men their brothers maim.

With bars they blur the gracious moon,
    And blind the goodly sun:
And they do well to hide their Hell,
    For in it things are done
That Son of God nor son of Man
    Ever should look upon!

The vilest deeds like poison weeds
    Bloom well in prison-air:
It is only what is good in Man
    That wastes and withers there:
Pale Anguish keeps the heavy gate,
    And the Warder is Despair

For they starve the little frightened child
    Till it weeps both night and day:
And they scourge the weak, and flog the fool,
    And gibe the old and grey,
And some grow mad, and all grow bad,
    And none a word may say.

VI

In Reading gaol by Reading town
    There is a pit of shame,
And in it lies a wretched man
    Eaten by teeth of flame,
In burning winding-sheet he lies,
    And his grave has got no name.

And there, till Christ call forth the dead,
    In silence let him lie:
No need to waste the foolish tear,
    Or heave the windy sigh:
The man had killed the thing he loved,
    And so he had to die.

And all men kill the thing they love,
    By all let this be heard,
Some do it with a bitter look,
    Some with a flattering word,
The coward does it with a kiss,
    The brave man with a sword!

WILLIAM BUTLER YEATS

William Butler Yeats was born in Dublin in 1865. Poet, playwright
and critic, he was a founder member of The Abbey Theatre in his
native city. *The Wanderings of Oisin* (1889) immediately
established his reputation. He won the Nobel Prize in
1923 and died in 1939.

WILLIAM BUTLER YEATS

A Pity Beyond All Telling

'If a powerful and benevolent spirit has shaped the destiny of this world we can better discover that destiny from the words that have gathered up the heart's desire of the world.' Yeats found them in English, in Ireland. The publication in 1889 of William Butler Yeats's first book of poetry, *The Wanderings of Oisin*, was a seminal moment, not only in Irish literature but in Irish political history. The Gaelic League, started in 1893 by Douglas Hyde, had as its express purpose the continuation of the Celtic tradition in the language of Gaelic. Yeats, whose first book was based on the ancient Fenian cycle, would from then on bring Irish mythology to the Irish people in the English language: the language in which, Yeats pointed out, 'modern Ireland thinks and does its business'.

Roy Foster's essential, magisterial, two-part biography of Yeats, *The Apprentice Mage* and *The Arch-Poet*, weaves from poetry, personality and history a tale of creation – not only of a poet but of a literature and a society. Yeats was born in 1865 (his brother Jack is the celebrated painter) to John Butler Yeats, the son of rectors in the Church of Ireland, and to Susan Pollexfen, whose shipbuilding family came from Sligo. It was she who filled his head with the strange visions and the folklore of the area – which is perhaps why Joyce said of him, 'He had a surrealist imagination few painters could match.' As Foster shows us, Yeats learned early that art is what matters. His father, a solicitor, gave up his practice to study painting in London. Yeats went, not very happily, to Godolphin School (now Godolphin and Latymer) in Hammersmith, where, bizarrely, he became the best high diver in the school. He returned to Dublin, studied art and finally, in one of literature's luckiest volte-faces, decided on poetry. In Yeats, as Foster tells us, all the great gifts combine: 'the feeling for syllable and rhythm' that is essential to what Eliot called 'the auditory imagination', the visual sensibility of the trained painter; and the alchemist's power to transform language, so that it steals us away, with otherworld words, to the 'Land of Heart's Desire'.

In Irish literature Yeats resembles a tidal wave. The tide was not only poetical. In 1904, he set up the National Theatre of Ireland, the Abbey Theatre, with Lady Gregory. In his Nobel speech to the Swedish Academy in 1923, he chose as his subject not poetry, but the Irish dramatic movement. 'I would not be here were I not the symbol of that movement. When we thought of the plays we would like to perform we thought of what was romantic and poetical, for the nationalism we had called up – like that every generation had called up in moments of discouragement – was romantic and poetical.'

Well, up to a point. Yeats, the artist who claimed the 'romantic and poetical' for Irish nationalism, also, with his genius for spotting genius in others, brought to the Abbey Theatre Synge's *The Playboy of the Western World* and O'Casey's *The Plough and the Stars*. The Abbey audience was possibly the most hypersensitive in history. The plays were provocative. They rioted, frequently. Yeats fought back. He harangued them from the stage – 'You have disgraced yourselves, again' – and he persevered. This strength of character and courage in the face of prejudice, which was noted by Eliot, is fundamental to his astonishing achievements. As a senator he was to endeavour to get a 'bill of divorcement' through the Irish Senate. He failed. The fact that he tried at all is astonishing. Finally, he refused to allow himself to be destroyed by the agony of his unreciprocated, lifelong obsession with Maud Gonne, an obsession that would have felled lesser men.

She exploded into his life in 1889 just after the publication of *The Wanderings of Oisin*. Foster charts her tempestuous journey through the life of the poet. She was young, twenty-two, tall, with 'flaming' hair, but it was her passion that 'began all the trouble of my life'. She took possession of his soul – when the soul is lost to a woman, all is lost – and she inspired some of the greatest love poetry ever written. He had found the love of his life; she had found a poet for the cause. She was magnificent, brave and dangerous, with a fanatical love of Ireland – although not Irish herself – and was twice imprisoned for her activities. She described the British Empire as 'the outward symbol of Satan in the world'. Understatement was not her thing. Yeats wrote of her, 'She lived in storm and strife, / Her soul had such desire / For what proud death may bring / That it could not endure / The common good of life.' And therein lies the pity. Her fanaticism swept away much that was good in her life. His enduring love, expressed in poems of genius, gave us the strange poetry of the exultant, broken heart.

She married Sean MacBride, a revolutionary as extreme as she – Foster tells us they spent part of their honeymoon 'allegedly reconnoitring assassination attempts for an impending Royal visit to Gibraltar'. The confirmation of their marriage was, Yeats said, 'like lightning through me'. Their union was a disaster and they separated after five years. Sean MacBride was executed with the leaders of the 1916 rebellion.

In his fifties Yeats married Georgie Hyde-Lees, with whom he had two adored children, Anne and Michael. He was 'capable of experience' and, in embracing life with passion and courage in both the private and the public spheres, he did what no poet has ever done before or since: he wrote some of his greatest work in his sixties and seventies. 'Maturing as a poet,' Eliot wrote, means 'maturing as a whole man ... out of his [Yeats's] intense experience he now expressed universal truths. An artist, by serving his art with his entire integrity, is at the same time rendering the greatest service he can to his country and to the whole world.' Ireland owes him.

William Butler Yeats is buried in the Sligo he loved, beneath 'bare Ben Bulben's head'. His epitaph reads, as he requested: 'Cast a cold eye / On life, on death. / Horseman, pass by.'

The Poems

'The Pity of Love' has one of the loveliest lines in poetry: 'A pity beyond all telling / Is hid in the heart of love.' More provocatively, in 'The Tower' Yeats posed another question about love: 'Does the imagination dwell the most / Upon a woman won or woman lost?' In 'The Folly of Being Comforted' it seems that either way, there 'ain't no cure for love'. It survives the loss of beauty, youth, vitality – and rages on. 'O heart! O heart! If she'd but turn her head, / You'd know the folly of being comforted.'

In 'Friends' the gentle beauty of Olivia Shakespeare, with whom he had an affair after falling in love with Maud Gonne (to follow Maud Gonne meant one was always second), is praised, as is the indomitable spirit of Lady Gregory. And the third friend in this famous poem, what of Maud Gonne? Twenty-three years after he'd met her he writes that when he thinks of her 'up from my heart's root / So great a sweetness flows / I shake from head to foot'. Long, long love. 'Women, Beware Women,' wrote Thomas Middleton. What do they want? The utterly impossible, as Freud probably knew. In 'Before the World was made' the narrator searches in mirror after mirror for her mythical, mystical face. She is not in quest of a Lacan-like moment of psychological insight but of the power that would entice her lover to 'love the thing that was / Before the world was made'. It's a little-known poem and undeservedly so.

The poem 'Easter, 1916' was inspired by the tragic military failure of the rebellion, of which Yeats wrote to Lady Gregory: 'I had no idea that any public event could so deeply move me ... all the work of years has been overturned.' The patriotic self-sacrifice of MacDonagh and MacBride, Connolly and Pearse, led to the poem that presages the birth of a nation. The iconic line 'A terrible beauty is born' contains both warning and blessing. The word 'terrible', I believe, requires equal weight with the word 'beauty'. The rhythms and repetitions in the poem seem to keep pace almost irresistibly with the destiny of the men. The lines 'Too long a sacrifice / Can make a stone of the heart' sound another note of ambivalence, which was possibly the reason that Maud Gonne was less than impressed by the poem.

'The Municipal Gallery Re-visited' is, he said, 'a poem about the Ireland we have all served, and the movement of which I have been a part'. He had just visited the gallery and, as he looked at the portraits of so many old friends, memories of old loves flooded in: 'Think where man's glory most begins and ends / And say my glory was I had such friends.'

'Adam's Curse' reminds us, as he once wrote, that 'we achieve, if we do achieve, in little sedentary stitches as though we were making lace'. Often in secret, 'All that is beautiful in art is laboured over' in 'the hidden hours unnoticed by bankers, schoolmasters and clergymen'. 'Yet if it does not seem a moment's thought, / Our stitching and unstitching has been naught.' And love? 'We sat grown quiet at the name of love ... I had a thought ... That you were beautiful, and that I strove / To love you in the old high way of love.'

'The Circus Animals' Desertion', written late in life, is one of the greatest poems ever to deal with the creative tension between art and life. Yeats says, 'Maybe at last being but a broken man / I must be satisfied with my heart', and continues: 'Now that my ladder's gone / I must lie down where all the ladders start / In the foul rag and bone shop of the heart.' Where else?

Before the World was made

If I make the lashes dark
And the eyes more bright
And the lips more scarlet,
Or ask if all be right
From mirror after mirror,
No vanity's displayed:
I'm looking for the face I had
Before the world was made.

What if I look upon a man
As though on my beloved,
And my blood be cold the while
And my heart unmoved?
Why should he think me cruel
Or that he is betrayed?
I'd have him love the thing that was
Before the world was made.

Easter, 1916

I have met them at close of day
Coming with vivid faces
From counter or desk among grey
Eighteenth-century houses.
I have passed with a nod of the head
Or polite meaningless words,
Or have lingered awhile and said
Polite meaningless words,
And thought before I had done
Of a mocking tale or a gibe
To please a companion
Around the fire at the club,
Being certain that they and I
But lived where motley is worn:
All changed, changed utterly:
A terrible beauty is born.

That woman's days were spent
In ignorant good-will,
Her nights in argument
Until her voice grew shrill.
What voice more sweet than hers
When, young and beautiful,
She rode to harriers?
This man had kept a school
And rode our wingèd horse;
This other his helper and friend

Was coming into his force;
He might have won fame in the end,
So sensitive his nature seemed,
So daring and sweet his thought.
This other man I had dreamed
A drunken, vainglorious lout.
He had done most bitter wrong
To some who are near my heart,
Yet I number him in the song;
He, too, has resigned his part
In the casual comedy;
He, too, has been changed in his turn,
Transformed utterly:
A terrible beauty is born.

Hearts with one purpose alone
Through summer and winter seem
Enchanted to a stone
To trouble the living stream.
The horse that comes from the road,
The rider, the birds that range
From cloud to tumbling cloud,
Minute by minute they change;
A shadow of cloud on the stream
Changes minute by minute;
A horse-hoof slides on the brim,
And a horse plashes within it;
The long-legged moor-hens dive,
And hens to moor-cocks call;
Minute by minute they live:
The stone's in the midst of all.

Too long a sacrifice
Can make a stone of the heart.
O when may it suffice?
That is Heaven's part, our part
To murmur name upon name,
As a mother names her child
When sleep at last has come
On limbs that had run wild.
What is it but nightfall?
No, no, not night but death;
Was it needless death after all?
For England may keep faith
For all that is done and said.
We know their dream; enough
To know they dreamed and are dead;
And what if excess of love
Bewildered them till they died?
I write it out in a verse—
MacDonagh and MacBride
And Connolly and Pearse
Now and in time to be,
Wherever green is worn,
Are changed, changed utterly:
A terrible beauty is born.

PART II
THE POET IN THE GARDEN

CREATING THE GARDEN

'The Book of Life,' Oscar Wilde said, 'begins with a man and a woman, in a garden.' He omitted to mention the serpent, and thereby hangs a tale ...

Every story should have a beginning, a middle and an end – though, as one author remarked, not necessarily in that order. In that defiant spirit, we will end the reading at the beginning: in the Garden of Eden, which became Milton's and our Paradise Lost.

From the moment God created that garden, eastward of Eden as the Bible tells us, and then ruthlessly threw us out of it, the garden here on earth became the plain man's real paradise. We play God when we create a garden large or small, though, as those of us who are married to a gardener can testify, it takes a lot longer than the seven days in which God created the entire universe. There is always work in progress.

Perhaps the fascination in creating a garden lies in the metaphoric power of the garden: the budding, the flowering, maturing and withering of spring, summer, autumn and winter, reflecting the natural rhythms of life. The great dream of resurrection, promised as spring follows winter – begins afresh, begins afresh.

How could the writer resist? Poetic sensibility is particularly intense in the garden and few poets, if any, have resisted, which made the selection and construction of this evening challenging.

Right from the beginning, garden images are woven through the poetic canon.

Aeneas' search in the *Aeneid* for the sacred tree with its golden bough, which allows him to follow Proserpine into the underworld, is echoed in Swinburne's nineteenth-century 'Garden of Proserpine', where we give thanks that 'no life lives for ever; / That dead men rise up never; / That even the weariest river winds somewhere safe to sea'.

According to the Bible, Christ was betrayed in the garden of Gethsemane. Centuries later, Kipling sets another night of agony, and he echoes the line from the Bible in 'It didn't pass – it didn't pass', in a French garden called Gethsemane.

In the erotic Song of Solomon, the woman's body is 'A garden enclosed ... a spring shut up, a fountain sealed ... Let my beloved come into his garden, and eat its pleasant fruits.' Picking up that theme, the sixteenth-century poet Thomas Campion sings, 'There is a garden in her face, / Where roses and white lilies grow.'

Octavio Paz saw 'the other face of being': the feminine void.

Shakespeare's *Othello* tells us 'Our bodies are our gardens, to the which our wills are gardeners.' He also draws political lessons from the garden. The gardener in *Richard II* counsels 'like an executioner, / Cut off the heads of too-fast-growing sprays, / That look too lofty in our commonwealth'. So, learn the lesson of the flowers – or, as Voltaire intones in *Candide*, 'We must cultivate our garden.'

Three of the greatest poems of all time did not open in palaces or within four walls, however humble.

Dante famously began his early-fourteenth-century masterpiece, *The Divine Comedy*, in a dark wood.

'Of Man's first disobedience, and the fruit / Of that forbidden tree' are the opening lines of Milton's *Paradise Lost*.

T. S. Eliot, the greatest poet since Milton, according to Ted Hughes, began the seminal poem of the twentieth century, *The Waste Land*, with 'April is the cruellest month.'

We are going to start this evening with Love in the Garden, and I can assure you that it is less pastoral than you might imagine.

'Down by the Salley Gardens' was published in 1889, when Yeats was twenty-four. A few months later, Maud Gonne exploded into the Yeats household, and in a single afternoon she took possession of his soul and of his heart. The debate continues as to her possession or not of his body. However, it is safe to say that from that moment he never, ever took love easy, which is the theme of 'Down by the Salley Gardens'.

After that, to another Maud. What is it about Mauds that they cause such havoc?

Like Maud Gonne, the fictional Maud of Tennyson's eponymous poem is also tall and stately. Her lover waits all night, calling 'Come into the garden, Maud' while she dances away with a more acceptable suitor. As you can imagine, this will end in tears.

Tennyson, who was the master of melancholia, really gets the marvellous sense of hope and despair of the lover as he is waiting.

Will she come? Is she mine? Yes, she is mine. And it's beautiful, it's hopeful, it's heartbreaking, and I think the closest thing in literature that I can think of is perhaps the story of poor Michael Furey, waiting in a garden to catch a glimpse of his beloved, which cost him his life in Joyce's astonishing short story 'The Dead'.

Many believed Blake, the eighteenth-century mystic, to have been insane. Wordsworth agreed, but said 'there is something in the madness of this man which interests me more than the sanity of Lord Byron'. In 'The Garden of Love', from *Songs of Experience*, Blake attacks the constraints placed by the Church on sexual love: a well-known Blakean theme, as in *Songs of Innocence*, where he is asked 'Why a tender curb upon the youthful burning boy?'

Donne's dark and bitter poem, 'Twicknam Garden', resonates with sexual symbolism and with self-disgust bordering on Poe, like horror. 'I do bring / The spider Love, which transubstantiates all.' 'Make me a mandrake,' he cries – a narcotic plant, the root of which was once thought to resemble a human form and to shriek when pulled.

This poem is full of rage and guilt and self-disgust. This may be because Donne was born into a fiercely Catholic family. His uncle was the leader of the Jesuit mission in England. His younger brother died in prison for harbouring a priest. Donne himself renounced Catholicism, and eventually became Dean of St Paul's and one of the great preachers of his age. Before he died, in 1631, he had his portrait drawn wearing a funeral shroud and standing on a funeral urn as he believed he would appear when rising from the grave at the Last Judgement. One hopes he will not be disappointed.

We then have a ten-word haiku by Oshima Ryota, called 'And Then ...'. It required two eminent English poets to translate these ten words. It was worth it, because it is really stunning.

We end Love in the Garden with a warning from the American writer Dorothy Parker, of the limitations of sending the beloved one perfect rose.

Come into the Garden Maud
Alfred, Lord Tennyson

Come into the garden, Maud,
    For the black bat, night, has flown,
Come into the garden, Maud,
    I am here at the gate alone;
And the woodbine spices are wafted abroad,
    And the musk of the rose is blown.

For a breeze of morning moves,
    And the planet of Love is on high,
Beginning to faint in the light that she loves
    On a bed of daffodil sky,
To faint in the light of the sun she loves,
    To faint in his light, and to die.

All night have the roses heard
    The flute, violin, bassoon;
All night has the casement jessamine stirred
    To the dancers dancing in tune;
Till a silence fell with the waking bird,
    And a hush with the setting moon.

I said to the lily, 'There is but one
    With whom she has heart to be gay.
When will the dancers leave her alone?
    She is weary of dance and play.'
Now half to the setting moon are gone,
    And half to the rising day;
Low on the sand and loud on the stone
    The last wheel echoes away.

I said to the rose, 'The brief night goes
    In babble and revel and wine.
O young lord-lover, what sighs are those,
    For one that will never be thine?
But mine, but mine,' so I sware to the rose,
    'For ever and ever, mine.'

And the soul of the rose went into my blood,
    As the music clashed in the hall;
And long by the garden lake I stood,
    For I heard your rivulet fall
From the lake to the meadow and on to the wood,
    Our wood, that is dearer than all;

From the meadow your walks have left so sweet
    That whenever a March-wind sighs
He sets the jewel-print of your feet
    In violets blue as your eyes,
To the woody hollows in which we meet
    And the valleys of Paradise.

The slender acacia would not shake
    One long milk-bloom on the tree;
The white lake-blossom fell into the lake
    As the pimpernel dozed on the lea;
But the rose was awake all night for your sake,
    Knowing your promise to me;
The lilies and roses were all awake,
    They sighed for the dawn and thee.

Queen rose of the rosebud garden of girls,
    Come hither, the dances are done,
In gloss of satin and glimmer of pearls,
    Queen lily and rose in one;
Shine out, little head, sunning over with curls,
    To the flowers, and be their sun.

There has fallen a splendid tear
    From the passion-flower at the gate.
She is coming, my dove, my dear;
    She is coming, my life, my fate;
The red rose cries, 'She is near, she is near;'
    And the white rose weeps, 'She is late;'
The larkspur listens, 'I hear, I hear;'
    And the lily whispers, 'I wait.'

She is coming, my own, my sweet,
    Were it ever so airy a tread,
My heart would hear her and beat,
    Were it earth in an earthy bed;
My dust would hear her and beat,
    Had I lain for a century dead;
Would start and tremble under her feet,
    And blossom in purple and red.

Twicknam Garden
John Donne

Blasted with sighs, and surrounded with tears,
    Hither I come to seek the spring,
And at mine eyes, and at mine ears,
    Receive such balms as else cure every thing.
    But O! self-traitor, I do bring
The spider Love, which transubstantiates all,
And can convert manna to gall;
And that this place may thoroughly be thought
True paradise, I have the serpent brought.

'Twere wholesomer for me that winter did
    Benight the glory of this place,
And that a grave frost did forbid
    These trees to laugh and mock me to my face;
    But that I may not this disgrace
Endure, nor yet leave loving, Love, let me
Some senseless piece of this place be;
Make me a mandrake, so I may grow here,
Or a stone fountain weeping out my year.

Hither with crystal phials, lovers, come,
    And take my tears, which are love's wine,
And try your mistress' tears at home,
    For all are false, that taste not just like mine.
    Alas! hearts do not in eyes shine,
Nor can you more judge women's thoughts by tears,
Than by her shadow what she wears.
O perverse sex, where none is true but she,
Who's therefore true, because her truth kills me.

And Then . . .

Oshima Ryota
Translated by Geoffrey Bownas and Anthony Thwaite

Bad-tempered, I got back:
Then, in the garden,
The willow tree.

One Perfect Rose

Dorothy Parker

A single flow'r he sent me, since we met.
   All tenderly his messenger he chose;
Deep-hearted, pure, with scented dew still wet –
   One perfect rose.

I knew the language of the floweret;
   'My fragile leaves', it said, 'his heart enclose.'
Love long has taken for his amulet
   One perfect rose.

Why is it no one ever sent me yet
   One perfect limousine, do you suppose?
Ah no, it's always just my luck to get
   One perfect rose.

GARDENING

'All gardening is landscape-painting,' Pope famously wrote, and how to create a garden is the subject of his witty epistle to Richard Boyle, Earl of Burlington. Here he warns of the perils of excess, of the over-designed parterre or terrace, and gathers in for praise or blame Le Nôtre, Versailles and the architect Inigo Jones.

Pope was not a lyric poet, more a prose poet, as one critic remarks. But then again, if your body is ruined at twelve by a tubercular infection of the spine, it might kill the lyric spirit.

In 1718 he moved with his mother to Twickenham and devoted much of his time to his garden and grotto. He knew what he was talking about.

Dylan Thomas follows with the great 'Fern Hill'. Born in 1914 in Swansea, the wild poet, lover and drinker who married the gloriously named Caitlin Macnamara, was, despite all that, a disciplined artist.

There is some mythology that it was all terribly easy for him, but his work sheets show a man who continually laboured over every line, so anyone who thinks that he just rolled out of bed in a drunken haze after a night of passionate lovemaking and dashed off a masterpiece like 'Fern Hill', one of the greatest celebrations of a country childhood ever written, is alas, wrong.

Larkin wrote 'The Mower' in 1979 – a kind of poetic *Death on the Lawn*, the famous American novel. It's much kinder than normal Larkin. It's clever. As A. L. Rowse once asked about Larkin, was he too clever to live? Larkin also had a pathological fear of death. That is not just my opinion; it's an actual doctor's clinical assessment. Many of his friends during that time had been very seriously ill.

This poem is about death, and the fear of death.

Incidentally, in 1979 Larkin, a D. H. Lawrence fanatic (he liked to wear a T-shirt decorated with a print of Lawrence), had a nice vision while mowing the lawn: death on the lawn.

Gerard Manley Hopkins, like Blake, was an ecstatic born into a family of High Anglicans, but became a Catholic. And like all ecstatics wished, I think, to be a saint. He became a Jesuit and burnt his poems but, thank heavens, many of them remain. His work was turned down as incomprehensible, even by Catholic journals. Eventually his genius, his search for a unifying sacramental view of human life so clear in 'Pied Beauty', made him one of the nineteenth century's great poets.

Then we come to one of the loveliest poems ever written: John Keats's 'Ode to a Nightingale'. Keats, who supposedly, in Byron's very unkind line, died of a bad review, was mercilessly attacked and deeply wounded by the viciousness of those who called him part of 'the Cockney School'. It's almost unbearable to think that he died aged only twenty-five from tuberculosis. However, like all brilliant writers, he knew. He wrote to his brother: 'I think I shall be among the English Poets after my death.' And he was right.

That we are now familiar with Andrew Marvell is almost a literary miracle.

His poems were published in 1681, a few years after his death, but it was not until after the First World War, in Herbert Grierson's biography and T. S. Eliot's essays on him, that he became really well known. His oblique, ironic and enigmatic way of treating a poem was more acceptable to a modern audience. He was born out of his time.

'Thoughts in a Garden' is one of the greatest contemplative poems ever written, in which he gathers up almost all of life 'To a green thought in a green shade'.

The Mower
Philip Larkin

The mower stalled, twice; kneeling, I found
A hedgehog jammed up against the blades,
Killed. It had been in the long grass.

I had seen it before, and even fed it, once.
Now I had mauled its unobtrusive world
Unmendably. Burial was no help:

Next morning I got up and it did not.
The first day after a death, the new absence
Is always the same; we should be careful

Of each other, we should be kind
While there is still time.

Pied Beauty
Gerard Manley Hopkins

Glory be to God for dappled things—
    For skies of couple-colour as a brinded cow;
        For rose-moles all in stipple upon trout that swim;
Fresh-firecoal chestnut-falls; finches' wings;
    Landscape plotted and pieced—fold, fallow, and plough;
        And áll trádes, their gear and tackle and trim.

All things counter, original, spare, strange;
    Whatever is fickle, freckled (who knows how?)
        With swift, slow; sweet, sour; adazzle, dim;
He fathers-forth whose beauty is past change:
        Praise him.

Thoughts in a Garden
Andrew Marvell

How vainly men themselves amaze
To win the palm, the oak, or bays,
And their uncessant labours see
Crown'd from some single herb or tree,
Whose short and narrow-vergèd shade
Does prudently their toils upbraid;
While all the flowers and trees do close
To weave the garlands of repose!

Fair Quiet, have I found thee here,
And Innocence thy sister dear?
Mistaken long, I sought you then
In busy companies of men:
Your sacred plants, if here below,
Only among the plants will grow:
Society is all but rude
To this delicious solitude.

No white nor red was ever seen
So amorous as this lovely green.
Fond lovers, cruel as their flame,
Cut in these trees their mistress' name:
Little, alas! they know or heed

LIFE SAVING

How far these beauties hers exceed!
Fair trees! wheres'e'er your barks I wound,
No name shall but your own be found.

When we have run our passions' heat,
Love hither makes his best retreat:
The gods, that mortal beauty chase,
Still in a tree did end their race;
Apollo hunted Daphne so
Only that she might laurel grow;
And Pan did after Syrinx speed
Not as a nymph, but for a reed.

What wondrous life in this I lead!
Ripe apples drop about my head;
The luscious clusters of the vine
Upon my mouth do crush their wine;
The nectarine and curious peach
Into my hands themselves do reach;
Stumbling on melons, as I pass,
Ensnared with flowers, I fall on grass.

Meanwhile the mind from pleasure less
Withdraws into its happiness;
The mind, that ocean where each kind
Does straight its own resemblance find;
Yet it creates, transcending these,
Far other worlds, and other seas;
Annihilating all that's made
To a green thought in a green shade.

Here at the fountain's sliding foot,
Or at some fruit-tree's mossy root,

Casting the body's vest aside,
My soul into the boughs does glide;
There, like a bird, it sits and sings,
Then whets and combs its silver wings,
And, till prepared for longer flight,
Waves in its plumes the various light

Such was that happy Garden-state
While man there walk'd without a mate:
After a place so pure and sweet,
What other help could yet be meet!
But 'twas beyond a mortal's share
To wander solitary there:
Two paradises 'twere in one,
To live in Paradise alone.

How well the skilful gard'ner drew
Of flowers and herbs this dial new!
Where, from above, the milder sun
Does through a fragrant zodiac run:
And, as it works, th' industrious bee
Computes its time as well as we.
How could such sweet and wholesome hours
Be reckon'd, but with herbs and flowers!

GARDENS OF THE IMAGINATION

Our next section is gardens of the imagination.

The first poem is one of the most mysterious poems Eliot wrote, and it has baffled readers for years.

It's called 'Usk'. And when we talk of the white hart in this, we are not talking about the heart here in the chest, we are talking about the male deer.

What is the 'white hart behind the white well'? What exactly does he mean by 'Gently dip, but not too deep'? It's a very haunting poem.

The poem after that has an Eliot connection. It's called 'Rose Garden'. It is inspired by the unforgettable lines from *Four Quartets*: 'Footfalls echo in the memory / Down the passage which we did not take / Towards the door we never opened / Into the rose-garden.'

I was thrilled to find this poem. It is brilliant, but try as we might we cannot establish the author, so if any of you recognise it please let us know.

'Dedication to my Wife' is the only personal poem Eliot ever wrote, and it speaks of the imaginary rose garden in which perhaps we would all wish to live. Its last line is particularly moving.

Then a poem of the imagination by Edward Thomas, entitled 'For These'. Edward Thomas's poem is a garden of hope, somewhere, if fate is kind. Well, fate wasn't kind to Edward Thomas. He was killed at Arras, and much of his work was published posthumously. In a text called *The Strange Death of Edward Thomas*, the authors recount the following: 'The Germans were in retreat and the British soldiers were shouting and dancing, almost believing they had won the war when 2nd Lieutenant Edward Thomas stepped out of the dugout as the German fired one last shell. It missed him but came so close the blast of air stopped his heart. There was not the slightest sign of injury.'

'The Song of Wandering Aengus', an early Yeats poem set in a hazel wood, is a kind of surrealist poem, and Joyce said very cleverly of Yeats that he had an imagination no surrealist painter could ever equal. This is one of the poems that illustrate this brilliantly.

We end this section with *Kubla Khan*, by Samuel Taylor Coleridge. Charles Lamb described him as 'an Arch angel a little damaged'. Now here we do have the masterpiece dreamed in an opium dream.

It was dreamed as a three-hundred-line poem, but Coleridge was famously interrupted by a person from Porlock and only fifty-four lines remained in his memory. But what lines ... As long as poetry is read or listened to, it will delight and thrill us.

Usk
T. S. Eliot

Do not suddenly break the branch, or
Hope to find
The white hart behind the white well.
Glance aside, not for lance, do not spell
Old enchantments. Let them sleep.
'Gently dip, but not too deep.'
Lift your eyes
Where the roads dip and where the roads rise
Seek only there
Where the grey light meets the green air
The Hermit's chapel, the pilgrim's prayer.

For These
Edward Thomas

An acre of land between the shore and the hills,
Upon a ledge that shows my kingdoms three,
The lovely visible earth and sky and sea
Where what the curlew needs not, the farmer tills:

A house that shall love me as I love it,
Well-hedged, and honoured by a few ash trees
That linnets, greenfinches, and goldfinches
Shall often visit and make love in and flit:

A garden I need never go beyond,
Broken but neat, whose sunflowers every one
Are fit to be the sign of the Rising Sun:
A spring, a brook's bend, or at least a pond:

For these I ask not, but, neither too late
Nor yet too early, for what men call content,
And also that something may be sent
To be contented with, I ask of Fate.

Kubla Khan
Samuel Taylor Coleridge

In Xanadu did Kubla Khan
A stately pleasure-dome decree:
Where Alph, the sacred river, ran
Through caverns measureless to man
Down to a sunless sea.
So twice five miles of fertile ground
With walls and towers were girdled round:
And there were gardens bright with sinuous rills
Where blossom'd many an incense-bearing tree;
And here were forests ancient as the hills,
Enfolding sunny spots of greenery.

But O, that deep romantic chasm which slanted
Down the green hill athwart a cedarn cover!
A savage place! as holy and enchanted
As e'er beneath a waning moon was haunted
By woman wailing for her demon-lover!
And from this chasm, with ceaseless turmoil seething,
As if this earth in fast thick pants were breathing,

A mighty fountain momently was forced;
Amid whose swift half-intermitted burst
Huge fragments vaulted like rebounding hail,
Or chaffy grain beneath the thresher's flail:
And 'mid these dancing rocks at once and ever
It flung up momently the sacred river.
Five miles meandering with a mazy motion
Through wood and dale the sacred river ran,
Then reach'd the caverns measureless to man,
And sank in tumult to a lifeless ocean:
And 'mid this tumult Kubla heard from far
Ancestral voices prophesying war!

The shadow of the dome of pleasure
Floated midway on the waves;
Where was heard the mingled measure
From the fountain and the caves.
It was a miracle of rare device,
A sunny pleasure-dome with caves of ice!

A damsel with a dulcimer
In a vision once I saw:
It was an Abyssinian maid,
And on her dulcimer she play'd,
Singing of Mount Abora.
Could I revive within me,
Her symphony and song,
To such a deep delight 'twould win me,
That with music loud and long,
I would build that dome in air,
That sunny dome! those caves of ice!
And all who heard should see them there,
And all should cry, Beware! Beware!

His flashing eyes, his floating hair!
Weave a circle round him thrice,
And close your eyes with holy dread,
For he on honey-dew hath fed,
And drunk the milk of Paradise.

A WALK THROUGH THE WOODS

In this next section, we are going to take a walk through the woods.

There is a very short poem by Goethe, the great genius of German culture. Poet, playwright, scientist, botanist, 'the wisest of our time', as Carlyle described him. We found this short poem, twenty lines in total, in which a flower talks to him and says: 'Shall I be gather'd / Only to fade?' And he decides not to pluck it; he digs it out by the root and takes it home.

This little poem is a gem. It reminds me of what I consider the best description of the tragedy of *Hamlet*, which is Goethe's: 'a great deed laid upon a soul unequal to the performance of it ... an oak-tree planted in a costly vase ... the roots spread out, the vase is shivered to pieces.'

Next, 'The Trees'. Again, a gentler Larkin, with the lovely line 'Begin afresh, afresh, afresh.'

Then we have the first middle-aged male crisis: Dante.

Dante made the spiritual visible, according to Eliot. In *The Divine Comedy*, written in 1307, is probably the first literary examination of the middle-age crisis which leads, as these things often do, to hell.

In 'The Road Not Taken', Robert Frost also finds himself perplexed in a wood. It's an evocative poem that illustrates life's choices. How they are often irrevocable.

Then to Rupert Brooke's 'The Soldier'. In 1915, Winston Churchill wrote: 'Rupert Brooke is dead ... this life has closed at the moment when it seemed to have reached its springtime ... Only the echoes and the memory remain; but they will linger.' He was right. Well, there is a corner of so many green fields where British soldiers lie all over Europe.

Then, we come to a little known, quite remarkable poem, 'High

Wood', written by a Canadian poet, Philip Johnstone. It's an extraordinary leap of the imagination in which he sees what will happen to 'this patch of wood' well into the future.

At the Battle of Loos, of Johnstone's regiment fifty-four officers and 7054 men died. Twelve Victoria Crosses were awarded to the regiment during their service in France and Flanders. He survived, returned to Cranleigh School where he had previously taught and eventually, like Donne and Gerard Manley Hopkins, took holy orders, and at the age of fifty he settled in York. Here he translated the York Mystery Plays and was awarded the OBE for his work on the York Minster archives. He died in 1968.

Found

Johann Wolfgang von Goethe

Once through the forest

Alone I went;
To seek for nothing

My thoughts were bent.

I saw i' the shadow

A flower stand there
As stars it glisten'd,

As eyes 'twas fair.

I sought to pluck it,—

It gently said:
'Shall I be gather'd

Only to fade?'

With all its roots

I dug it with care,
And took it home

To my garden fair.

In silent corner

Soon it was set;
There grows it ever,

There blooms it yet.

High Wood
Philip Johnstone

Ladies and gentlemen, this is High Wood,
Called by the French, Bois des Fourneaux,
The famous spot which in Nineteen-Sixteen,
July, August and September was the scene
Of long and bitterly contested strife,
By reason of its High commanding site.
Observe the effect of shell-fire in the trees
Standing and fallen; here is wire; this trench
For months inhabited, twelve times changed hands;
(They soon fall in), used later as a grave.
It has been said on good authority
That in the fighting for this patch of wood
Were killed somewhere above eight thousand men,
Of whom the greater part were buried here,
This mound on which you stand being ...
Madame, please,
You are requested kindly not to touch
Or take away the Company's property
As souvenirs; you'll find we have on sale
A large variety, all guaranteed.
As I was saying, all is as it was,
This is an unknown British officer,
The tunic having lately rotted off.
Please follow me – this way ...
the path, sir, please
The ground which was secured at great expense
The Company keeps absolutely untouched,
And in that dug-out (genuine) we provide

LIFE SAVING

Refreshments at a reasonable rate.
You are requested not to leave about
Paper, or ginger-beer bottles, or orange-peel,
There are waste-paper-baskets at the gate.

PARADISE LOST

We are now going to take a very short section from *Paradise Lost* by Milton.

Paradise Lost was actually going to be a play, and it was going to be called 'Adam Unparadised'.

Critics say that Milton changed his mind because he realised the weight of Shakespeare was such that, instead of trying to compete, he would write the great long epic poem.

Milton's purpose, stated in Book I, is to 'justify the ways of God to men'. And as Goethe once wrote, the devil is God's best excuse.

Milton was a sect, if you like, of his own. He makes you feel that he was puritanical, or misogynistic, but that is just not true. He fought very hard for divorce, for example, he believed in sexual intercourse before marriage, which in his time made him notorious.

In the section we are going to hear, Satan has already persuaded Eve that she must eat of the fruit. She knows she shouldn't, she has been told she shouldn't, but she does. And after she has eaten it, and she now has knowledge, she thinks to herself, Now why should I share the knowledge with Adam? Wouldn't it be nice to keep it to myself and just for once be the superior being?

But eventually, off she goes to Adam, and she tries to persuade him. The minute he sees her he knows what she has done, and she is doomed, and in a rather moving passage he resolves to join her in this doom. 'Flesh of flesh / Bone of my bone thou art, and from thy state / Mine never shall be parted'. He eats the fruit, and then come the beautiful lines: 'some sad drops / Wept at completing of the mortal sin / Original', which is the first great sin.

Immediately carnal desire inflames him and Eve responds, and

Milton says 'in lust they burn'. They are off to a shady bank in the garden, which he beautifully describes.

This first sexual encounter leads to the first post-coital guilt, which leads to the first post-coital blame game and row in which Adam berates her – If only you'd listened to me!

The rows continue on, as indeed they do for eternity, and when we leave them, they are in the male–female row that continues to this day.

So we join Eve in the garden. She has eaten the fruit . . .

Paradise Lost

[excerpt]

           Adam the while
Waiting desirous her return, had wove
Of choicest flow'rs a garland to adorn
Her tresses, and her rural labours crown,
As reapers oft are wont their harvest queen.
Great joy he promised to his thoughts, and new
Solace in her return, so long delayed;
Yet oft his heart, divine of something ill
Misgave him; he the falt'ring measure felt;
And forth to meet her went, the way she took
That morn when first they parted; by the Tree
Of Knowledge he must pass, there he her met,
Scarce from the tree returning; in her hand
A bough of fairest fruit that downy smiled,
New gathered, and ambrosial smell diffused.
To him she hasted, in her face excuse
Came prologue, and apology too prompt,
Which with bland words at will she thus addressed.

        Hast thou not wondered, Adam, at my stay?
Thee I have missed, and thought it long, deprived
Thy presence, agony of love till now
Not felt, nor shall be twice, for never more
Mean I to try, what rash untried I sought,
The pain of absence from thy sight. But strange
Hath been the cause, and wonderful to hear:

This tree is not as we are told, a tree
Of danger tasted, nor to evil unknown
Op'ning the way, but of divine effect
To open eyes, and make them gods who taste;
And hath been tasted such: the serpent wise,
Or not restrained as we, or not obeying,
Hath eaten of the fruit, and is become,
Not dead, as we are threatened, but thenceforth
Endued with human voice and human sense,
Reasoning to admiration, and with me
Persuasively hath so prevailed, that I
Have also tasted, and have also found
Th' effects to correspond, opener mine eyes,
Dim erst, dilated spirits, ampler heart,
And growing up to godhead; which for thee
Chiefly I sought, without thee can despise.
For bliss, as thou hast part, to me is bliss,
Tedious, unshared with thee, and odious soon.
Thou therefore also taste, that equal lot
May join us, equal joy, as equal love;
Lest thou not tasting, different degree
Disjoin us, and I then too late renounce
Deity for thee, when Fate will not permit.
Thus Eve with count'nance blithe her story told;
But in her cheek distemper flushing glowed.
On th' other side, Adam, soon as he heard
The fatal trespass done by Eve, amazed,
Astonied stood and blank, while horror chill
Ran through his veins, and all his joints relaxed;
From his slack hand the garland wreathed for Eve
Down dropped, and all the faded roses shed:
Speechless he stood and pale, till thus at length
First to himself he inward silence broke.

O fairest of Creation, last and best
Of all God's works, creature in whom excelled
Whatever can to sight or thought be formed,
Holy, divine, good, amiable or sweet!
How art thou lost, how on a sudden lost,
Defaced, deflow'red, and now to death devote?
Rather how hast thou yielded to transgress
The strict forbiddance, how to violate
The sacred fruit forbidd'n! Some cursèd fraud
Of Enemy hath beguiled thee, yet unknown,
And me with thee hath ruined, for with thee
Certain my resolution is to die;
How can I live without thee, how forgo
Thy sweet converse and love so dearly joined,
To live again in these wild woods forlorn?
Should God create another Eve, and I
Another rib afford, yet loss of thee
Would never from my heart; no no, I feel
The link of nature draw me: flesh of flesh,
Bone of my bone thou art, and from thy state
Mine never shall be parted, bliss or woe.
So having said, as one from sad dismay
Recomforted, and after thoughts disturbed
Submitting to what seemed remédiless,
Thus in calm mood his words to Eve he turned.
      Bold deed thou hast presumed, advent'rous Eve,
And peril great provoked, who thus hath dared
Had it been only coveting to eye
That sacred fruit, sacred to abstinence,
Much more to taste it under ban to touch.
But past who can recall, or done undo?
Not God omnipotent, nor Fate, yet so
Perhaps thou shalt not die, perhaps the fact

Is not so heinous now, foretasted fruit,
Profaned first by the serpent, by him first
Made common and unhallowed ere our taste;
Nor yet on him found deadly; he yet lives,
Lives, as thou saidst, and gains to live as man
Higher degree of life, inducement strong
To us, as likely tasting to attain
Proportional ascent, which cannot be
But to be gods, or angels demi-gods.
Nor can I think that God, Creator wise,
Though threat'ning, will in earnest so destroy
Us his prime creatures, dignified so high,
Set over all his works, which in our Fall,
For us created, needs with us must fail,
Dependent made; so God shall uncreate,
Be frustrate, do, undo, and labour lose,
Not well conceived of God, who though his power
Creation could repeat, yet would be loath
Us to abolish, lest the Adversary
Triúmph and say; Fickle their state whom God
Most favours, who can please him long? Me first
He ruined, now mankind; whom will he next?
Matter of scorn, not to be given the Foe.
However I with thee have fixed my lot,
Certain to undergo like doom; if death
Consort with thee, death is to me as life;
So forcible within my heart I feel
The bond of nature draw me to my own,
My own in thee, for what thou art is mine;
Our state cannot be severed, we are one,
One flesh; to lose thee were to lose myself.
    So Adam, and thus Eve to him replied.
O glorious trial of exceeding love,

Illustrious evidence, example high!
Engaging me to emulate, but short
Of thy perfection, how shall I attain,
Adam, from whose dear side I boast me sprung,
And gladly of our union hear thee speak,
One heart, one soul in both; whereof good proof
This day affords, declaring thee resolved,
Rather than death or aught than death more dread
Shall separate us, linked in love so dear,
To undergo with me one guilt, one crime,
If any be, of tasting this fair fruit,
Whose virtue, for of good still good proceeds,
Direct, or by occasion hath presented
This happy trial of thy love, which else
So eminently never had been known.
Were it I thought death menaced would ensue
This my attempt, I would sustain alone
The worst, and not persuade thee, rather die
Deserted, than oblige thee with a fact
Pernicious to thy peace, chiefly assured
Remarkably so late of thy so true,
So faithful love unequalled; but I feel
Far otherwise th' event, not death, but life
Augmented, opened eyes, new hopes, new joys,
Taste so divine, that what of sweet before
Hath touched my sense, flat seems to this, and harsh.
On my experience, Adam, freely taste,
And fear of death deliver to the winds.

    So saying, she embraced him, and for joy
Tenderly wept, much won that he his love
Had so ennobled, as of choice to incur
Divine displeasure for her sake, or death.
In recompense (for such compliance bad

Such recompense best merits) from the bough
She gave him of that fair enticing fruit
With liberal hand: he scrupled not to eat
Against his better knowledge, not deceived,
But fondly overcome with female charm.
Earth trembled from her entrails, as again
In pangs, and Nature gave a second groan;
Sky loured, and muttering thunder, some sad drops
Wept at completing of the mortal sin
Original; while Adam took no thought,
Eating his fill, nor Eve to iterate
Her former trespass feared, the more to soothe
Him with her loved society, that now
As with new wine intoxicated both
They swim in mirth, and fancy that they feel
Divinity within them breeding wings
Wherewith to scorn the earth: but that false fruit
Far other operation first displayed,
Carnal desire inflaming; he on Eve
Began to cast lascivious eyes, she him
As wantonly repaid; in lust they burn:

AFTERWORD

Maurice Saatchi

On 24 October 2011 the Dean of Westminster allowed Josephine Hart the unprecedented honour of a memorial poetry reading in Westminster Abbey, beside Poets' Corner.

When the Dean, Sir John Hall, was asked whether such an event might be possible, his reply was that it would be 'very appropriate'.

So it was that members of Josephine Hart's repertory company of great actors – Eileen Atkins, Bono, Kenneth Cranham, Charles Dance, Joanna David, Emilia Fox, Edward Fox, Julian Glover, Jeremy Irons, Felicity Kendal, Damian Lewis, Helen McCrory, Ian McDiarmid, Elizabeth McGovern, Roger Moore, Dan Stevens, Harriet Walter and Dominic West – came to Westminster Abbey for a reading of T. S. Eliot's poems, 'The Love Song of J. Alfred Prufrock', 'Portrait of a Lady' and 'The Hollow Men'. They were directed by her mentor Michael Grandage who, a year before, had told her he could fill the Donmar theatre with her poetry for a week. And he did.

Josephine Hart spoke of her 'absolute respect' for actors, and dedicated her last book to the 'mysterious art' of the actor.

No mystery there.

Kind people. Generous people. Brilliant people.

Josephine Hart agreed with T. S. Eliot that we understand the poet's work better if we are introduced to the poet's life. That is the origin of this book of her introductions to the Josephine Hart Poetry Hours at the British Library, the National Theatre, the Donmar, the American

Embassy, the Irish Embassy, Harvard University and the New York Public Library. So perhaps I may attempt an introduction to Josephine Hart. Here is what I said that night in Westminster Abbey . . .

Josephine Hart had definite views about definite things, including poetry.

Josephine Hart said, 'Without reading, life would have been less bearable and infinitely less enjoyable.'

Josephine Hart described reading Eliot for the first time as 'a physical shock'.

The only book I put into her coffin, with her own, was *The Collected Works of T. S. Eliot*.

Her view of poetry would have been well expressed in these Post-It notes, found later, of the speech she never gave, to the opening night she never attended, of her Poetry Week at the Donmar Warehouse:

> Public performance of the great poetry of the dead poets read by great actors should be the norm in London. The British Library said yes. And now Michael Grandage has given us a week. We have an amazing cast. And what poets! You have the list. And we're sold out! Thank you audience!

The record seems to show that the last words Josephine Hart ever wrote were on this Post-It note:

> Rehearsing my text all day . . . INTROS

For an explanation of Josephine Hart's view that poetry is a force for good in a human life, I recommend her Royal Life Saving Institution certificate, awarded to her age thirteen. The citation reads:

> For practical knowledge of rescue, releasing oneself from the clutch of the drowning, and for the ability to render aid in resuscitating the apparently drowned.

For Josephine Hart, poetry is life saving.

Josephine Hart had definite views about other things, like ... God. Love. Memory. And Death.

Josephine Hart described her relationship with poetry as 'a long love affair, which started with a *coup de foudre* in a House of God':

> In the beginning was the Word, and the Word was with God, and the Word was God.

Josephine Hart said this was the first line of pure poetry she ever heard, and that it remained to her, perfect.

She learned about God from the nuns of the Convent of St Louis near her home town of Mullingar, in the middle of Ireland.

The nuns taught Josephine Hart to read. Sometimes too well. She was often caught and punished for taking a torch and a book under her bedclothes.

The nuns taught Josephine Hart to sing. To her rendition of 'Do Re Mi', Sister Columba said, 'Sit down child and never sing again.'

The nuns taught Josephine Hart 'a literary hierarchical system of Orwellian precision. Novels good. Plays better. Poetry best.'

The nuns showed Josephine Hart the difference between a mortal and a venial sin. When Gregory Peck kissed Audrey Hepburn in

Roman Holiday, the nuns shook the projector.

From the nuns, Josephine Hart learned that confession to God is a shining shield over your chest, to keep you pure and clean.

Age fourteen, this is what she wrote:

We stand for God, and for his glory. The Lord Supreme and God of all, strengthen our Faith, Redeemer. Guard us when danger is nigh. To thee we pledge our lives and service. Strong in a Faith that ne'er shall die.

But in Josephine Hart's case, it did die. She despaired ... on the night the priest came to their house to ask if she wanted to, or would he, tell her parents that her younger brother had died in the accidental explosion at their house. At that point, the last her brother had said to her was:

Turn me over. Don't let mama see me.

So it was that Josephine Hart walked along the corridor to her parents' room.

Josephine Hart also had definite views about love. She said it is: 'The extreme emotion. The incandescent experience.'

Josephine Hart was sure that 'dying for love' is celebrated in the iconography of the cross, that 'God had sent His dearly beloved son down to earth to die for our sins. And thus prove His love for us.'

For Josephine Hart, 'Love is sacrifice. And sacrifice is a sign of love.'

Josephine Hart says her mind was formed 'in a benediction of this most beautiful concept'.

It follows that Josephine Hart much approved John Bayley's version of marriage:

A giant glass bell jar descended over the married couple and they were never heard of again.

According to Josephine Hart, there is only one force powerful enough to get under the bell jar. She called it 'the moral landscape of memory'.

She meant the same as Eliot:

The awareness of things ill done and done to others' harm which once you took for exercise of virtue.

After the death of Josephine Hart's brother, age one, her sister, age eight, and her other brother, age fifteen, Josephine Hart's mother was among the first patients to be given electric shocks to erase memory. It was called ECT. Electro Convulsive Therapy.

This may be why Josephine Hart wrote 'I worry about the future of my past.' And that 'before us lies yesterday'.

Josephine Hart had a name for such sentiments, based on her home town of Mullingar: 'Mullingaritis'.

For those so afflicted, of which I am myself a victim, to 'move on' after a death, is a monstrous act of betrayal. To 'come to terms with' an act of unforgivable selfishness.

I come at last, to the end.

Josephine Hart had definite views about death.
Josephine Hart kept a file, called 'Death'.
She liked, in particular, two versions.
In Auden, that, after witnessing the amazing sight of a boy, Icarus, falling from the sky into the sea:

The expensive delicate ship ... had somewhere to get to and sailed calmly on.

And how, in Robert Frost, after the boy's arm was cut off in the sawmill, about the boy's workmates, that they:

Since they were not the one dead, turned to their affairs.

But Josephine Hart's version of death was much darker than either Auden or Frost.
For Josephine Hart, death is a double-dealer.
First, it gives you your physical death.
Then, according to Josephine Hart, your real death. When there is nobody left on the planet who remembers you.
She called that 'oblivion'.

By March, Josephine Hart could not eat or drink.
She was attached to tubes and wires twelve hours a day.
From that state, on 15 April, she got up to go to the National Theatre with her actors, all of whom are here, to perform the Romantic poetry of Keats, Byron and Shelley.
After that, she gave a dinner for her actors and her friends.
Then, she went back to her attachments.

There have been many examples of great courage by actors on the stage of the Olivier. This must be one of them.

Her attention then turned to the Donmar, on 30 May:

The Donmar! The Donmar!
You have to get me to the Donmar!
By then she was quite weak.
On Saturday, I went to John Bell & Croyden to buy her a wheelchair.
Steel. Chrome. Black.
Top of the range.
Top of the range.
Very chic.
It would be a Hollywood entrance.
We agreed, an ambulance would be no good.
A black cab!
With a ramp!
Two nurses put on her lucky shoes, and she was wheeled across Harley Street in the rain into the cab.
She went on stage for rehearsals for a few minutes, but she was too tired and went back to the dressing room. Fifteen minutes before curtain up, I said to her, 'We must go back to the hospital.'
To my astonishment, she agreed.
After that, about the last Josephine Hart had to say was, 'I just want to rest. I'm out there with the boys.'
Some time later, I received a letter:

I am the taxi driver who took your courageous wife to the opening of the poetry week at the Donmar Warehouse Theatre.
I have never been so deeply touched by someone's sheer fortitude and determination, and I was totally overcome by this.
That chance encounter has changed my view of life

Josephine Hart always said: 'It's over in a second.'

I said these were childhood terrors.

But she knew better. She said, 'I am doomed.'

Many of you have praised Josephine Hart for her spare prose. Her precise use of words.

Well, out of nowhere, they finished Josephine Hart with only three words:

Malignant

Advanced

Inoperable

But I can do better.

I will finish Josephine Hart for you. Right here and now. Once and for all. With three much better words.

VIVACITÉ

Josephine Hart was Ladies' Breaststroke Champion of Mullingar, age fifteen.

Years later, to see Josephine Hart's powerful breaststroke in water, is a sight of unparalleled female beauty.

The word means 'the vigour of hardy plants'.

VOLUPTÉ

Beautiful décolletage. Shoulders. Legs.

The boys in Mullingar particularly admired Josephine Hart's legs. They had a phrase for it:

Beef to the heel. The Mullingar heifer.

VOLONTÉ

It means:

Will.

Josephine Hart never shed a tear. She said, 'The little army of nod-ules is taking me over.'

I pray for you all that your daughter, sister, mother, lover . . . will never speak, or hear, lines like these.

Josephine Hart said to her doctor, 'I have terminal cancer . . . Right?'

'Yes.'

'I am in the terminal stage of terminal cancer. Right?'

'Yes.'

'How long?'

'Three weeks.'

Josephine Hart said poetry, once it entered into her mind, surfaced at times of need, and became a lifeline.

And it did.

Josephine Hart said:

For a girl with no sense of direction, poetry was a route map through life.

And it was.

Josephine Hart said, it all started in a House of God.

So, dear, dear Josephine Hart.

Here we are again:

In my beginning is my end

~

Since then, thanks to her two Colonels-in-Chief, Angharad Wood and Monique Henry, the Josephine Hart Poetry Foundation has continued her purpose.

Poetry can't cure cancer, but it can save your life until you die.

The philosophy behind the Josephine Hart Poetry Hour can be simply expressed in three parts:

First, the life of the poet

Josephine Hart agreed with T. S. Eliot that:

The poet always writes out of his personal life; in his finest work out of its tragedy, whatever it may be, remorse, lost love or loneliness.

So far, in the later Poetry Hours, Josephine Hart's narrator has been played by Melvyn Bragg, David Hare, Alan Yentob, Roy Foster, Simon Callow, Richard Eyre and Tom Stoppard.

Second, the poets read aloud

According to Josephine Hart, poetry startles us into a more full sense of life. It is a trinity of Sound, Sense and Sensibility, and what Robert Frost called 'the sound of sense', will be lost unless we hear it.

Seamus Heaney, as an undergraduate at Queen's, found that on hearing Eliot's *Four Quartets* read by the actor Robert Speight, 'what had been perplexing when sight-read for meaning only was hypnotic when read aloud'.

Yeats in his seventies said he had spent his life 'clearing out of poetry every phrase written for the eye alone, and bringing it all back to syntax that is for the ear alone'.

Auden put it more bluntly:

No poem which is not better heard than read is good poetry

And third, poetry read by great actors

Again, she agreed with Eliot that:

Poetry should be read to us by skilled readers ... the feeling for syllable and rhythm penetrating far below the conscious level of thought and feeling, invigorating every word.

What followed, says Professor Ron Schuchard at London University, is an amazing twenty-eight-year programme of poetry readings at the British Library, Harvard, the New York Public Library, the Donmar Warehouse and the National Theatre.

Josephine Hart thought that to see and hear Harold Pinter as Larkin, Jeremy Irons as Satan, Roger Moore as Kipling, Bono as W. B. Yeats, Elizabeth McGovern as Plath, Dominic West as Wilde and Eileen Atkins and Edward Fox as T. S. Eliot is as good a theatrical experience as anyone could wish for.

These poets and actors provide a revelation in one line, which it would take a lifetime to learn. Love, loss, fear, envy, erotic obsession – they are all there.

Josephine Hart thought the technology of the app could match the live impact of the Poetry Hours, and bring them to life for a whole new generation.

So, just after the beginning of the app, and shortly before the diagnosis of her own end, she started work with the leading experts in mobile technology for the iPhone, iPad and Android to create the most advanced poetry site on the internet. With the help of Lennie Goodings, her revered Editor-in-Chief at Virago, that initial effort has been developed, and Apple kindly allowed it to be named The Poetry App. So far, this free app has had almost twenty thousand downloads from around the world. It allows people to decide for themselves whether to view, listen or read poetry (or all three at once), in a way no film, CD or book alone could ever do. Josephine Hart was certain this was how young people would discover that poetry gives voice to experience in a way no other art form can.

They can build their own virtual library, fill their bookcases with beautiful leather-bound copies of their favourite poems (including their own), and take them down from their own shelves whenever they please.

This is why the Boston School District in America now gives iPads free to its students – to relieve the burden on the state of buying heavy textbooks, and the burden on students' backs of having to carry them around.

These American students happily look and listen to you while operating their iPads without even looking down at the screen. They have evolved a completely new way of learning, which does not involve a book, a torch or a bed.

It is visual, not linear. The idea of a mouse scrolling through vertical lines of text seems ancient to them. Research among British two-year-olds confirms the point – they are puzzled when presented with a laptop or desktop screen. They reach out their hand to move the screen up, down, sideways, in and out, but . . . nothing happens. In future, the Poetry App will show audio and video of the Josephine Hart Poetry Hours within hours of the live events.

The Foundation has also established five Josephine Hart Scholarships at the Guildhall.

The Josephine Hart prize at the Guildhall for the Best Performance of a Poem by an Actor was presented at the British Library on 18 June 2012, to Edwin Thomas, by Felicity Kendal.

The Josephine Hart Prize for the Best Film of a Poem by a Director, at RADA, will be awarded next year.

A bursary has been created in her name by Professors Schuchard and Gould at the University of London.

Jean Cardot from the Institut de France is the legendary sculptor of two of the iconic statues in Paris – of Charles de Gaulle in the Champs Élysées, and Winston Churchill in the Avenue Winston Churchill. He is creating a 3.5-metre bronze statue of Josephine Hart, to be unveiled next year.

Maurice Saatchi
London, 2012

Copyright Acknowledgements

Sylvia Plath: 'Daddy' and 'Lady Lazarus' from *Ariel* (1965), reprinted by permission of the publishers, Faber & Faber Ltd.

Edward Thomas: 'For These', reprinted by kind permission of Mrs R. Vellender.

William Butler Yeats: 'Before the World was Made' and 'Easter, 1916' from *The Collected Poems of W B Yeats*, edited by Richard J Finneran (Macmillan, 1983), reprinted by permission of A P Watt Ltd on behalf of Michael B. Yeats.

Although we have tried to trace and contact copyright holders before publication, in some cases this has not been possible. If contacted we will be pleased to rectify any errors or omissions at the earliest opportunity.

Picture Credits

W. H. Auden: Getty Images

Elizabeth Bishop: © Bettmann/Corbis

Robert Browning by George Frederic Watts: © National Portrait Gallery, London

Lord Byron: © Illustrated London News Ltd/Mary Evans Picture Library

Emily Dickinson: Getty Images

T. S. Eliot: © National Portrait Gallery, London

John Keats: © National Portrait Gallery, London

Rudyard Kipling: Roger Viollet/Getty Images

Philip Larkin: © estate of Fay Godwin/British Library/National Portrait Gallery, London

Marianne Moore: Getty Images

John Milton: Mary Evans Picture Library

Sylvia Plath: © Bettmann/Corbis

Percy Bysshe Shelley: Mary Evans Picture Library

Robert Frost: courtesy of Dartmouth College Library, Special Collections

Robert Lowell by Alfred Eisenstaedt/*Life* magazine: Time & Life Pictures/Getty Images

Christina Rossetti: © Lebrecht Images

Walt Whitman: © National Portrait Gallery, London

Oscar Wilde: © National Portrait Gallery, London

William Butler Yeats: © National Portrait Gallery, London